FROM CAMELOT
TO JOYOUS GUARD

Justice Neale Carman

FROM CAMELOT TO JOYOUS GUARD

The Old French
La Mort le Roi Artu

———

translated by
J. NEALE CARMAN

edited with an introduction by
NORRIS J. LACY

THE UNIVERSITY PRESS OF KANSAS
Lawrence/Manhattan/Wichita

© Copyright 1974 by The University Press of Kansas
Printed in the United States of America

Library of Congress Cataloging in Publication Data

Mort Artu. English.
   From Camelot to Joyous Guard.

   Translation of Mort Artu.
   Includes bibliographical references.
   1. Lancelot—Romances. 2. Arthurian romances.
I. Carman, Justice Neale, 1897-1972, tr. II. Title.
PQ1496.M75E5 1974   843'.1   73-18242
ISBN 0-7006-0121-X

Justice Neale Carman
1897–1972

Professor J. Neale Carman was a member of the faculty of the University of Kansas for 49 years and Chairman of the Department of Romance Languages from 1957 to 1962. His research activities were numerous and varied. They fall principally into two categories: studies of linguistic distribution in the state of Kansas, and Arthurian literature. For many years he examined the survival of foreign languages throughout the state of Kansas. These investigations resulted in many articles, of which a few titles are: "Babel in Kansas," *Bureau of Government Research Publications* VI (1951); "Continental Europeans in Rural Kansas 1854–1861," *University of Kansas Publications, Social Science Studies* XI (1954); and *Germans in Kansas,* published by the Carl Schurz Memorial Foundation in Philadelphia in 1961. The culmination of this body of research was a three-volume linguistic atlas, *Foreign Language Units in Kansas.* The first volume was published by The University of Kansas Press in 1962. The second and third volumes are available on microfiche from The University Press of Kansas (Vol. II, *Account of Settlement and Settlements in Kansas*; Vol. III, *European and American Background*).

In Dr. Carman's second research area his publications were equally significant. They include two books: *The Relationship of the "Perlesvaus" and the "Queste del Saint Graal,"* University of Kansas Humanistic Studies, 1936; and *A Study of the Pseudo-Map Cycle of Arthurian Romance to Investigate Its Historico-Geographic Background and to Provide a Hypothesis as to Its Fabrication,* The University Press of Kansas, 1973. Three articles were presented in the *Publications of the Modern*

02065

Language Association and four in *Romance Philology:* "The Sword Withdrawn in Robert de Boron's 'Merlin' and in the 'Queste del Saint Graal,'" *PMLA* LII (1938); "The Symbolism of the 'Perlesvaus,'" *PMLA* LXI (1946); "The Conquests of the Grail Castle and Dolorous Guard," *PMLA* LXXXV (1970); "Was Pelles the Fisher King?" *RPh* III (1950); "Prose 'Lancelot' III, 29," *RPh* VI (1953); " 'Purgatorio' I and II, and the 'Queste del Saint Graal,'" *RPh* IX (1955); "New Light on 'Le Roman de Cassidorus,'" *RPh* XXI (1967).

Another article, "The 'Perlesvaus' and the Bristol Channel," was published in *Research Studies* XXXII (1964). Dr. Carman's most recent article, "South Welsh Geography and British History in the *Perlesvaus*," appeared in *A Medieval French Miscellany*, University of Kansas Humanistic Studies, 1972. Of his many published reviews, examples may be found in *RPh* XV (1961); XVI (1963); XXIII (1969).

A dedicated teacher, Dr. Carman early prepared a textbook for use in beginning French classes, *Elementary French* (New York: Farrar and Rinehart, Inc., 1943). This text was widely used for years. Dr. Carman was also a poet. A collection of his poetry, *On the Margin of a Scholarly Career*, was published as a tribute to him on his retirement in 1967.

Dr. Carman's studies were always the result of painstaking research and reflection as well as original interpretation of factual data. During his long career Dr. Carman made countless contributions of importance to the University of Kansas as a teacher and an administrator and to the academic world as a research scholar.

FOREWORD

It is scarcely an exaggeration to say that, at the time of his death, J. Neale Carman was as active as at any time in his career; in fact, his retirement several years ago simply gave him more time for his work. In addition to this translation, he had recently completed *A Study of the Pseudo-Map Cycle of Arthurian Romance*, published by The University Press of Kansas (1973). During the preceding year he had published a substantial article on the *Perlesvaus* and had read a paper at the 1972 Nantes congress of the International Arthurian Society. We can add to this his continued interest in linguistic studies, his work on his memoirs, and notes for a study he was preparing on the "Master Plan" of the Lancelot-Grail Cycle. Given his interests and his activity, I think his friends will agree that the publication of one of his manuscripts is an entirely appropriate memorial.

I should perhaps clarify my own part in this publication. Professor Carman had completed the translation of the text, and after typing and corrections, little remained to be done beyond seeing it properly through the press. I put together his preface from fairly extensive notes. The introduction is mine (although I base part of the "Early History of Lancelot" on Carman's notes). I have kept the introduction intentionally brief, limiting myself to essential information and to a few basic observations about the *Mort Artu* or the cycle it belongs to. I include in my introduction a brief concordance, which will facilitate the efforts of a reader wishing to consult the critical edition of the Old French original.

Aid and offers of aid came from a number of Professor Carman's colleagues and friends; I am most grateful to them all. In particular, I wish to express my deep gratitude to my colleague Professor Barbara M. Craig and to the University of Kansas Endowment Association. Besides preparing the necrology, Professor Craig provided extensive editorial and personal aid during my absence from the University during part of 1973. Her generosity is most appreciated. The Endowment Association provided financial support for the publication of this volume, in recognition of Neale Carman's long and valuable service to the University. I am happy to acknowledge that support, and particularly the efforts of Mr. Irvin E. Youngberg of the Endowment Association.

N. J. L.

PREFACE

The title for this translation of the Old French *Mort Artu* was chosen in order to avoid any confusion with the translation by Sir Thomas Malory. The merits of Malory's work are to most tastes greater than those of its Old French model, but their merits are not the same, for Malory did more than translate. I shall not try to compare the two works; I present this translation in part as an aid in studying the English author; in great part, though, because, despite shortcomings, the *Mort Artu* is important ideologically in ways not always perceptible in Malory's product.

Despite the Old French title of the romance, its principal hero is not Arthur but Lancelot; its unity comes from the transfer of a tragic fault from Lancelot to Arthur to Gawain and back to Arthur, with Lancelot, cleansed of the fault, remaining as the last survivor. In retrospect, after the reader has completed the reading of *From Camelot to Joyous Guard*, that title should not seem inappropriate.

The problems offered by the *Mort Artu* to the translator are not those ordinary to such a task. Usually one must seek an equivalent to what an author has set down, without neglecting all the nuances of his phrases but without resorting to prolixity to capture them. In the *Mort Artu*, however, the author's conceptions and his emotional implications are sealed within a vocabulary much more restricted than that of other writers of similar importance, even of his own age. Thus the translator's problem is, without boiling down the author's diffuseness and losing essential flavors in the boiling, to achieve enough variety of expression so that readers of the twentieth century, sensitive to clichés and irked by monotonous repetition, will not be driven from the extraction of the romance's meaningful marrow.

A particular problem facing the translator is the use of key words which denote traditional concepts or psychological states. Two such key expressions are *fole amour* and *outrage*. The phrase *fole amour* is used several times to describe the character of the amours of Lancelot and Guenevere during the period that the romance covers. Sometimes I have translated these two words by "guilty love," sometimes by "mad love,"

ix

depending on the meaning of the particular phrase. Both the notions of madness and guilt are included, but a guilt caused not so much by the existence of the love as by intemperate and imprudent indulgence in it; it is mad in the sense that it is uncontrolled by reason or by usual standards of conduct. The word *outrage* occurs four times, two of those in the repetition of Gawain's epitaph; the word also describes Gawain's conduct through the last half of the romance. I have translated it as "mad hatred," because the fault took that form in Gawain. The author applies the word once to Arthur in his last days, and there too, "mad hatred" is appropriate. The word *outrage* could also have qualified Mordred's conduct; in him the madness originates in thirst for power and in lust.

Fole amour and *outrage* are indeed key expressions, but the author does not discourse upon them; he shows their workings in action. Though he is not above moralizing discourse and indulges in it *à propos* of "Fortune," *fole amour* and *outrage* are vastly more important in his work than the inconstancies of Fortune. The translator must give to these concepts neither more nor less emphasis than the author put into their dramatization.

On the other hand, the translator must of course exercise great care in his rendering of the most commonplace sentences as well. How often should he eliminate the eternally recurring double negatives and leave a simple affirmation? Infrequently, I decided. How often should the many equivalents of absolute superlatives be reduced to the positive degree? Again I decided against frequent excisions. How often should synonyms be sought so as to avoid the monotony of repetition? I decided to seek variety as often as there was no alteration of meaning and no probability that I was destroying the author's effort to attain a rhetorical effect. The treatment of the word *sire*, as used in direct address, will serve as an illustration. When *sire* referred to King Arthur, and to Mordred as a usurping king, the English "sire" has been used. In a few cases, I have used "sir"; as a general thing I have used "my lord." *"Mes sires"* is regularly used with Gawain's name and occasionally with two or three other names; I have translated it as "sir."

I have introduced a minimum of archaisms. At points a reader may be shocked by the modern flavor of some English borrowing from Latin, but while the vocabulary I have used is somewhat larger than the author's, I have made a real effort to avoid Latin derivatives of which the equivalent does not appear in Old French. On the other hand, I have favored words of Anglo-Saxon origin as reproducing in English the simplicity of speech found in the *Mort Artu*. In a few cases I do admit occasional archaisms of vocabulary: I do say "swoon" instead of "faint" or "lose consciousness," but you will not find one "quoth." I might say something similar regarding grammatical constructions; usually I have written "I do not know"; occasionally, "I know not," but never "he went not."

I have tried to achieve a verbal art—or lack of art—similar to that of this early French prose. A somewhat greater freedom is permissible in dealing with medieval prose than with the product of later authors, because we cannot be sure just what the medieval author wrote. Each scribe in copying his manuscript made changes of his own, so that no two manuscripts are precisely the same. Probably the best is enough different from the original to allow a translator the same freedom that the scribe took with the manuscript he was copying—so long as the translator does not follow the practice of certain scribes in interpolating and excising portions of the text.

J. N. C.

CONTENTS

Foreword **vii**

Preface **ix**

Introduction **xv**

From Camelot to Joyous Guard

I

The Tournament of Winchester   3

II

The Wound and the Maid   14

III

The Queen's Anger   22

IV

Tourneying and Recovery   27

V

Morgan   38

VI

Love and Anguish   45

VII

Poisoned Fruit and a Wound   51

VIII

Death, Rescue, and Reconciliation   59

IX

Adultery and Rescue   72

X

Preparations for War   86

XI

Joyous Guard   92

XII

Parting   102

XIII
Invasion   **109**
XIV
Treason   **114**
XV
Gaunes   **120**
XVI
The Duel   **126**
XVII
From War to War   **135**
XVIII
The Last Campaign   **148**
XIX
The Death of King Arthur   **161**

INTRODUCTION

From the chronicle of Geoffrey of Monmouth to the chronicle-romance of Wace and the poems of Chrétien de Troyes, Arthurian literature had an auspicious infancy and came quickly to maturity. But in a number of ways the most remarkable monument of the Arthurian corpus was the vast prose cycle of the thirteenth century. Variously known as the Prose *Lancelot*, the Lancelot-Grail, the pseudo-Map Cycle, or the Vulgate Version of Arthurian Romance, it is impressive by size alone: in the text published by Sommer, it runs to several thousand pages in quarto format.[1] A long work is not necessarily a good work, of course, but in this case the quality and the historical importance of the cycle make it well worth the patience and the considerable time it demands of readers.

The Lancelot-Grail Cycle

The cycle comprises five separate but related works: the *Estoire del Saint Graal,* a *Merlin* romance and its sequel, the *Lancelot* proper, the *Queste del Saint Graal,* and *La Mort le Roi Artu* (or *Mort Artu*). The authorship of these works has long been a subject of controversy, scholars having dismissed as false their attribution, made in the text itself, to Walter Map. Refuting the suggestion that the cycle was the work of an indefinite number of writers, Ferdinand Lot contended that a single author composed the entire Prose *Lancelot* within a period of four or five years. He was forced to such a conclusion partly by the precise chronology at work throughout the romances, partly by the narrative unity achieved in the cycle by the use of the technique he called *entrelacement.* This term designates a method of composition (since recognized as quite usual in medieval narrative) whereby uncompleted themes disappear from the work, only to reappear later, perhaps several times, often after hundreds of pages. As a result, an elaborate web of connections extends throughout the cycle, not only backward, as the text refers to earlier themes or epi-

---

[1] The editions and studies referred to in this introduction (with the exception of Carman's, for which see n. 2) are documented in my Bibliographical Note.

sodes, but also forward, in anticipation of things to come. All these narrative threads are woven so skillfully through the romances and kept so carefully separate that to Lot it seemed that it could only have been done by a single person. Later, after further contributions by other scholars (like Pauphilet, who distinguished the authorship of the *Queste* from that of the other romances), Jean Frappier proposed the theory now accepted, at least in its broad outlines, by most scholars. He posited the existence of a person whom he calls the "Architect" of the cycle, who planned and outlined the last three romances and who was probably the author of much or all of the *Lancelot* proper. The composition of the *Queste* and the *Mort Artu* conformed generally to the plan established by the Architect. The *Estoire* and the *Merlin* were not part of the original plan; they were composed later and then added to the beginning of the cycle, perhaps much in the same way that poets impressed by the exploits (and the literary success) of an epic hero would invent the story of his youth. As Frappier put it, the *Estoire* was a late addition which "supplied a portico for the edifice."

More recently, J. Neale Carman developed a detailed hypothesis concerning the "Master Plan" of the cycle, the changes it underwent, and the persons responsible for it. According to his hypothesis,

> . . . the romances of the cycle were written by authors debating the value of courtly love, under the patronage of powerful figures, probably Eleanor of Aquitaine about 1200, and later the Marshal family. As outlined from the beginning, the Prose *Lancelot* proper was to be the work of writers convinced of the value of courtly love, and the *Queste* and the *Mort Artu* of men ready to show it as evil—destructive first spiritually and then socially. The latter part of the *Lancelot*, though written by the champions of courtly love, was to introduce the machinery needed for the two later romances. Under the superintendence of the patrons, a number of the authors probably worked out together a plan which all followed, though their work may have been done in scattered places and at different times. Thus, the last part of the *Lancelot* may have been written before or after the other two romances, the *Queste* before or after the *Mort Artu*. Their agreement was caused by the plan that they were instructed to follow; their disagreements arose from the need of filling out details, from imperfect understanding of the provisions of the plan, and from some rebellions (though not usually to the point of rejecting

outer conformity). The plan was fuller at some points than others, sometimes sketchy, sometimes quite detailed.[2]

Despite the usefulness of the theories mentioned here, the question of authorship remains largely unresolved. Inspiration, tone, style, and in some cases fact vary from romance to romance, and it seems clear that we owe the Vulgate Cycle to several authors. They remain nameless, but their identity is less important for our present purposes than the way they worked, adding muscle and flesh to a narrative skeleton given them by one or more planners.

La Mort le Roi Artu

The work presented in this volume as *From Camelot to Joyous Guard* is *La Mort le Roi Artu*, the conclusion, composed around 1230, of the Lancelot-Grail Cycle. Readers will find it to be a work of remarkable unity, economy, and directness, with very few digressions from the author's theme—the destruction of Arthur and the Round Table. The author conceived of his subject primarily in dramatic terms, with events linked tightly together in an inexorable cause-and-effect relationship. Moreover, the author transfers emphasis from courtly conventions and traditional patterns of behavior to a mature and often penetrating literary psychology, examining characters' motives and reactions and depicting events which result from the interplay of strong passions.

It is in the *Mort Artu* that the various threads from the earlier romances are tied up. This was a complex task, and one aspect of it will illustrate the author's method. The author was following the direction set by the other parts of the cycle, but he also had to deal with the accounts of Arthur's downfall offered earlier by Geoffrey and Wace. He easily and expertly welded the two accounts together, thus remaining faithful to both while offering a coherent explanation for the fall. His solution, as Frappier has pointed out, was to offer both a distant and an immediate cause for the ruin of the Round Table: it was brought about specifically, as in the chronicles, by Mordred's treason, but it is ultimately due to the illicit passion which existed between Lancelot and Guenevere and which eventually worked its destructive influence on their entire world.

---

[2] See the final chapter of his *A Study of the Pseudo-Map Cycle of Arthurian Romance* (Lawrence: The University Press of Kansas, 1973). The major elaboration of his hypothesis, however, and the quotation given here are from unpublished notes for a study of the cycle. The passage quoted is from an introductory paragraph and cannot suggest the preciseness of his conclusions. I nonetheless considered his ideas sufficiently important to make general reference to them here.

It has been suggested by some that the author's language and style were not equal to his vision. His rhetorical and lexical range is admittedly not wide, and the reader may frequently be bothered by his repetitions. In some cases, a character's reactions may strike us as being unrealistically bland; for example, when Arthur is told of Lancelot's and Guenevere's sin, he becomes pale, responds that "ce sont merveilles," and falls silent. Nothing more. And after their long, passionate, and tragic love affair, Lancelot's reaction to Queen Guenevere's death is noted in a single sentence (he was "most grieved and tormented"), before the poet turns his attention to other matters. Frappier admits that the style of the *Mort Artu* can be dignified and dramatic, but he finds it frequently monotonous, and he concludes that "this 'Twilight of the Gods' needs all the resources of an orchestra and the thunder-peal of organs; one has to be content with a flute." Many readers will doubtless share his judgment, but perhaps we should not go quite as far as he in criticizing this low-keyed Twilight of the Gods. Restraint and understatement are capable of conveying a sense of urgency and tragedy; the author obviously preferred the persuasive force of the drama itself to the emotive power of rhetoric. He clearly was *not* a master stylist, and it is easy to wish that he were; but his economy of narration and his strong sense of the dramatic go far toward creating, in the *Mort Artu*, an admirable and effective conclusion to the history of the Arthurian world.

Early History of Lancelot

It is a peculiar characteristic of Arthurian literature that much of it, whether in the poems of Chrétien de Troyes or in later romances, is not really about Arthur. The king and the Arthurian court provide a focal point for the narration and a standard of conduct for the knights, but it is someone else's story. So is it with the *Mort Artu:* as the title predicts, we will hear of the king's death, but in reality, the romance is a continuation of the story of Lancelot. In fact, the last sentence of the *Mort Artu* identifies the entire cycle as the *Estoire de Lancelot*.

As I have suggested, the romances of the cycle are separate and, to a degree, self-contained, and readers who approach the *Mort Artu* without having read the romances which precede it generally have little difficulty following the events of the last days of the Round Table. Nonetheless, narrative and thematic threads attach this work to the others, and it may be helpful to offer here a quick summary of Lancelot's early history.[3]

---

[3] Professor Carman's manuscript preserved notes on this subject, apparently intended to serve as part of the preface or introduction. For that reason, and for the sake of convenience, I have edited and completed them for use here.

Lancelot of the Lake was the son of Ban, King of Benwick. Just before his death, Ban lost his kingdom, as did his brother, the ruler of the adjoining kingdom of Gaunes. Much later King Arthur's forces regained both kingdoms for their rightful heirs, so that in the *Mort Artu* these kingdoms (in what became Western France) were the possessions of Lancelot and his cousins, Lionel and Bohort. King Ban also had a bastard son, Hector, who was thus Lancelot's half-brother. Throughout the *Mort Artu* these four, Lancelot, Bohort, Lionel, and Hector, are a firm group, often referred to as the "kindred of Ban."

Lancelot was the first to come to the kingdom of Logres (that is, England) to join King Arthur and the knights of the Round Table. There he received knighthood as a youth, and as a youth he was stricken with love for Queen Guenevere. His first exploit, which established him as "the best knight in the world," was his taking of the castle of Dolorous Guard, which he renamed Joyous Guard. The castle remained his permanent possession. When he took it, one of the marvels that he accomplished was the raising of the tombstone under which he was to be buried.

Lancelot's love for Guenevere was for a long time only distant worship. It was still in that state when Galeholt, Lord of the Distant Isles, became his fast friend. The friendship was so great that when Galeholt was about to conquer King Arthur, Lancelot was able to persuade him instead to become Arthur's liege man. It was through their friendship, also, that Galeholt brought Guenevere and Lancelot together. Even after the first kiss, there was a delay before the fateful adultery was accomplished. The love, which would go on undiscovered into the time of the *Mort Artu*, became more feverish as time passed, but Lancelot and Guenevere never lost the affection and admiration they had for Arthur.

At one point there appeared at court a woman who claimed to be Guenevere and whose wiles were such that she convinced Arthur. Guenevere was sent away with Lancelot to Galeholt's kingdom. The wrath of God destroyed the False Guenevere; the Pope, through the Archbishop of Canterbury, made Arthur take back his mate, and he was content with her.

Lancelot remained always faithful to Guenevere, though other women loved him. Once, however, he did lie with the daughter of the rich Fisher King, after being tricked into thinking she was Guenevere. The result of this deception was Galahad, the perfect grail knight. The Fisher King himself, Lord of the Grail Castle, was a party to the trickery that put Lancelot into his daughter's bed.

The great knight Gawain, King Arthur's nephew, figured at an early point in the history of Lancelot, but we hear of his brothers only shortly

before the episode that produced Galahad. There were four of them be-
sides Gawain, all sons of King Arthur's sister, the wife of King Lot.
Guerrehet is never a striking figure in the story. The virtues of Gaheriet,
Gawain's favorite among them, are evident from the start. Agravain is
not presented as entirely admirable, but he did nothing venomous until
he became a spy in the final romance. Though not all Mordred's acts are
bad, we learn that he is the great villain before the *Mort Artu* begins. His
most despicable act was the murder of the hermit who told him that
Arthur had fathered him incestuously and who predicted his future role.

Arthur had another relative worthy of condemnation—his sister
Morgan the Fay, who by turns, or perhaps simultaneously, loved and hated
Lancelot. The latter resisted her blandishments and was her victim at
times. Once she had him imprisoned, whereupon to pass the time he
painted the history of his love for Guenevere on the walls of his chamber.
The details of this event are repeated in the *Mort Artu*.

When Galahad reached the age to be knighted by his father, the
quest of the Holy Grail began. During the grail hero's short lifetime
(which ended soon after he achieved the grail), he was "the best knight
in the world," but after his death, that title returned to Lancelot, who held
it throughout the *Mort Artu*. During the quest of the grail, events
showed Gawain to be a great knight with a generous soul, but flawed and
sinful; Lancelot was brought to a sense of the sinfulness of his adultery,
was truly repentant, and fell from grace only when he returned to court
at the beginning of the *Mort Artu*.

Bibliographical Note

The text of the entire cycle was made available, though not in a true
critical edition, by the publication, in seven volumes, of H. O. Sommer's
The Vulgate Version of the Arthurian Romances (Washington: The
Carnegie Institution, 1908–1916); volume VI contains the *Mort Artu*.
Editions of the *Mort Artu* were prepared by J. D. Bruce (Halle: Nie-
meyer, 1910) and by Jean Frappier (Paris: Droz, 1936; 3rd edition,
Geneva, 1964).

The two volumes of Bruce's *The Evolution of Arthurian Romance,
from the Beginnings down to the Year 1300* (Gloucester, Mass.: Peter
Smith, 2nd ed., 1928; reprinted 1958) provide a useful study of much of
Arthurian literature; part III (ch. 3–6) treats the Vulgate Cycle. Another
comprehensive treatment of the Arthurian matter, this time in the form
of a "collaborative history," is *Arthurian Literature in the Middle Ages*,
ed. R. S. Loomis (Oxford: Clarendon Press, 1959). Jean Frappier pre-

pared the section on the Vulgate Cycle, which constitutes ch. 22 of the work. Among the major critical examinations of the cycle and the *Mort Artu* are Ferdinand Lot's *Etude sur le Lancelot en prose* (Paris: Champion, 1918) and Frappier's *Etude sur la Mort Artu*, published by Droz (Geneva) in 1961. Frappier's *Etude*, among other works, will prove more than adequate as a source of additional bibliographical information.

Translator's Source

The present translation was based on the critical edition prepared by Jean Frappier and published by Droz. Specifically, Professor Carman worked from the second edition (1954), which incorporates some corrections and slight modifications but otherwise reproduces the 1936 text.

Concordance

Unlike the Carman translation, which is divided into nineteen major sections or chapters, Frappier's critical edition of the Old French text is composed of 204 shorter sections, varying in length from a brief paragraph to several pages. The following table will assist the reader of this translation who wishes to consult the corresponding passage in the original. The Roman numerals designate the chapters of the English version; the Arabic figures identify Frappier's section numbers (*not* his pages). In some cases where the Carman chapters begin after the first line of the corresponding section in French, the correct line number is given.

Carman's Chapter	*Frappier's Section*
I. The Tournament of Winchester	1
II. The Wound and the Maid	22
III. The Queen's Anger	31
IV. Tourneying and Recovery	37
V. Morgan	48
VI. Love and Anguish	55
VII. Poisoned Fruit and a Wound	62
VIII. Death, Rescue, and Reconciliation	70
IX. Adultery and Rescue	85, l. 20
X. Preparations for War	98
XI. Joyous Guard	107
XII. Parting	117
XIII. Invasion	124, l. 7
XIV. Treason	134
XV. Gaunes	144

XVI. The Duel   147, l. 26
XVII. From War to War   159
XVIII. The Last Campaign   176
XIX. The Death of King Arthur   191, l. 2

FROM CAMELOT
TO JOYOUS GUARD

I
The Tournament of Winchester

After Master Walter Map had put into writing the *Adventures of the Holy Grail* as completely as seemed proper to him, his lord King Henry opined that what he had done was not enough, unless he recorded the end of those whom he had brought to mind, how those had died whose prowess he had celebrated in his book. And therefore he began this last part. And when he had assembled it, he called it *The Death of King Arthur*, because at its end it related how King Arthur was wounded at the Battle of Salisbury and how he parted from Girflet, who remained in his company so long that after him there was no man who saw the king alive, and Master Walter begins thus this last part.

When Bohort had come to court within the city of Camelot from such distant lands as are the areas of Jerusalem, he found many there who greeted him with great joy, for all the knights and ladies greatly desired to see him. And when he had related Galahad's demise and the death of Perceval, all those at court were grief-stricken, but took comfort as best they could. Then the king caused to be set down in writing all the adventures that the fellowship in the quest of the Holy Grail had told at court; and when he had done this, he said: "Lords, look among you to see how many of your companions we have lost in this quest." And they looked about at once, and found that by count they lacked thirty-two, and of all these there was not one who had not died in combat.

The king had heard a report that Sir Gawain had killed many; so he had him come before him and he said to him:

"Gawain, I require of you by the oath you made me when I knighted you that you tell what I shall ask."

"Sire," said Sir Gawain, "you have pressed me so urgently that I would in no wise fail to answer you even if it were to my shame, the greatest which ever befell a knight of your court."

"Now I ask you how many knights you believe that you have killed in this quest."

Sir Gawain stood in thought a little, and the king said again:

3

"By my head, I wish to know, because some go about saying that you have killed so many that it is a marvel."

"Sire," said Sir Gawain, "you wish to be certain of my great misfortune; I shall tell you, for I see I must. I tell you truly that with my hand I killed eighteen, not that I was a better knight than any other, but misfortune turned more upon me than upon any of my companions. Know well that it was not because of my knightly qualities, but because of my sin; now, you have made me tell my shame."

"Truly, fair nephew," said the king, "this was in fact a real misfortune, and I know well that it befell you because of your sins. But still tell me whether you think you slew King Baudemagu."

"Sire," he said, "I killed him, there is no denying it. I have never done aught that pained me so."

"Truly, fair nephew, if it pains you, it is no wonder. So help me God, I am much afflicted, for by his loss my household is weakened more than by that of four of the best who died in the quest."

King Arthur spoke these words concerning King Baudemagu, whereby Gawain was much more discomfited than he had been before.

The king, seeing that the adventures of the kingdom of Logres were so nearly completed that very little more could happen, had a tournament cried on the meadows at Winchester, because he in no way wished that his knights should give up bearing arms.

Now, though Lancelot had behaved chastely by the counsel of the holy man to whom he had confessed when he was in quest of the Holy Grail, and though he had completely renounced Queen Guenevere, as the tale has related before, as soon as he had come to court, not one month passed before he was smitten and inflamed as much as he had ever been at any time, so that he fell back into sin with the queen just as he had done earlier. And if he had before carried on that sin so prudently and secretly that no one had perceived it, now he behaved with such folly that Agravain, Sir Gawain's brother, who had never loved him and watched his goings and comings more closely than any other, perceived it. He paid such great heed, that he found out the whole truth, that Lancelot loved the queen with sinful love, and the queen loved him too.

The queen was so beautiful that all marveled, for at that time, when she was a good fifty years old, she was so fair a lady that in the whole world one could not have found her equal; wherefore there were knights who said, because her beauty never failed her, that she was the fount of all beauty.

When Agravain had learned about the queen and Lancelot, he was most joyful, more because of the harm that he thought would come to

Lancelot from it than because he might take vengeance for the king's shame. It happened that this was the week during which the tournament was to take place at Winchester; King Arthur's knights went there in great numbers. But Lancelot, who had a desire to be there in such a way that no one should know him, said to those who were around him that he was so ill that he could not go there at all, but he wished Bohort and Hector and Lionel to go and the knights of their company. They answered that they would not go, since he was so ill. He said to them:

"I desire and command you to go; you will depart in the morning, and I will stay behind."

"My lord," they said, "since it is your pleasure, we shall go; but we should have liked to stay with you to keep you company."

He said that he did not wish them to do so. So they said nothing further.

The next morning Bohort and his company left the city of Camelot. When Agravain learned that Bohort and his knights were going and Lancelot was staying, he thought at once that it was because he wished to go in to the queen when they had left. Then he went to his uncle the king and said:

"Sire, I would give you a piece of advice if I did not think it would grieve you. Know that I speak so as to avenge your shame."

"My shame?" said the king. "Is it so serious a matter as to concern my shame?"

"Yes, sire," said Agravain, "and I will tell you how." Then he drew him aside and said into his ear: "Sire, the fact is that Lancelot loves the queen with sinful love and the queen loves him. Because they cannot come together at will when you are here, Lancelot is staying behind, and will not go the tournament at Winchester; instead he has sent his retinue, so that when you have left tonight or tomorrow he may at his good leisure speak to the queen."

On hearing these words, King Arthur could not believe them true, rather he believed it must be a lie, and answered:

"Agravain, fair nephew, never say such a thing, for I would not believe it, for I know well that Lancelot would not think of it at all, and if he ever thought it, the force of love made him do so, against which reason and good sense can never hold out."

"What, sire!" said Agravain, "you will do nothing more?"

"What do you wish me to do?"

"Sire, I should like you to have him watched until they can be caught together; then you would know the truth, and would believe me more readily another time."

"Do as you like," said the king, "for you will not be thwarted by me."
Agravain said that he asked nothing more.

That night Arthur thought much of what Agravain had said, but he did not take it greatly to heart, for he could not easily believe that it was true. In the morning he prepared to go to the tournament and bade numerous knights to bear him company. The queen said to him:

"Sire, I should be glad to go see this tourney if it were your pleasure; indeed, going would please me a great deal, for I have heard there will be many knightly deeds."

"My lady," said the king, "this time you will not go." So she said no more. He had her stay behind on purpose to test Agravain's lie.

When the king had set out with his companions to go to the tournament, they talked much among themselves of Lancelot, and said that he would not go now to this meeting. Lancelot, as soon as he knew that the king and those who were bound for Winchester had set out, rose from his bed, made ready, went to the queen and said to her:

"My lady, if you were willing to allow it, I would go to this tournament."

"Why," she asked, "did you stay behind the others?"

"My lady," he said, "because I wanted to go all alone and come to the tournament in such wise that neither strangers nor those close to me would know me."

"Go ahead then," she said, "if you like; I am willing."

He departed forthwith from her presence, went back to his residence and remained there till night.

In the evening, when night had fallen, as soon as all were abed in the city of Camelot, Lancelot came to his squire and said to him:

"You must mount and ride with me, for I wish to go see the tournament at Winchester. We shall travel only at night, for on no account should I be willing to be recognized along the way."

The squire carried out his commands; he got ready as fast as he could, and brought out Lancelot's best horse, for he saw that his lord wished to bear arms in this tournament. When they were out of Camelot and had got on the right road to Winchester, they rode all night without ever resting.

The next day, when it was light, they came to a castle where the king had lain that night, and Lancelot stopped there only because he did not wish to ride in the daytime, lest perchance he be recognized. When he came up close to the castle, he rode with his head down so low that he could hardly be known; he did this because of the king's knights who were issuing from within; he was very sorry that he had arrived so soon.

6

King Arthur, who was still leaning on a window sill, saw Lancelot's horse. He recognized it as one that he had given him, but he did not recognize Lancelot, for his head was down too low. Nonetheless, in the castle town at a crossing in the street, where Lancelot raised his head, the king looked at him and saw who he was, and pointed him out to Girflet.

"Did you see Lancelot, who yesterday gave us to understand that he was ill, and now he is here at this castle?"

"Sire," said Girflet, "I will tell you why he did it; he wishes to be at this tournament without anyone's knowing him; that is why he did not want to come with us, be very sure of that."

And Lancelot, who was unaware of all this, was already well inside the castle town with his squire and had entered a house, and had forbidden his man to name him to anyone there, if anyone should ask who he was.

The king, who was still at the window waiting for Lancelot to go by, remained there until he was sure that Lancelot had stayed in the town. Then he said to Girflet:

"We have lost Lancelot, for he has already taken shelter."

"Sire," said Girflet, "that may well be. Know that he is riding only at night so as not to be recognized."

"Since he wishes to hide, let us conceal him, too; take care to tell no mortal man that you have seen him on this road, and I shall not speak of it. Thus he can well be hidden, for only we two have seen him."

Girflet swore that he would never speak of it.

So the king quitted the window and departed with his retinue, and Lancelot stayed behind in the residence of a well-to-do gentleman who had two sons, very strong and handsome, newly knighted by King Arthur's own hand. And Lancelot looked at the knights' two shields and saw that they were solid vermilion without emblems upon them. It was then the custom that no new knight, during the first year after he had received the order of knighthood, should bear a shield that was not all one color; if he did otherwise, it was against his code. Then Lancelot said to the lord of the manor:

"Sir, I should like to beg of you as a favor that you lend me one of the shields to bear at that meet at Winchester along with its covering and all its fittings too."

"Sir," said the gentleman, "have you no shield?"

"None that I wish to bear," he said; "for if I bore it, it might be recognized sooner than I wished; rather I will leave mine here with you and my arms, too, until I come back this way."

The worthy man said at once: "Take whatever you like, sir, for by

7

chance one of my sons is so ill that he cannot bear arms at this tournament, but the other will set out at any moment to go there."

At these words the knight who was to go to the meet came in. And when he saw Lancelot, he showed him a warm countenance, because he seemed to him a man of merit, and he asked him who he was. Lancelot told him that he was a knight from a foreign land neighboring the kingdom of Logres, but he never would tell him his name, nor discovered aught else to him about his background, but he told him that he was going to the assembly at Winchester and that on that account he had come to this place.

"Sir," said the knight, "it has turned out well for you, for I too wished to go there; now we will travel together and bear each other company."

"Sir," said Lancelot, "I would not ride by day, for the heat then does me hurt, but if you desired to wait until evening, I would bear you company; however, in no wise would I ride before nightfall."

"Sir," said the knight, "you seem to me a man of such valor that I will do all you like; I will tarry all day for love of you, and forthwith, at whatever hour you please, we will go off together."

Lancelot thanked him much for his company.

That day he remained there and was served and made comfortable with all that one can honor and serve an esteemed man. The people who lived there asked him much about himself; but they could never find out anything except what the squire told the host's daughter, who was very beautiful and inquired of him insistently who his master was. He, who saw her of such great beauty, did not wish to hide everything from her because that would seem churlish on his part, and so he said to her:

"My lady, I cannot reveal all to you, for I should perjure myself and might anger my master, but without fail what I can discover to you without a misdeed, I will tell you. Know that the knight is the best in the world, I give you my word loyally."

"God be my witness," said the maiden; "you have told me much and have satisfied me with those words."

Then the maiden came straightway to Lancelot, knelt before him and said:

"Noble knight, give me a boon by the faith you owe her whom you love best."

And when Lancelot saw on her knees before him so beautiful a damsel and so attractive as this one was, it was a matter of sore regret to him, and he said to her:

"Ah! young lady, rise to your feet. Know truly there is nothing on

8

earth that I can do that I would not do at your request, for you have conjured me too warmly."

She rose at once, and said to him: "Sir, a hundred thousand thanks for your consent. And do you know what you have granted me? You have consented to wear at this tournament my right sleeve instead of another insignia, and you will do deeds of arms for love of me."

When Lancelot heard this request, he was greatly downcast and still he did not dare contradict her, since he had given his word. Nevertheless, he was much grieved at what he had granted, for he knew well that if the queen learned of it, she would bear him such a great grudge because of it that he would never again find peace with her. But in spite of all, as he had promised, he would keep his word and take the risk, for otherwise he would be disloyal if he did not do for the damsel what he had covenanted with her. The damsel brought him the sleeve at once attached to a pennon and begged that he would do such deeds of arms at the tournament for love of her that she would consider her sleeve well employed.

"And know truly, sir," she said, "that you are the first knight of whom I ever made a request for anything, and I would not have made it, either, but for the great goodness that there is in you."

And he answered that for love of her he would do so much that he would never be blamed for it.

So Lancelot stayed all day there; in the evening, after dark, he left the gentleman's house, said goodbye to him and the damsel, had his squire carry away the shield that he had got there, and left his own. He and his company rode all night till the next day a little before sunrise they came to a spot near Winchester.

"Sir," said the knight to Lancelot, "where would you like us to put up?"

"If anyone," said Lancelot, "should know of some good quiet house near the tourneying grounds where we might be in privacy, I should think myself well cared for with it, for I had rather not go into Winchester."

"On my word," said the knight, "it has fallen out well for you; near here, off the highway, on the left, is a seat that belongs to my aunt, a gentlewoman who will give us good quarters and who will show great pleasure at seeing us in her house."

"On my word," said Lancelot, "I will go there gladly."

Soon they left the highway and went straight and quietly in the direction of the lady's house. And when they had alighted there and the lady saw it was her nephew, you never saw such great joy as she showed, for she had not seen him since he had become a new knight. She said to him, "Fair nephew, where have you been that I do not see you any more, and where did you leave your brother? Is he is not coming to this tournament?"

"No, aunt," he said, "he cannot, for we left him at home a little indisposed."

"And who," she said, "is this knight who has come with you?"

"So help me God, my aunt," he said, "I know not who he is except that he seems a noble man to me; because of the goodness that I think is in him, I will go in his company to the tournament tomorrow and we shall bear arms alike and horse trappings too."

The lady came at once to Lancelot, spoke him well and honored him, and presently took him to a room and had him lie down and rest on a very rich bed, for she had been told that he had ridden all night long. Lancelot was there throughout the day and had a great plenty of everything good. That night the squires looked after their master's arms to see that nothing was amiss. The next day, as soon as it was light, Lancelot rose and went to hear mass in the chapel of a hermit who had a shelter near there in a grove. When he had heard mass and said his prayers as Christian knights should, he came back to his lodgings, then breakfasted with his companion. Lancelot had sent his squire into Winchester to find out who would help those inside the town and who would be in the party from outside. The squire was so diligent in gathering the news and returning quickly that he was back at the manor before Lancelot had begun to arm himself. And when he came to his master, he said to him:

"Sir, there are a great many people both inside and out, for knights have come from all directions, those from afar as well as those of the company of the Round Table who are there."

"And do you know," said Lancelot, "which side Bohort and Lionel and Hector have taken?"

"Sir," he said, "with those within and rightfully, for otherwise they would not show that they were knights of the Round Table, if they were not on that side."

"And who is outside?" said Lancelot.

"Sir," the man said, "the king of Scotland, the king of Ireland, the king of Wales, the king of North Wales, and many other men of high degree, but still they do not have as good people as those within, for they are all foreigners gathered up from one place or another. They are not accustomed to bearing arms like the men from the kingdom of Logres, are not at all such good knights."

Then Lancelot mounted, and said to his squire: "You shall not come with me, for, if you came, you would be recognized, and through you I too would be known, and that I would not like at all."

And the squire said he would gladly stay behind since his master so desired; really he would have preferred to go along. Lancelot departed at once with his companion and two squires that the knight had brought with him. So they rode till they came to the Winchester meadow which was already covered with jousters, and the tournament was so far along that the two parties were assembled separately. But Sir Gawain did not bear arms that day nor Gaheriet, his brother. The king had forbidden them to do so, because he knew well that they would come and he did not wish them to wound one another if it should happen in the jousting, for he would have greatly disliked for fighting or bad feeling to arise between them.

The king with a great company of knights had climbed the town's main tower to see the tournament; with him was Sir Gawain and his brother Gaheriet. The knight who had come with Lancelot said to him:

"Sir, which side shall we help?"

Lancelot replied: "Which seems to you the one who may get the worst of it?"

"Sir," said the knight, "the people outside, it seems to me, for those inside are very valiant men and good knights and skilled in bearing arms."

"Then," said Lancelot, "let us be with those outside, for it would not redound to our honor if we helped those who have the best of it." And his companion said that he was quite ready to do whatever Lancelot advised him to do.

Then Lancelot bore down upon his stirrups and rode into the mass and struck the knight that he first came upon so hard that he brought both him and his horse to earth. He rushed on to carry through his thrust, for his spear was not yet broken, reached another knight and struck him so that neither shield nor hauberk kept him from receiving a deep, bad wound in his left side, but he was not mortally wounded. The blow went straight, and Lancelot brought him down from his horse to earth so hard that he was dazed by his fall; then the spear flew to pieces. At this blow many knights stopped in the tournament and some said that they had seen the new knight strike a splendid blow.

"True," the others said, " 'tis the best that the hand of any single man has dealt today, and he will not succeed today in dealing such another."

And Lancelot's comrade made a run at Hector des Mares, whom he encountered as he came on; he struck him so that he broke his spear in the middle of his chest, and Hector struck him with such strength with a short thick lance that he brought down in a heap both him and his horse.

"Now you can see on the ground one of the brothers from Escalot Castle," everyone said.

The brothers were known by the name of the castle wherever they appeared, because they bore arms alike, so that the people at the tournament thought for sure that Lancelot was one of the two brothers of Escalot, because of the arms that he bore. When Lancelot saw his host borne to earth so hard before him, he was greatly wroth; he let run at Hector and held a good strong lance, but they did not know each other because they had changed their arms to try to remain unknown at the tournament. And Lancelot hit Hector so hard with all his might that he brought him to earth before Galegantin the Welshman. Sir Gawain, who knew Hector well since he had given him his armor, when he saw the blow, said to the king:

"Sire, by my head, that knight with the vermilion arms who is wearing a sleeve on his helmet is not the knight that I thought he was; he is someone else instead."

"And who do you think he is?" said the king.

"I do not know, sire," said Sir Gawain, "but he is a very mighty man."

Lancelot succeeded in remounting his companion and in getting him out of the press where it was greatest. Bohort who came through the tournament bringing down knights, and wrenching helmets from heads and shields from necks, rode till he met Lancelot in the crowd. He did not greet him, since he did not know him; instead, he struck him so hard and mightily with a strong stiff spear that he pierced shield and hauberk, and put his spear tip into his right side, and made a great, deep wound there. He came with such force and so well settled in the saddle that he hit Lancelot so hard that he brought him and his horse to earth, and at his fall the spear broke. He did not stay down long. His horse was strong, quick, and agile and was soon up. His wound did not keep him from rising quickly and mounting his horse though sweating with pain and humiliation. And he said to himself that it was no boy who had brought him down; till then no grown man had ever been able to do as much. But if Lancelot ever had the chance, the stranger would never have done a kindness that would receive its recompense so soon.

Forthwith Lancelot took a short thick spear that one of his squires was holding and made off at once toward Bohort. Room was quickly made for them when the others on the lots saw that they wished to joust on equal terms; they had already done so well at the tournament that they were held to be the two best on the field. Lancelot, charging at as great a speed as he could get from his horse, struck Bohort so hard that he bore his horse to earth with the saddle over his rump, for the girths and breast strap broke. And Sir Gawain, who knew Bohort well, when he saw him on the ground, said to the king:

"Certainly, sire, if Bohort is down, he suffers no great shame, for he did not know what to expect, and that knight who has made those two runs against him and Hector is a good knight, and by my head, if we hadn't left Lancelot sick in Camelot, I should say that he was there."

When the king heard this speech, he divined at once that it was Lancelot. He began to smile and said to Sir Gawain:

"By my head, fair nephew, whoever the knight may be, he has begun very well, but I believe he will do still better later; that is my opinion."

Lancelot, as soon as he had broken his lance, drew his sword and began to give great blows right and left, and bring down and kill horses, and wrench shields from necks and helmets from heads, and do deeds of prowess on every hand, so that no one saw him who did not consider it a great marvel. On the other hand, Bohort and Hector, who had risen and mounted again, began to do so well that no one could blame them. And before everyone on the field they did knightly deeds so evident that most of those of their party took example from their boldness in doing doughty deeds so as to win the tournament. Those two kept making Lancelot back up and come out again, for they were always in front of him, and hemmed him in so that he had to pass between them; that day they deprived him of many a good blow. It was no marvel, for he was very badly wounded and had lost a great deal of blood so that he was not easily at the height of his power, and they were both knights of great prowess. Nevertheless, whether they liked it or not, he accomplished so much by his prowess that the knights from the city were beaten back inside, and on both sides he carried away the tournament prize. Those from within lost much, and those outside won much. And when time to conclude came, Sir Gawain said to the king:

"Upon my word, sire, I do not know who the knight is who is wearing that sleeve on his helmet, but I should say that he has rightfully won this tournament, and that he should have the prize and the praise. And be sure that I shall never rest easy until I know who he is, for to my mind he has done too many knightly deeds."

"Certainly," said Gaheriet, "I do not think I know him. But I say truly that he is, to my knowledge, the best knight in the world, the best that I have ever seen, except only Lancelot of the Lake."

Lancelot's comrades spoke thus, and Sir Gawain ordered his horse to be brought, for he would like to go find out who that knight was so as to make his acquaintance. Gaheriet said the same thing. Then they came down from the tower and into the courtyard. As soon as Lancelot saw

13

that those within had lost everything, he said to the knight who had come with him:

"Sir, let us depart, for we can gain nothing by staying longer."

So they set off at once, riding hard. They left dead on the grounds one of their squires whom a knight had killed with a spear by mischance. The knight asked Lancelot where he would like to go.

"I would like," he answered, "to be in a spot where I might stay a week or more, for I am so sorely wounded that riding might greatly hurt me."

"Well," said the knight, "let us go back to my aunt's, where we lay last night, for there we shall be quiet, and it is not far from here."

Lancelot agreed to the proposal. They turned off at once into a copse, for Lancelot thought that someone from the king's household would follow him to find out who he was, for a great many knights had seen him at the tourney, both knights of the Round Table and others. So he and the knight rode away fast with one of their squires, and went on till they came to the manor where they had lain the night before. Lancelot dismounted covered with blood, for he was sorely wounded. When the knight saw the wound, he was much dismayed. He sent with all possible speed for an old knight who lived nearby and who made a business of healing wounds and certainly knew more about it than anyone then in the country. When he had seen the wound, he said that he thought that with God's help he could cure Lancelot, but it would not be soon, for the wound was large and deep.

II
The Wound and the Maid

So Lancelot found help for his wound, which was very fortunate for him, for if he had long delayed, he might well have died. Because of this wound that he had received at the hand of Bohort, his cousin, he lay six weeks where he was so ill that he could not bear arms nor leave the manor. But now the tale ceases to speak of him and goes back to telling of Sir Gawain and Gaheriet.

At this point the tale tells that when Sir Gawain and Gaheriet had mounted to follow the knight who had won at the tournament, they rode in the direction that they thought he had taken. When they had ridden two English leagues at such great speed that they would certainly have overtaken him if the knight and his companion had gone that way, they met two squires who were lamenting as they came and carrying in their arms a knight newly slain. Sir Gawain and Gaheriet rode straight up to them and asked if they had met two knights with vermilion arms of whom one was wearing on his helmet a lady's or damsel's sleeve. They answered that they had seen no knight armed in the way they described, but they had seen other knights coming from the tournament in great plenty.

"Sir," said Gaheriet to Sir Gawain, his brother, "you can now be sure that they did not come this way. If they had come by here, we would have caught up with them some time ago, for we have been riding fast."

"I am very sorry," said Sir Gawain, "that we are not finding them. I tell you so quite sincerely, for he is of a surety such a good knight and a man of such merit that I would have greatly liked to make his acquaintance, and if I had him here with me now, I should certainly never stop until I had brought him to Lancelot of the Lake, so as to acquaint them with each other."

Then they asked the squires who it was that they were carrying.

"Sir," they said, "he was a knight."

"And who wounded him in such a way?"

"Sir," said the squires, "a wild boar that he came upon on the edge of this forest." And they pointed to it a league away.

"On my word," said Gaheriet, "that is bad, for he has the appearance of a man who might have been a good knight."

Thereupon they left the squires and returned to Winchester. It was already dark night when they arrived. When the king saw Sir Gawain back, he asked at once if he had found the knight.

"No," said Sir Gawain, "no, we did not, for he took a different road from the one we followed."

At once the king began to smile, and Sir Gawain looked at him and said:

"Fair uncle, this is not the first time that you have laughed about it."

The king answered, "It is not the first time that you have looked for him, and it will not be the last, I am sure."

Then Sir Gawain perceived that the king knew him.

"Ah, sire, since you know him, you might tell who he is, if you please."

"Right now," said the king, "I shall not tell you, for since he wishes to conceal who he is, I would be downright base if I revealed his secret to you or anybody else. Therefore, my lips are sealed for the moment. You will lose naught thereby, for in good time you will know him."

"On my word," said Galegantin the Welshman, "I know not who he is, but this much I can tell you truly; he left the tournament very badly wounded and bleeding so that one could follow him by the red trail. The blood was flowing in a constant stream from a wound that Sir Bohort made in him while jousting."

"Is that really so?" asked the king.

"Sire," answered Galegantin, "yes; know it for the truth."

"Now know well," said the king to Bohort, "that you never made a wound in a knight during your whole life that you will ever repent of as you will of this one, and if he dies of it, unhappy the day you saw him."

Hector, who thought that the king had spoken out of ill will toward Bohort, sprang forward angry and full of resentment, and said to the king:

"Sire, if the knight dies, let him die. It is sure that no evil or cause of fear can come to us from his death."

The king made no reply; he began to smile, greatly pained and troubled that Lancelot had left the tournament wounded, for he was much afraid that he was in peril of death.

They spoke much that evening of the Knight of the Sleeve who had won at the tournament, and they were very desirous of knowing who he was. But that could not be, for they were not then to know more. The king concealed his knowledge so well within him that no news on this score was uttered from his mouth before they returned to Camelot. The next day they left Winchester; before leaving they had a tournament cried for Monday a month later at Tanebourc. That Tanebourc was a very strong castle very well situated at the entrance to North Wales. When the king left Winchester, he rode till he came to the castle named Escalot, that same castle where he had seen Lancelot. The king lodged in the fortress of the castle with a great company of knights. But by chance it fell out that Sir Gawain stayed in the house where Lancelot had lain, and they made his bed in the very room where Lancelot's shield hung. Sir Gawain did not go to court that evening, for he was a little ill; instead, he and his brother Gaheriet ate at his lodgings, also Mordred, and there were other knights with them to bear him company. And when they had sat down to supper, the damsel who had given Lancelot the sleeve asked Sir Gawain all about the tournament, if it had been good and well fought. Sir Gawain said to her,

"Fair damsel, I can tell you truly that it was the best-fought tournament that I have seen this long time. A knight won it whom I should like to resemble, for he is the most valiant man whom I have seen since I left Camelot. But I know not who he is, nor what his name is."

"My lord," asked the damsel, "what arms did the knight bear who won the tournament?"

"Fair damsel," answered Sir Gawain, "some that were all vermilion, and he had on his helmet a sleeve from I do not know what lady or damsel. I can tell you truly that, if I were a maid, I would wish the sleeve to be mine provided that he who wore the sleeve might be my lover, for never on any day of my life have I seen a sleeve better employed than that one was."

When the maiden heard this speech, she was very joyful, but she did not dare show her joy because of those before her. While the knights sat at table, the damsel served, for it was the custom at that time in the kingdom of Logres that if knights errant came to the home of some man of high degree, and if there was a damsel in this house, the nobler she was, the more it behooved her to serve them and not to sit at table until they had all had their food. And the damsel was so beautiful and so well made in every respect that no maid could be better. Sir Gawain looked upon her gladly as she served, and it seemed to him that the knight would be born lucky who with such a maid might have delight and satisfaction at will.

In the evening after supper it turned out that the lord of the place went to enjoy himself in a bit of meadow behind his house, and took his daughter with him. And when he arrived there, he found Sir Gawain and his company who were taking their pleasure there. They rose as he came up. Sir Gawain had him sit on his right and the maiden on his left; then they began to talk of many things. And Gaheriet drew their host away from Sir Gawain and began to question him on the customs of the castle, and the other told him all about them, and Mordred drew apart so that Sir Gawain might speak to the maiden if it pleased him. When Sir Gawain saw himself so placed that he could speak to the maiden, he spoke and begged for her love. She asked him who he was.

"I am," he said, "a knight; my name is Gawain and I am King Arthur's nephew. If it pleased you, I should love you in such a manner that, as long as our love endured, I should love no lady or damsel but you, and I would be your knight completely and ready to do your every wish."

"Ha! Sir Gawain," said the damsel, "do not joke so. I know well that you are too rich and powerful a man to love a damsel as poor as I. Nevertheless, if you fell in love with me now, I would be more sorry on your account than for any other reason."

"Damsel," asked Sir Gawain, "why would you be sorry on my account?"

"My lord," she replied, "because, if you so loved me so that your heart would break, you could not reach me in any way, for I love a knight whom I would not betray for anything in the world. I tell you truly that I am still a virgin and never had I loved until I saw him. But at once I fell in love with him, and asked him to do feats of arms at that tournament, and he said he would. He has done so much, out of his gracious-

17

ness, that people would rightfully shame the damsel who would leave him to take you; for he is no less a good knight than you, nor is he less a man of merit, and I do not say so to displease you. So, know that it would be pains wasted to ask for love from me, for I would do nothing for any knight in the world except for him whom I love with all my heart and will love every day of my life."

When Sir Gawain heard her who so proudly rebuffed him he answered, greatly vexed:

"Fair damsel, out of courtesy and for love of me, bring it about that I can prove in combat with him that I handle arms better than he. If I can conquer him with my weapons, leave him and take me."

"What, sir knight," she answered "do you think that I will behave so? Thus, I might cause the death of two of the most valiant men in the world."

"What, damsel," said Sir Gawain, "is he then one of the most valiant men in the world?"

"My lord," said the damsel, "not long ago I heard someone testify he was the best knight in the world."

"Damsel," asked Sir Gawain, "what is your friend's name?"

"My lord," the damsel answered, "I shall not tell you his name, but I will show you his shield which he left when he went to the tourney at Winchester."

"I should like to see the shield," he said, "for if he is a knight of the prowess that you say, I cannot help knowing him by his shield."

"You will see the shield," she said, "when you like, for it hangs in the room in front of the bed in which you will be tonight."

He replied that then in that case he would see it very soon. Then he rose at once and so did the others, when they saw that Sir Gawain wished to leave. He took the maiden by the hand and they entered the house; the others followed. And the maiden led him into the room where there was so much light and such an illumination from candles and torches that the whole chamber seemed afire. And she immediately showed him the shield and said to him:

"My lord, there is the shield that belongs to the man whom I love most in the world. Now look to see if you know him so as to learn if you could agree that he is the best knight in the world."

Sir Gawain looked at the shield and recognized that it belonged to Lancelot of the Lake. And he stepped back aghast and grieved at the words which he had said to the maiden, for he was afraid lest Lancelot should find it out. Still, if he could make his peace with the damsel he would consider himself well off.

"Damsel, for God's sake, do not take to heart what I have said, for in this matter I surrender. I grant you that you are right. And know that he whom you love is the best knight in the world, for there is no damsel in the world, however much she loved me, who would not, rightfully, leave me and cling to him. For he is a better knight than I am and handsomer and more attractive and a man of greater merit. If I had thought that it was he and that you had the courage to love one of such high station, certainly, I should never have dared to love you or to ask for your love. And yet I tell you truly that you are the damsel whom I would most have wished to love me, if there had not been so great an obstacle as there is. And certainly if it is true that Sir Lancelot loves you as much as I think you love him, never did a lady or damsel have such a treasure of love; and for God's sake, I beg you, if I have said aught that displeases you, to pardon me."

"Sir," she said, "gladly."

When Sir Gawain saw that the maiden had given her word not to tell Lancelot or anyone else anything that he had said, he said to her:

"I beg you to tell me what arms Sir Lancelot was bearing in the tournament at Winchester."

"Sir," she said, "he bore a vermilion shield with horse trappings of the same color and had on his helmet a silken sleeve that I gave him out of love."

"By my head, damsel," said Sir Gawain, "that is a good description, for he was there and I saw him there, just as you have described, and I am now more convinced that he loves you than I ever was before, for otherwise he would not have worn such a token. It is my opinion that you should greatly prize the love of a man of such merit. And I am certainly very glad to know it, for he has always been so secretive with everyone that at court no one was ever able truly to say that he loved a woman."

"So help me God, sir," she said, " 'tis so much the better, for you know well that public love cannot amount to much."

Then the damsel left the room, and Sir Gawain saw her to the door, and then went to bed. He thought much that night of Lancelot and said to himself that he did not believe that Lancelot would ever wish to place his heart anywhere, unless it were in a higher and more honorable spot than others:

"And still," he said, "I cannot rightly blame him if he loves this damsel, for she is so beautiful and attractive in every respect that if the highest man on earth had set his heart on her, he would have employed it well, I believe."

That night Sir Gawain slept but little, for he thought much of the damsel and of Lancelot, and in the morning, as soon as it was light, he woke and made all the others do so too, for the king had already sent word to Sir Gawain that he should mount, for he wished to leave the castle. When they were all ready, Sir Gawain came to his host, commended him to God, and thanked him much for the good cheer that he had shown him in his house. Then he returned to the damsel and said to her:

"Damsel, I commend you to God, and know that I am your knight wherever I may be, and there is no spot so inaccessible, if I were there and you sent for me in your need, that I would not come if I could. I beg you greet for me Sir Lancelot, for I believe firmly that you will see him before I do."

The damsel answered at once that just as soon as she should see him, she would greet him in Sir Gawain's name. Sir Gawain thanked her deeply. Mounting, he left the house and found in the courtyard his uncle, King Arthur, already on horseback and waiting for him with a great company of knights. They greeted each other and set off and rode away speaking of many things. Sir Gawain then said to the king:

"Sire, do you know who the knight is that won that tournament at Winchester, the one with the vermilion arms who was wearing the sleeve on his helmet?"

"Why do you ask?" said the king.

"Because," said Sir Gawain, "I don't believe you know him."

"Yes, I know him," said the king, "but you do not know him; though you ought to know him from his marvelous feats of arms, for nobody but he only could have done so much."

"Certainly," said Sir Gawain, "I should know him well, for I have seen him many times do as many doughty deeds, but his disguise as a newly made knight caused me to fail to recognize him. But I have since then learned enough so that I know truly who it was."

"And who was it?" said the king. "I will know, be sure, if you are telling the truth."

"Sire," he said, "it was Sir Lancelot of the Lake."

"That is true," said the king. "He came secretly to the tournament so that nobody knowing him would refuse to joust with him. Without a doubt he is certainly the man of the greatest merit in the world and the best knight alive. If I had believed your brother Agravain, I would have had him killed, and would have thus done a great felony and an act of very great disloyalty, so that the whole world would rightly have shamed me because of it."

"Truly?" said Sir Gawain. "Whatever did my brother Agravain say to you? Tell me."

"Yes, I will tell you," said the king. "He came to me the other day and told me that he marveled much how I had the will to keep Lancelot around me when he was disgracing me so greatly by bringing shame upon me through my wife. He said outright that Lancelot loved her madly in my very presence and that he had known her carnally and that I could be sure that it was for no other reason that he was staying at Camelot except to come to the queen whenever he liked after I had left to go to the tournament at Winchester; your brother Agravain would have had me believe this. And I would have considered myself now much shamed, if I had believed his lie. For now I know well that if Lancelot loved the queen wrongly, he would not have quitted Camelot as long as I was absent; rather he would have stayed to have his will of the queen."

"Certainly," said Sir Gawain, "Lancelot stayed behind only to come more secretly to the tournament. You may know all this for truth, and be careful never to believe a man who brings you such words, for I tell you truly that Lancelot has never thought of such love for the queen; rather, I tell you truly, he loves one of the most beautiful damsels in the world, and she loves him and is still a virgin. Beside, we know that he loved with all his heart King Pelles' daughter, who bore Galahad, the most excellent knight, he who put an end to the adventures of the Holy Grail."

"Certainly," said the king, "if it were true that Lancelot loved her deeply, I could not believe that he would have the heart to do such an act of disloyalty as to shame me through my wife, for in a heart that holds such high qualities treason could not force an entry except by the very greatest workings of the devil."

So spoke King Arthur concerning Lancelot. And Sir Gawain told him that he should be sure of it, for Lancelot never desired the queen with such mad love as Agravain affirmed.

"And furthermore, I tell you, sire," he said, "that I feel Lancelot so guiltless of this thing that there is no knight on earth so good but that, if he contradicted this fact, I would not go into the field against him to defend Lancelot."

"What would you say about it?" said the king. "Even if everybody kept telling me day after day and I saw things better than I have perceived them, I would not believe it."

Sir Gawain advised him very warmly not to quit that good state of mind. Then they left off speaking.

21

III

The Queen's Anger

Arthur and his company proceeded with short day's rides until they came to Camelot. When they had alighted, there were many who asked news of the tournament and its winner. But there was nobody, except the king, Sir Gawain, and Girflet, who could tell them the true facts, and those three did not yet wish to reveal them because they knew that Lancelot wanted to conceal himself. Sir Gawain said to the queen:

"My lady, we do not know precisely who won the tournament, for we think that it was a foreign knight, but we can tell you at least that he had vermilion arms and bore on his helmet like a pennant the sleeve of a lady or damsel."

The queen then decided at once that it was not Lancelot, for she did not believe that he would wear anybody's token at the tournament, unless she herself had given it to him. So she said no more except to ask of Sir Gawain:

"Was Lancelot not at the tournament?"

"My lady," he said, "if he was there and I saw him, I did not recognize him, and if he had been there, I am sure that he would have won the tournament, and besides we have seen his arms so many times that, if he had come, unless he came secretly, we could have recognized him."

"And I tell you," said the queen, "that he went there as secretly as he could."

"And I tell you, my lady," said Sir Gawain, "that, if he was there, he was the knight with vermilion arms who won the tournament."

"It was not he," said the queen, "know that for sure, for he is not so closely bound to any lady or damsel as to wear her token."

Then Girflet came forward and said to the queen:

"My lady, know truly that the knight with the vermilion arms who wore the sleeve on his helmet was Lancelot; for when he had won the day and left, I went after him to know who he was; and still I doubted it, because he was so disguised. I went until I saw him plainly in the face, where he was riding off badly wounded with a knight armed like him, for they both had the same sort of arms."

"Sir Gawain," said the queen, "do you believe that he is telling the truth? By the faith you owe my lord the king, tell me what you know about it, if you do know anything."

"My lady," he said, "you have conjured me so urgently that I would hide nothing that I knew. I tell you for a fact that it was he, in flesh and blood, who had vermilion arms and wore the sleeve on his helmet and won the tournament."

When the queen heard these things, she grew silent and went off to her room with tears flowing from her eyes. She lamented much and said to herself:

"Ah, God, I have been so villainously betrayed by the man in whom I thought all loyalty was lodged, for whom I had done so much that for love of him I had brought shame on the man of greatest merit in the world. Ah, God! who will discover loyalty in any knight, in any man, when disloyalty has found lodgment in the best of all the good men?"

Thus spoke the queen to herself, for she truly believed that Lancelot loved her whose sleeve he had borne at the tournament and that he had deserted her. She was in such distress that she did not know what counsel to follow for herself, except that she would take vengeance on Lancelot or on the damsel, if she could in any wise, so soon as she should have a chance. The queen was much grieved by the news that Sir Gawain had brought her; she would not have believed that Lancelot would have the heart to love another than her. All day long she was downcast and forsook laughter and play.

And the next day Bohort came to court and Lionel and Hector and their company from the tournament. When they had alighted at the king's residence where they had lodging and shelter every time they came to court, Hector began to ask all those who had stayed behind with the queen when they went to the tournament where Lancelot had gone, for they had left him when they departed.

"Sir," they said, "he set off from here the day after you did, in such wise that he took along with him just one squire; it has befallen that we have never seen or heard of him since."

When the queen learned that Lancelot's brother and cousins had come, she sent for Bohort, and said to him:

"Bohort, were you at that tournament?"

"Yes, my lady," he said.

"And did you see your cousin Lancelot?"

"No, my lady, for he was not there."

"By my head," said the queen, "yes, he was."

"Save your grace, my lady, he was not. If he had been there, he could not have failed to talk to me, and I must have recognized him."

"Know for a fact," said the queen, "that he was there; as witness, he

23

had vermilion arms with no device and wore on his helmet a lady's or damsel's sleeve, and it was he who won the tournament."

"In God's name," said Bohort, "I should wish above everything that the man of whom you speak was not my cousin, for they say he left the tournament very badly wounded from a wound that I gave him in the left side when we tilted against each other."

"Cursed be the hour," said the queen, "that you did not kill him, for he has acted so disloyally toward me that not for anything in the world would I have believed it possible."

"How is that, my lady?" said Bohort.

Then she told him the story just as she thought it was, and when she had spoken her whole mind, Bohort answered:

"Don't believe, my lady, that it is as you think it to be before you know the facts better. For, so help me God, I could not believe that he would play you false in such a way."

"I tell you truly," she said, "that some lady or damsel has under-handedly given him a potion or enchanted him so that never again in his life will he be in my good graces, nor I in his. If by some chance he came back to court, I would deny him quarters with my lord the king and would forbid him ever to be so bold as to set foot in them."

"You will do whatever you decide, my lady," said Bohort, "but never-theless I tell you for certain that my lord never undertook to do such things as you lay to his score."

"He showed it clearly at the tournament," said the queen, "I am sorry that the truth is so evident."

"If it is as you tell me, my lady," said Bohort, "he never did anything that made me so sorry, for to whomever he might do evil, to you he should in no way do evil."

All that week and the following one Bohort and his company stayed in King Arthur's abode. They were very quiet and pensive, more than they usually were because of the queen whom they saw greatly angered. Within that period nobody came to court bringing news of Lancelot or who had seen him near at hand or far away. King Arthur marveled much thereat.

One day the king and Sir Gawain were at the windows of the great hall together, speaking of many things until the king said to Sir Gawain:

"I marvel much, nephew, where Lancelot is staying so long. I have not seen him away from my court for such a space this long time."

When Sir Gawain heard him, he began to smile and said to the king:

"Know now that the place where he is is not wearisome for him, for if it were wearisome, he would not put off coming, and if it pleases him,

24

we should not marvel thereat, for it ought to please the richest man in the world if he had placed his heart as I think Lancelot has placed his."

When the king heard this speech, he was very anxious to know what it meant; so he required Sir Gawain to tell him the truth about it on the faith and oath that he had made him.

"I shall tell you the truth, sire," said Sir Gawain, "as I understand it, but let it be a secret between us two, for if I thought it would be told anywhere else, I would not tell you a thing about it."

And the king told him that from then on nothing would be known about it.

"I tell you truly, sire," said Sir Gawain, "Sir Lancelot is staying at Escalot because of a damsel with whom he is in love, but know this for certain truth that she is one of the most beautiful damsels to be found in the kingdom of Logres. And she was still a virgin when we were there. For the great beauty that I saw in her I sought her love not long ago, but she put me off brusquely, and said that she was loved by a handsomer and better knight than I. I was greatly desirous to know who he was, and I insisted that she tell me his name, but she did not want to do any such thing, and nonetheless she told me that she would show me his shield. I answered that I asked nothing better and she showed it to me. I recognized it at once; I knew well that it was Lancelot's shield. And I asked her, 'Tell me, damsel, as a favor, when this shield was left here.' She answered that her friend had left it with her when he went to the tournament at Winchester, and he carried away the arms of a brother of hers which were all vermilion and that the sleeve he wore on his helmet was hers."

The queen was leaning in thought at another window and had heard the king and Sir Gawain talking. She came forward and said:

"Fair nephew, who is that maiden whom you consider so beautiful?"

"She is the daughter of the master of Escalot, my lady. If he loves her it is no wonder, for she is full of overflowing beauty."

"It is sure," said the king, "I could not have believed he would put his heart on a lady or damsel, if she were not of very high station, and I tell you truly, he is not delaying his return here on that account; rather he lies ill or wounded, if I know anything about the wound on his side that his cousin Bohort gave him at the tournament at Winchester."

"On my word," said Sir Gawain, "that might well be, and now I do not know what to think, except that, if he were ill, he would have let us know or at least have sent word to Hector, his brother, and his cousins who are staying here."

The king and queen and Sir Gawain talked long. The queen rose to leave them so grief-stricken and so angered that no woman could be more so; she believed sincerely that Sir Gawain was telling the whole truth concerning the damsel and Lancelot; and she went straight to her chamber and sent for Bohort to come talk to her, and he came at once. The queen said as soon as she saw him:

"Bohort, now I know the truth about your lord, your cousin. He is staying in Escalot with a damsel he loves. Now may we say that you and I have lost him, for she has put him in such a state that he could not leave her if he wished. This word came just now to my ears and those of my lord the king from such a knight that you would believe all he said if he were speaking to you. And know as fact that he affirmed it for truth."

"Well, my lady," said Bohort, "I know not who he is, this knight who told you this thing, but if he were the most veracious in the world, I know that he is a liar to advance such a thing; for I know well that my lord has such a noble heart that he would not deign to do it. I should like to beg you to tell me who that was who said this speech, for he will not be such but that before night I will make him held a liar."

"You shall know no more from me," she said, "but I can tell you that never again will Lancelot have peace from me."

"Certainly, my lady," said Bohort, "that grieves me, and since you have acquired such great hatred for my lord, our people ought not stay here. Wherefore, my lady, I take leave of you and commend you to God, for we shall go away in the morning. And when we have set out, we will seek our lord until we find him, please God. And when we have found him, we will not stay in this country, if it pleases him, in the court of any nobleman. If staying in this country does not please him, we will go over to our own lands to our people who are very desirous to see us, for they have not seen us this long time. And know truly," said Bohort, "that we should not have stayed in this country as we have if it were not for our love of my lord, and he would not have lingered so long after the quest of the Holy Grail except for you; and know truly that he has loved you more loyally than any knight ever loved a lady or damsel."

When the queen heard these words, no woman could have been more afflicted, and she could not help tears coming to her eyes. And when she spoke she cursed the hour that ever such news came to her, for "I am," she said, "in great trouble." Then she said again to Bohort:

"What, sir, will you leave me thus?"

"Yes, my lady," he said, "for I must."

Then he left the room and sought out his brother and Hector. He related to them the words that the queen had said to him and they were greatly afflicted. And they did not know whom to blame; they could only

26

curse the hour that Lancelot had ever come close to the queen. Bohort said to them:

"Let us take leave of the king, and let us go away from here. We will search for my lord until we have found him, and if we can take him to the kingdom of Gaunes or to that of Benwick, never will we have done such a good deed, for then we shall be in repose, if he can get along without the queen."

Lionel and Hector agreed to this proposal, and then they went to the king and asked his leave to go look for Lancelot. He gave it to them most unwillingly, for he liked to see them around him, especially on account of Bohort, who was then at the height of his renown, of better conduct and better knighthood than any knight who was in the kingdom of Logres.

IV
Tourneying and Recovery

The next day King Ban's kinsmen left court, and rode along the direct road to Escalot. When they had come there, they asked news of Lancelot everywhere that they thought they could find information, but never could they find anyone who could tell them news of him. They searched long up and down, but the more they asked, the less they learned. So they rode on eight days without ever being able to have news. When they saw this, they said:

"For no good will we wear ourselves out any longer, for we shan't find him now before the tournament, but he will come to it without fail, provided he is in this country and in possession of his powers."

So for this reason they put up at a castle which was called Athean, a day's journey from Tanebourc, and it was not more than six days till the tournament. The king of North Wales, who was staying at a fortress of his eight leagues from Athean, as soon as he knew that the kinsmen of King Ban were there, they who were the most famous in the world and of greatest prowess and knightly quality, he went to see them, for he desired greatly to make their acquaintance. And if it had been possible, he would have liked for them to be of his household at the tournament against King Arthur and his company. When they saw the king coming to see them, they considered it a great kindness, and they received him handsomely and courteously like men who knew how to behave so. They had him stay with them that night, and he begged them until they went off with him the next day to his fortress. So the king of North Wales kept them in his lodgings with great joy and honor till the day of the tournament and begged them so hard that they promised that in the jousting they would be on his side. The king was very joyful at this promise and thanked them over and over. But now the tale ceases here to speak of Bohort and his company and returns to speaking of Lancelot, who lay ill at the house of the aunt of the new knight from Escalot.

Now the tale tells at this point that when Lancelot had come there, he went to bed. He lay there a month or more ill with the wound that Bohort his cousin had given him at the tournament at Winchester. The knight who had been with him at the tournament expected nothing but death. It distressed him much, for he had seen so many good things in Lancelot that he prized him for his knightly merit above all those whom he had ever seen; he still did not know that it was Sir Lancelot. When the patient had lain there more than a month, it happened that the damsel who had given him the sleeve came there. When she saw that he was not yet healed, it pained her much and she asked her brother how the patient was doing. He answered:

"He is doing well, sister, thank God, considering what has happened. But, not a fortnight ago, there were times when I could not think that he would escape except through death. For his wound has been dangerous in the healing; that is why I really thought that he would die of it."

"Die!" cried the damsel, "may God spare him. It would certainly be a grievous pity, for after him there would be no best knight in the world."

"So you know who he is, sister?" said the knight.

"Yes, sir," she said, "very well. He is Sir Lancelot of the Lake, the best knight in the world; Sir Gawain, King Arthur's nephew, told me so himself."

"By my head," said the knight, "I am truly ready to believe that it may be he, for never did I see a man do as many deeds of arms as he did at the tournament at Winchester, nor was a lady's or damsel's sleeve ever better employed nor looked at so much as yours was."

The damsel stayed there with her brother until Lancelot was somewhat recovered, so that he could walk about there. When he was almost well and somewhat back to his handsome self, the damsel who stayed with him night and day loved him so much, because of the good things that were said about him and because of the manly beauty that she saw in him, that it seemed to her that she could not in any way live on if she did not have her will of him. So the damsel loved Lancelot as much as she ever could. When she could no longer be silent on what she was thinking, she came to him one day when she had prepared herself and decked herself out in her finest, and had put on the handsomest gown that she had;

without fail she was full of the greatest beauty. Thus attired she came before Lancelot and said to him:

"My lord, would not the knight whose love I asked be truly recreant if he rejected me?"

"If, young lady, he had his heart at his disposal so that he could do with it just what he liked, he would be truly recreant if he rejected you. But if matters stood so that he could not dispose of himself or his heart as he ordered, and he refused you his love, nobody should blame him. I am speaking about myself in the first place, for, so help me God, if you were of such a mind that you deigned to place your heart before me, and I could do with myself as I willed and pleased, as many another knight might, I am a man who would consider himself very, very fortunate, if you deigned to give me your love; for, so help me God, I have not seen this long time a lady or damsel that one should love better than one should you."

"What, my lord?" said the damsel. "Is your heart not so completely in your own power that you can do with it according to your will?"

"Young lady," he said, "I am carrying out my will, for my heart is where I desire it to be, and I would not want it to be anywhere but where it is, for nowhere could it be so well placed as it is where I have lodged it. May God grant that it never separates from this will, for after that, I could not live a day as happily as I do now."

"Certainly, my lord," said the damsel, "you have told me so much that I have become acquainted with a part of your heart's desires. I am very sorry that so it is, for from what you have now told me and given me to understand by this single speech you will cause my death soon. If you had told me a little less frankly, you would have placed my heart in a languor full of every good hope, and that hope would have made me live in all the joy and sweet delight where an amorous heart may dwell."

Then the damsel went to her brother and at once disclosed to him her whole mind; she told him that she loved Lancelot with such a great love that she had come to her death unless her brother should bring it about that she should have her will. He was sorrowful because of this and he said to her:

"You must put your longings elsewhere, sister, for you cannot reach this goal. I know well that our guest has placed his heart so loftily that he would not deign to descend to love so poor a maid as you, though now you are one of the most beautiful maidens anywhere. If you must love, you will have to bring your heart down lower, for from such a tall tree you could not pluck the fruit."

"Truly, brother," said the damsel, "it grieves me, and if it had pleased

God, I would that my heart had been given to some other knight before I saw him, but that cannot be now, for my destiny is that I shall die because of him. I will die from it, as you will see clearly."

Thus the damsel prophesied her death, and it came about just as she said, for it is certain that she died for love of Lancelot.

On the day of which we have last been speaking it happened that a squire who had come from Northumberland stopped for the night where Lancelot was. Lancelot had him brought in to him and asked him where he was going:

"I am going to Tanebourc, sir," he said, "where the tournament was set; it will take place three days from now."

"What knights will be there?" said Lancelot, "do you know?"

"The knights of the Round Table will be there, sir," he said, "and those who were at the assembly at Winchester, and to see the tournament, so they say, King Arthur will bring Queen Guenevere."

When Lancelot heard that the queen would be there, he was so troubled that it seemed to him he would die of pain; he began to be greatly excited, and when he spoke, he said so loudly that all those in his presence heard him:

"Ah, my lady, now you will not see your knight, for I languish here, doing naught else. Ah, knight who gave me this wound, God grant that I meet you in such wise that I recognize you. Certainly, I would not accept the whole world as a compensation for not making you die a cruel death."

Then he lay down because of the great pain he had, and in stretching out he opened his wound, and a burst of blood came out as great as if it were from a mortally wounded beast. He swooned straightway. When his leech saw him, he said to the squire:

"You have killed him with your words."

And he had him undressed and put to bed and strove mightily to staunch the bleeding, for otherwise he would have died right away. All that day Lancelot lay without opening his eyes or uttering a word; he was as though half dead. On the next day, he regained as much of his vigor as was possible, and pretended that he felt no illness nor pain, and that he was completely healed. He said to his physician:

"Master, thanks to God and to you, you have done so much for me and spent on me so much care and labor that I feel so well and so vigorous that from now on I can ride without hurting myself in any way. Therefore, I should like to beg the lady of this manor and my companion, this knight here who has done me such service during this sickness, that they give me leave to go see this tournament; the flower of all good knights in the world will be there!"

"Ah, my lord, what are you saying?" cried the worthy man. "Certainly, if you were mounted on the smoothest-riding horse on earth, know that the whole earth could not bring it about that you would not die before you had ridden the length of an English league, for you are still so very weak and ill that I see not how anyone but God can give you perfect health."

"Ah, fair sweet master," said Lancelot, "for the love of God will you not tell me something different?"

"Certainly not," the master replied, "naught except that you are dead if you move from here at this stage."

"On my word," said Lancelot, "if I do not go to the tournament at Tanebourc, I could not get well, but would die of sorrow, and if die I must, I would rather die as I ride than while I am languishing."

"You will do whatever your heart says you must do, for you would not give up anything for my sake, and since you do not wish to be guided by my counsel, I shall leave you completely, you and your company, for if you die in this pursuit, I want no one to say that it was through my ministrations, and if you regain your health—and God grant you may—I desire to be neither praised nor blamed."

"Ah, fair master," said Lancelot, "will you desert me thus, you who through this sickness have been of such great value to me and helped so much till now? How could you find it in your heart to do so?"

"On my word," said the Master, "I must leave from moral need, for I would in no wise wish that a man of such merit and such a good knight as you should die under my care."

"Fair sweet master," said Lancelot, "are you then telling me loyally that I would have to die if I left here at this point to go to the tournament which is to be held at Tanebourc?"

"I tell you loyally," said the worthy man, "that if the whole world were helping you, without God's special help, you would not be able to ride two leagues without dying on the way. But stay here with us for a fortnight, and I tell you loyally that by then I think I will have made you so healthy and sturdy with God's help that you will be able to ride safely wherever you like."

"Master," said Lancelot, "I will stay with such an agreement, but so sorrowful and vexed that no one could be more so."

Then he turned toward the squire who was beside him, the one who had brought him news of the tournament and whom he had retained to bear him company in the morning, thinking really he would go to the tournament with him, and he said to him:

"Fair sweet friend, go away now, for I must stay, it seems. And when you reach the tournament at Tanebourc and see Sir Gawain and my lady Queen Guenevere, greet them for me in the name of the knight who won the tournament at Winchester, and if they ask you how I am, say nothing to them of my condition nor where I am."

And the man said that he would carry out the message. Straightway he mounted his horse and left and rode until he came to the tournament. And that squire was somewhat acquainted with the king of North Wales. So he went to that king's court and stayed there the night before the tournament was to take place. When night had come, Sir Gawain went to the quarters of the king of North Wales, entered and stayed there to see Bohort and his company and to speak with them. They received him joyfully and festively. The squire served wine, and as he knelt before Sir Gawain to give him the wine, he began to smile broadly, for he remembered about the knight with the foolish notion about coming to the tournament. When Sir Gawain saw the smile and noted it, he concluded that it had a cause. He drank the wine, and as soon as he had drunk it, he said to the squire:

"I beg you to tell me what I am about to ask."

And the squire said that he would gladly tell if he knew the answer; "Ask confidently."

"I ask you," said Sir Gawain, "why you began to smile just now."

"On my word," said the squire, "I was remembering about the maddest knight I ever saw or heard of. He was wounded nearly to death, and sick as he was, he wanted to come to the tournament, whether his physician would let him or not. And he was still so badly off that scarcely could anyone draw a word from his mouth. Does it not seem to you that was great folly?"

"Ha, my friend," said Sir Gawain, "when did you see the knight of whom you speak?"

"I tell you that to my knowledge he is a man of very great merit, and I think I know well that if he were in his usual power, he would not have easily refrained from being here."

"Now may God give him health," said Sir Gawain, "for it is certainly too bad when a valiant man has an illness that prevents his doing deeds of prowess."

"I swear to you in God's name, my lord," said the squire, "I know not who he is, but I dare to tell you that I heard him testified to as the best knight in the world, and besides he told me when I left him yesterday morning, to greet you in the name of him who won the tournament at Winchester, and to my lady the queen he also sends wishes of good health."

When Sir Gawain heard these words, he knew at once that it was Lancelot. He said to the squire:

"Tell me, my friend, in what spot you left the knight of whom you speak."

"I will not tell you, my lord," said the squire, "for I would be doing a misdeed."

"At the very least you told us," said Sir Gawain, "that he is wounded."

"If I told you so, my lord," said the squire, "I repent my words and I have already discovered to you much more than I should, but nevertheless I beg you out of friendship that, if you see my lady the queen before I do, you greet her in the name of him of whom I told you."

Sir Gawain said that he would very gladly do so.

The three cousins were much dismayed by these words which they heard the squire saying; they perceived that he was speaking of Lancelot, who was thus greeting the queen and Sir Gawain. So they pressed the squire hard to tell them where he had left him. And he answered that he would tell them no more for any prayer they made.

"At least," they said, "you can tell us where you left him."

And he told them another place from the one where he left him. And they said that they would go look for him after the tournament until they found him.

The next day knights from four kingdoms assembled beneath Tanebourc against those of the Round Table. And many a fine tilt was made with lances, and many a fine blow struck with swords. You could have seen the meadow covered with foreigners who came against those of the kingdom of Logres and against those of the Round Table, who were renowned for prowess and boldness. But the kinsmen of King Ban and Bohort and Sir Gawain surpassed all who were there. When the king saw and knew that Lancelot had not been there, he was much grieved, for he had come there to see Lancelot and talk to him more than for any other reason. By the common consent of nearly everyone he had another tournament announced for the end of a month on the meadow at Camelot. All those of the place agreed to it. So the tournament concluded in this way, for nothing more was done at that time.

That day the king said to Bohort that he should come to court, he and his company. Bohort said that he would not do so before he learned news of Lancelot which should be true. The king did not dare urge him longer. Sir Gawain told the queen what the squire had said of Lancelot and how he wanted to come to the tournament, but his physician did not let him because he was too ill. But the queen could not believe that he had been so long in recovery; rather she believed truly that the damsel whom Sir Gawain had praised so highly to her was the reason for his lingering and that he had stayed with her, and she thought that he had so long delayed coming to court for no other reason. So she hated him so mortally that there was no shame that she did not wish to see him suffer. But on account of Bohort and his company who had left the court because of the lack of Lancelot she had such great regret and was in such distress at having thus lost them that she did not know what would become of her. She would have been greatly pleased if it could have been that they should come back, for she loved their company so much, because of the great comfort that they gave her, that she prized no other people so much as she did them. And at her privy council she said sometimes that she knew no knight in the world so worthy nor so capable of holding a great empire as was Bohort of Gaunes. For love of him it pained her greatly that all his companions did not stay at court.

The king remained at Tanebourc three days to rest. He sent word to Bohort and all his company who were staying with the king of North Wales that they should come see him. And they said that they would not go and never again would they enter his court before they had learned true news of Lancelot. The day after he had sent them this message, the king left Tanebourc and rode toward Camelot with those of his household. That same day Bohort and his companions left the king of North Wales. Sir Gawain went with them and said he would never quit their company before they had found Lancelot. So they rode in the direction that the youth had taught them, for they had left him. But when they had come there, they found nobody able to give them news of Lancelot. Then Sir Gawain said to Bohort:

"Sir, I would advise in open counsel that we go to Escalot; for in that castle I know a place where I think they will inform us about what we are seeking."

"My lord," said Bohort, "I wish we were there, for I long for us to find my lord and cousin."

So they set out and rode till evening and lay that night beside a grove. The next day as soon as it was light, they mounted and rode through the chill, and they traveled so much with their days' stints that they arrived at Escalot. Sir Gawain dismounted at the place where he had lain earlier and took Bohort into the room where he had left Lancelot's shield. He found it still hanging there. Then he said:

"Sir, have you ever seen this shield before?"

Bohort said that he had left Camelot while that shield was there when he went to the tournament at Winchester. Then Sir Gawain sent word to the host of the place to come speak with him. And he came without delay. Sir Gawain said to him:

"Fair host, I beg you as a great favor, and beseech you by the faith you owe whatever you most love in the world to tell me where the knight is who left this shield here, for I am quite sure that you know well where he is, and can tell us if you wish. If you are of such a mind that you will not do it for our prayers, be sure that we will harm you and make war upon you if we can bring it about."

"If I thought," said the worthy man, "that you were asking for his good, I would give you the information, but otherwise I would in no wise do it."

"I give you my oath," said Sir Gawain, "upon all I hold from God, that we are men in the world who love him most deeply and who would do most for him. Because we have not seen him for a long time nor know whether he is in good health or bad, we go seeking him and have searched for him more than a week."

"Only stay here today," said the worthy man, "and tomorrow I will tell you where you can find him. If you wish, I will give you one of my young fellows from here who will teach you the road."

That night the companions stayed there in great joy and in holiday humor and were easier in mind than was usual with them because of the news that they had learned. The next day, as soon as they saw daylight, they rose, and when they came into their host's hall, they found him up. The knight who was ill when Lancelot came there was quite well, and said that he would go with them and bear them company to the place where the knight whom they were seeking was. They said that it was very pleasing to them. Then they mounted and departed from there all together. They commended their host to God and hastened to ride till they came toward evening to the manor of the lady where Lancelot had stayed. He was then so far along on the road to good health that he could walk around there to amuse himself. When they came there, they dismounted at the gate. Lancelot was in the middle of the court where he was walking for pleasure and conversing with the gentleman who had undertaken to heal him. He was followed by the knight who had been with him at the tournament, who had borne him constant company in his illness, for he had not left him from morning till night. When they had alighted in the courtyard and Lancelot recognized them, ask not if he was delighted. He ran straight to Bohort to tell him that he and Hector and Lionel and

Sir Gawain were welcome. To the latter he showed marvelous joy. Then he said to them all:

"Fair sirs, you are most welcome."

"God bless you, my lord. The great desire that we had to see you and the great fear because you had not been at the tournament at Tanebourc, put us in quest of you. Thank God, it has turned out well for us, for with less trouble than we thought we have found you. But, for God's sake, tell us about yourself and how you have done, for we heard a few days ago that you were very seriously ill."

"Really," he said, "thanks to God, all is very well with me now, for I am well on the way to good health, but it is true that I have been very sick and suffered much anguish and have been as though in peril of death. So they give me to understand."

"Where do you think you caught this illness, my lord?" said Bohort.

"I know well," he said, "that I took it at the Winchester tournament from a great wound that a knight gave me at a jousting. The wound was much more dangerous than I thought, and it is still evident, for I am not so completely healed from it yet that I could ride comfortably tomorrow."

"Since you are on the way to good health, sir," said Sir Gawain, "I will not be concerned about past pain, for that is not now an overgreat worry. But now tell me when you think you will be in such shape that you will be able to come to court."

"Certainly soon, please God," he replied.

And the worthy man who had cared for him addressed Sir Gawain: "My lord," he said, "know that without any fail he will be healed within a week so that he can ride and bear arms as mightily as he did not long ago at the tournament at Winchester."

They answered that they were very happy with this news.

The next day, as they sat at dinner, Sir Gawain said laughingly to Lancelot:

"Did you ever find out who the knight was who gave you this wound?"

"No, of a certainty," said Lancelot, "but if I could find out and by chance come across him in some tournament, I think that he would never have done anything that would not be fully paid back to him so soon, for before he left, I would make him feel whether my sword could cut steel, and if he has drawn blood from my side, I would draw as much or more from his head."

Then Sir Gawain began to clap his hands and display the greatest joy in the world. He said to Bohort:

"Now we shall see what you will do, for you are not threatened by the greatest coward in the world. If he had threatened me so, I would never be at ease until I had made peace with him."

When Lancelot heard these words, he was astounded and said:

"Bohort, was it you who wounded me?"

Bohort was so grieved that he did not know what to say, for he did not dare admit it and he could not deny it, but nevertheless answered:

"My lord, if I did it, I am sorry and nobody should blame me for it, for at the time Sir Gawain speaks of, if you were he whom I wounded, you were so disguised that I would never have known you in those arms because they were such as a new knight would have, and you have borne arms more than twenty-five years. That is why I failed to recognize you. So it seems to me that you should not hold it against me."

Lancelot answered that he would not, since things had so fallen out.

"In God's name, brother," said Hector, "I can praise you for that day's work, for you made me feel hard earth in an hour when I had no need to do so."

Lancelot responded, laughing, "you will never complain about me concerning that day without my complaining much more of you; for now I know that you and Bohort are the two knights who at that tournament took away the most from my will to do things, for you were so forward that you aspired to nothing except to do me harm and shame me. I think I would have carried off the prize that day, but you two took it from me. I will tell you that I have never found anywhere two knights who gave me so much trouble as you two, you will never hear me speak of it again; instead I forgive you."

"You know now," said Sir Gawain, "how well they can wield lances and swords."

"That is certainly true," he said, "I had a good test of it, and I still bear such signs of it as are quite evident."

They spoke much that day of that thing, and Sir Gawain took the floor again gladly because he saw that Bohort was as much ashamed and downcast as if he had done the greatest misdeed in the world. They stayed the whole week there in great joy and merrymaking, glad to see Lancelot on the way to health; as long as they were there, Bohort did not dare reveal to him what he had heard the queen say, for he feared that he would be too much tormented thereby if he heard the cruel words that she had said of him. But now the tale ceases to speak of them and returns to King Arthur.

V

Morgan

In this part the tale tells that when King Arthur had left Tanebourc with the queen he rode the first day as far as a castle of his which was called Tauroc; that night he lay there with a great company of knights, and the next day he sent word to the queen that she should go on to Camelot. The king remained at Tauroc and stayed there three days. When he left, he traveled into a forest. In that wood Lancelot had formerly been imprisoned two winters and a summer, held by deceitful Morgan who was still there, and with her many people who bore her company in every season. The king went into the wood with his household, and he was not in the best of health. They went astray so that they were completely lost. They went on thus until night had fallen. Then the king stopped and asked his household:

"What shall we do? We have lost our way!"

"Sire," they said, "it will be better to stay here than to go on, for we would only wear ourselves out, since there is in this wood no house or refuge that we know of. We have a great deal of meat; so we will pitch your pavilion in this meadow and we will rest the remainder of the day. Tomorrow, please God, when we have been set on our way, we will find a road that will take us out of the wood as we desire."

The king agreed to this. As soon as they had begun to set up his pavilion, they heard a horn very near them which sounded twice.

"On my word," said the king, "there are people near here. Go see what this is."

Sagremor the Desreez immediately mounted his horse, and went off straight in the direction where he had heard the sound of the horn. He had not gone far when he found a great strong tower closely battlemented and surrounded on all sides by a very high wall. He dismounted and came to the gate and called. When the porter heard people at the gate, he asked who it was and what they wished.

"I am," the answer was, "Sagremor the Desreez, a knight whom my lord, King Arthur, who is nearby in the wood, has sent here. He sends word to those in this castle that he wishes to stop in it for the night. So, be ready to receive him as you should, for I shall bring him here right away with all his company."

"Fair sir," said the porter, "wait a little, if you please, until I have spoken to my lady, who is up there in her room. I will come back immediately, and you will hear her answer."

"What!" said Sagremor, "Is there no lord here?"

"No," the fellow answered.

"Well, go quickly and come back quickly," said Sagremor, "for I do not wish to stay here."

The young fellow climbed the stairs and came to his lady and told her his message just as Sagremor had said it, that King Arthur wanted to be there that night. As soon as Morgan heard those words, she was most joyful and answered the young man:

"Go back quickly and tell the knight to bring the king, for he will be received as well as we can."

The porter returned to Sagremor and told him what his lady had said. Then Sagremor left the gate and rode till he came back to the king, and said to him:

"Sire, you have been fortunate, for I have found you quarters where you will be lodged tonight according to your desire, so they say."

When the king heard this, he said to those with him:

"Let us mount and go straight in that direction."

When the king had said this, everybody mounted. And Sagremor led them in that direction. When they came to the gate, they found it open. They entered and saw that the spot was so beautiful, so delightful, so rich, and so well sheltered that never in their whole lives had they seen such a fine dwelling nor so well situated, it seemed to them. There was within a very great provision of candles, from which the light was so bright that they marveled what it could be, nor within was there a wall which was not covered with silken cloths. And the king asked Sagremor:

"Did you see any of this equipment just now?"

"On my word, sire," he answered, "I did not."

And the king crossed himself because of his astonishment, for he had never seen a church or abbey more richly encurtained than the courtyard of that castle.

"I give you my word," said the king, "I would not be surprised if there were great riches within, for outside there is a very great display."

King Arthur dismounted and all the others in his company did, too. When they entered the great hall, they met Morgan and with her a hundred attendants, knights, and ladies bearing her company and they were all dressed so richly that never at any festival that he had held in his life had King Arthur seen people so richly costumed as everyone was throughout the room. And when they saw the king come in, they shouted with one voice:

"Sire, be welcome here, for never has so great an honor befallen us as befalls us because you are stopping here."

The king answered with a wish that God might grant them all joy. They took him at once and led him to a room so beautiful and rich that never, it seemed to him, had he seen any as beautiful and delightful.

As soon as the king was seated and had washed his hands, the tables were set with all speed. They caused everyone who had come in the king's company to sit down, provided that they were knights. And then damsels began to bring in dishes as if they had really foreseen a month earlier the king's coming with all his companions. Nor had the king ever in his life seen such a plenty of rich gold and silver vessels as these were. If he had been in the city of Camelot and had done his best to have great riches in food, he would have had no more than he had that night at that table, nor finer, and he would not have been served more fittingly. They marveled where such great plenty could come from.

When they had eaten a great deal according to their desires, the king listened and heard in the next room all the various instruments that he had ever heard of in his life. They were played so very sweetly together with one another that he had never heard a melody which was so sweet or pleasant to hear. And in that room there was such a great light that it seemed too much. It was not long before he saw two very beautiful damsels issue from it carrying two gold candlesticks with two great burning tapers. They came before the king and said:

"Sire, if it were your pleasure, it would be now time to rest in accordance with your need, for a great part of the night is spent, and you have ridden so far that you are worn out, we think."

The king responded, "I would like to be already in bed, for I have great need of it."

"Sire," they said, "we have come here to convey you to your bed; for we have been so commanded."

"I am quite willing," said the king.

Then the king got up at once, and they went off to the very room where Lancelot had formerly stayed so long; in that room he had painted the story of his and Queen Guenevere's love. In that room the damsels put King Arthur to bed and when he was asleep, they left and came to their lady.

Morgan thought a great deal about King Arthur, for she was longing to apprise him of the affair between Lancelot and the queen; on the other hand she feared that, if she revealed the truth and Lancelot heard that the king knew it through her, the whole world could not prevent him from killing her. She thought long that night about the matter, that is, if she should tell him or keep silent; for, if she told him, she risked death, if Lancelot could learn of it, and if she concealed the matter, she would never again be in as good a situation as she was right then to tell him. She thought about it all till she fell asleep. In the morning, as soon as it was light, she got up and went in to the king, greeted him handsomely and said to him:

"Sire, I ask a boon from you as recompense for all the services that I ever did for you."

"I grant it," said the king, "if it is anything that I can grant you."

"You can grant it to me very well," she said, "and do you know what it is? It is that you stay on here the rest of the day and tomorrow, and know that if you were in the best city that you have, you would be no better served nor in greater comfort than you will be here, for you will never be able to tell us anything that you will not have."

He replied that he would stay, since he had promised to.

"Sire," she said, "you are in the house where in this world one would most desire to see you, and know there is not a woman on earth who loves you more than I do, and I ought to do so truly, if blood love is not wholly lacking."

"Who are you, my lady," said the king, "who loves me so much as you say?"

"Sire," she said, "I am your nearest blood friend; my name is Morgan, and I am your sister; and you should know me better than you do."

He looked at her and recognized her, jumped out of bed, and showed the greatest joy in the world, and he told her that he was most happy at this adventure which God had given unto him.

"For I tell you, sister," said the king, "that I thought you were dead and gone from this world. Since it pleases God that I have found you safe and sound, I will take you with me to Camelot, when I leave here, and henceforth you will stay at court and be a companion to Queen Guenevere, my wife, and I know well that she will be very happy and filled with joy when she knows the truth about you."

"Do not require that of me, brother," she said, "for I give you my earnest word that I will never again go to court, but without fail, when I leave here, I will go to the Isle of Avalon where the ladies live who know all the enchantments of this world."

The king dressed and got into proper array at once; then he sat on his bed, and had his sister sit beside him. He began to ask her about her life. She told him part of it, and concealed a part. So they remained there in conversation till the hour of prime.

That day the weather was very fine and the sun had risen bright and clear so that it shone in and lighted everything, making the room brighter than it was before. They were quite alone, for they found great pleasure in speaking together without others present. When they had asked each other about their ways of life, it happened that the king began to look around him and saw the paintings and figures that Lancelot had painted while he was staying there in prison. King Arthur knew quite enough of reading so that he could understand writing somewhat. When he had seen the letters with the figures which set forth the meaning of the portraits he began to read them, and read till he knew plainly that that room was painted with the deeds of Lancelot and with the feats that he had accomplished while he was a newly made knight. The king saw nothing whatsoever that he did not recognize as true from the news that people brought him every day at court about Lancelot's knightly feats, just as soon as he had done a deed of prowess.

Thus the king began to read the works of Lancelot through the paintings that he saw. When he saw the figures which depicted the relations with Galeholt, he was greatly surprised and grew quite thoughtful; he began to look at that thing and said to himself in an undertone:

"On my word, if the meaning of these letters is true, then Lancelot has brought shame upon me with the queen, for I see very clearly that he has entered into relations with her. If it is true, as this writing testifies, it is a thing that will bring me the greatest grief I ever had, for Lancelot could not disgrace me more than by bringing shame upon me with my wife."

Then he said to Morgan, "I beg you, sister, to tell me the truth about what I shall ask you."

She answered that she would do so gladly, if she knew it.

"Swear that you will," said the king, and she gave her oath.

"Now I require of you," said the king, "by the faith that you owe me and that you have pledged me here, that you will tell me whom these pictures portray, if you know the truth. Do not depart from it for any reason."

"Ah, my lord," said Morgan, "what are you saying and what do you ask me? Certainly, if I told you the truth about it, and he who made the paintings found it out, nobody but God could ever be a guarantor against his killing me."

"In God's name," said the king, "you must tell me and I give you my word as a king that you will never be revealed by me."

"My lord," she said, "is there nothing that you would consider to allow me not to tell you?"

"Certainly not," said the king, "you must tell me."

"I will tell you then so exactly that I will not lie by a single word. It is true," said Morgan, "I do not know whether you yet know it, that

Lancelot has loved Queen Guenevere since the first day that he received the order of knighthood, and for love of the queen, when he was a new knight, he did all the deeds of prowess that he did. You could have known this at the Castle of Dolorous Guard when you came there first and you could not set foot in it, for they made you stop by the river. When you sent a knight there, several times, he could not enter it. But as soon as Kay, who was the queen's knight, went there, he entered. You did not notice this as many did."

"Certainly," said the king, "I did not perceive it; but still it happened just as you say. But I do not know whether it was for love of the queen or on my account."

"Sire," she said, "there is more."

"Go ahead," said the king.

"Sire," she said, "he loved my lady the queen so much that no mortal man could love a woman more; but he never let her know it through word of his or through any other, and he endured such hardships for love of her that he did all the knightly deeds that you see here portrayed. For a long time he but languished, as one loving but not loved, without daring to declare his love until he became a friend of Galeholt, the son of the Giantess, the day that he bore black arms and won the assembly at arms set by you two, as the pictures that you see here set forth. When he had made peace between you and Galeholt in such wise that the honor was all yours, and when Galeholt saw that he was daily growing worse and had lost all taste for meat and drink, so fervently did he love the queen, then he urged him so much and begged him so much that Lancelot made him understand that he loved the queen and that he was dying on account of her. Galeholt pleaded with him not to be dismayed about this thing, for he would bring it about that his friend should have his desires of the queen. And just as he had promised, he did for him, for he begged the queen so hard that she granted everything to Lancelot and put him in possession of her love with a kiss."

"You have told me a great deal," said the king, "for I see my shame very clearly and Lancelot's treason. But now tell me who painted these pictures."

"Truly, sire," she said, "Lancelot painted them. I will tell you when. Do you remember two tournaments when the knights of the Round Table said that they would not go into the tests where Lancelot was with them because he always carried off the prize? And he turned against them and made them leave the field and by might made them quit the city of Camelot. Do you remember that?"

"Certainly I do," said the king. "It still seems to me that I see the

43

tournament, for never since, wherever I have been, have I seen one knight do deeds of arms as he did that day. But why have you asked me?"

"Because," she said, "when he left court that time, he was lost over a year and a half so that nobody knew where he was."

"True," said the king, "you are right."

"I tell you," she said, "that then I held him in prison two winters and a summer, and then he painted the pictures that you see here. I would still hold him in prison so that he would never again come out on any day in his life, if he had not done what he did, the greatest piece of deviltry that ever a man did in this world."

"What was that?" said the king.

"On my word," she said, "he broke the bars of that window with his hands."

Then she showed him the irons that she had had mended. Then the king said that no man, but a devil, had done that thing. The king looked long at the work on the chamber walls and thought hard thoughts; he stood long without saying a word. When he had thought a long time, he said:

"Agravain too told me about this thing not long ago, but I did not believe him; instead, I thought that he was lying, but this thing here brings my heart to greater certainty than before. Therefore, I tell you I shall never again be easy before I know the whole truth. And if it is as these paintings testify, that Lancelot has brought on me such disgrace as to shame me through my wife, I will work at the matter until they are caught together in the act. Then if I do not do such justice that people will speak of it forever after, I declare that I will never wear a crown again."

"Certainly," said Morgan, "if you did not act so, God and man should heap shame upon you, for there is no king, no man, who suffers such shame to be done him."

They spoke long about this matter that morning, the king and his sister. Morgan urged him to take vengeance for this shame very soon. And he swore as a king that he would do so with such cruelty that it would be talked of forever after, if he could bring it about that he caught them together in the act.

"It will hardly be long," said Morgan, "before they are found together, if people keep a sharp lookout."

"I shall do so much," said the king, "that if they love each other with a mad love, as you tell me, I will have caught them together, before this month is out, if Lancelot chances to come to court within that time."

That day the king stayed with his sister, and the next day, and the whole week; she hated Lancelot more than any other man because she knew that the queen loved him. So, as long as the king was with her, she never gave up urging him to avenge his shame when he should come to Camelot, if he could find a chance.

"There is no need to beg me, sister," said the king, "for I would not desist for the half of all my kingdom from doing all that I have undertaken in this matter."

The king remained there the whole week, for the spot was beautiful and agreeable and full of wild animals of which the king killed so many during the week that he worked hard at it. But now the tale tells no more of him and Morgan, save to say that he would let nobody enter the room in all the time that he was there on account of the painting which openly portrayed his shame. He would not for anything let others know the truth except himself, for he feared shame too much and that the word would get out elsewhere.

VI
Love and Anguish

At this point the tale tells that Bohort and Sir Gawain and the other companions stayed so long with Lancelot that he was quite well and as strong as he had been before. As soon as he felt that he was back in shape and was no longer afraid to bear arms, he said to his physician:

"Doesn't it seem to you that I can hereafter do with my body what I like without harm to my wound which lasted so long?"

"I tell you truly," the good man said, "that you are quite recovered and need no longer heed the illness that you have had."

"That news pleases me," said Lancelot, "for now I can go away when I like."

The companions that day had a great celebration with much joy. In the evening Lancelot said to the lady of the manor that he would go away the next day and thanked her deeply for her hospitality and the good cheer that she had given him at her manor. Afterward he had her given so much of his property, also to the good man who had healed him, that they were well off for the rest of their lives. That same day the two brothers from Escalot prayed Lancelot to be taken into his company as knights under his banner; they would not leave for any other lord. He received them very gladly, for they were both worthy men and good knights; he spoke to them thus:

"Gentlemen, I receive you among my companions, but I shall often go far away from you, so much alone that you will have no news of me until I return."

"It does not matter, my lord," they said, "if only we can claim to be of your household and you will consider us your knights."

He said he would gladly do so and would give them lands and estates in the kingdom of Benwick or in the kingdom of Gaunes. Thus, they became his knights.

That same day the damsel who was the sister of the two brothers from Escalot came to Lancelot and said to him:

"You are going away, sir, and your return will be a matter of chance. Because no messenger should be so well credited as the lord himself, I shall tell you my need which is great. I wish you to know truly that I shall come to my death, if I am put aside by you in this matter."

"To your death, young lady?" said Lancelot. "You will certainly never die of anything I can help you with."

Then the damsel began to weep many tears; she said to Lancelot:

"Truly, sir, I can say that unlucky was the day I saw you."

"Why so, young lady?" said Lancelot; "tell me."

"Sir," she said, "as soon as I saw you, I loved you beyond any love that a woman's heart could give a man, for, ever since, I have not been able to drink or eat, nor to sleep, nor to rest; instead I have from then till now been tortured in mind and have suffered every grief and every misfortune night and day."

"It was madness," said Lancelot, "to long after me in such a manner, especially since I tell you that my heart does not belong to me, and that, if I could act according to my will, I should consider myself lucky if a young lady like you deigned to love me. And from this hour you ought not to long for me, for you may know well that I meant by such words that I would not love you or any other woman, save only her upon whom I had set my heart."

"Ah, sir," said the damsel, "shall I find no other counsel in you in the matter of this mischance?"

"Truly, no, young lady," said Lancelot, "for I could alter things neither through death nor life."

"Sir," she said, "I am grieved, and know well that I have come to my death; by death my heart will be separated from love of you. And such will be the guerdon of the good company my brother has borne you, ever since you came into this country."

46

Then the damsel quitted him and went to her bed to such a fate that never afterward did she rise from it, except dead, as the tale will relate without concealment. Lancelot, who was much pained and worried by what he had heard the damsel say, was that night more downcast and quieter than was usual, whereat all his companions wondered much, for they were not used to see him so sad.

That day Bohort sent the knight who had healed Lancelot to the king of North Wales with the message that he should think of the knight in such a way that he would be grateful to him, for the knight had done much for him. The next day, as soon as it was light, Lancelot left there with all his company and commended the lady of the manor to God. And when they had set out, they journeyed on till they came to the city of Camelot and alighted in the court of the main palace.

At the hour that Lancelot entered it, the queen was at the window and as soon as she saw him, she left the window out of which she was leaning and went to her bedchamber. As soon as Sir Gawain had dismounted, he entered the queen's room and found her on her bed where she was lying with the face of an angry woman. Sir Gawain greeted her. She rose to meet him and told him he was welcome.

"My lady," he said, "we bring you Lancelot of the Lake who has been out of these parts a long time."

She answered that she could not speak to him then, for she felt too ill. Sir Gawain left the room forthwith and went off to the others in his company and said to them:

"Gentlemen, know that the queen is indisposed. We cannot speak to her. But let us rest here until the king comes, and if he wearies us, we can go hunting in the woods of which there are a great many near here."

They all agreed.

That night Bohort spoke to the queen and asked her what was wrong with her.

"I have no disease," she said, "but I lack all desire to enter that room as long as Lancelot is there, for I have no eyes with which I can look at him nor a heart that consents to my speaking to him."

"What, my lady!" said Bohort, "do you hate him then so much?"

"Yes, I do," she said, "I hate nothing in the world at this moment as I hate him, and never on any day of my life did I love him as much as I hate him now."

"My lady," he said, "that is a pity for us and all our kindred. I regret deeply that the affair is going thus because people who had not deserved it will suffer from it. Fortune never brought about the love of you two, as I see it, except for great damage to us. For I see that my lord and

47

cousin, who is the best and handsomest in the world, is confident that he can get the better of anyone unless one thing takes away the possibility from him, that is, your anger. But without fail your displeasure can turn him away from all good adventures, for, if he knew the words that you have said here, I truly think that I could not reach him in time to keep him from killing himself. It is, to my mind, a very great pity when he who is the best among the good loves you so desperately and you hate him."

"If I mortally hate him," said the queen, "he deserves it."

"What should I say on this subject, my lady?" said Bohort. "I never saw a man of merit who was long in love with a woman who was not in the end put to shame on that account. And if you wished to look at the ancient deeds of the Jews and Saracens, one could show you some of those who true history testifies were shamed through woman. Consider the story of King David; you may find there that he had a son, the hand-somest creature that ever God formed. That son began a war against his father at the instigation of a woman, and he died vilely on that account. Thus you can see that the handsomest man among the Jews died because of a woman. And afterward you can see in that same history that Solomon, to whom God gave such wisdom—beyond what heart of man could understand he gave him knowledge—he denied God because of a woman, and was shamed and committed follies. And Samson the Strong, who was the strongest man in the world, came to his death because of one. Hector the valiant and Achilles, who for deeds of arms and chivalry had praise and esteem above all knights of olden days, both these men died and were killed and more than a hundred thousand men with them. And all this was done because of a woman whom Paris took by force in Greece. And in our own times, it was not five years ago that Tristram died on that account, the nephew of King Mark, who so loyally loved Isolt the Fair that never in his life did he wrong her. What more should I say? Never did a man attach himself firmly to a woman but that he died of it.

"And know that you will do much worse than other women have done, for you will cause to perish in a single knight all the excellent graces through which a man can rise in earthly honor and through which he is called blessed with grace, that is, beauty and prowess, boldness and chivalry, nobility of heart.

"My lady, you can maintain all these virtues in my lord so completely that not one will be missing, for you know well that he is the handsomest man in the world, and the most valiant, and the hardiest and best knight that anyone knows of. Along with this he comes of such a noble line on both his father's and his mother's side that nobody in the world knows a more noble man than he is. But just as he is now clothed and covered

48

with every good virtue, just so will you strip off his garments and leave him naked. You may truly say that by this deed you will take the sun away from the stars; that is, the flower of the world's knights from among the knights of King Arthur. By this act, my lady, you can see clearly that you will damage this kingdom and many another more than ever a lady did through the body of a single knight. Such is the great good that we expect from your love."

The queen responded thus to Bohort:

"If the outcome were what you predict, no other would lose so much as I, for I would lose body and soul. Now leave me in peace, for at this moment you will find no other answer."

"My lady," said Bohort, "you will never hear me speak of it again, unless you speak first to me about it."

Bohort then left the queen and came to Lancelot and said to him in private when he had drawn him aside far from the others:

"My advice is, sir, that we go away from here, for we can do no good staying here, as I see it."

"Why?" said Lancelot.

"My lord, my lord," said Bohort, "my lady the queen has forbidden you her quarters, you and me and all those who will come there in your name."

"Why?" said Lancelot, "do you know?"

"Yes," he said, "I know well, and I shall tell you when we are out of here."

"Let us mount then," said Lancelot. "You will tell me what it is, for I long to know."

Then Lancelot approached Sir Gawain and said to him:

"We have to leave here, my lord, I and all my company, and go attend to an affair of mine that I cannot put off. When you see the king, greet him for me, and tell him I shall return as soon as I can."

"God forbid," said Sir Gawain, "that you leave here in this manner; instead, you will wait for my lord the king."

Lancelot said that he would not. He and his company took horse at once; Sir Gawain rode out a long way with them, and said:

"On this meadow at Camelot there will be very soon a great and wonderful tournament. See that you be there, for there will be few knights left in the kingdom of Logres who are not there."

He said he would come if it were within his personal power. So they separated and Sir Gawain came back to Camelot, vexed that Lancelot had left so soon. Lancelot rode on till he came to the forest of Camelot. When they were within it, he asked Bohort to tell him why the queen was angry at him.

"I will tell you, my lord," he said. Then he began to tell about the sleeve that Lancelot had borne at the tournament at Winchester because of which the queen became greatly wroth and said, "You will never again find peace with me."

When he had told him everything, Lancelot stopped and began to weep in anguish, so that nobody could draw a word from him. After he had been in this condition a long time, he answered:

"Ah, Love! These are the rewards for serving you. Anyone who gives himself up completely to you cannot escape without death. Such is the reward you give for loving loyally. Oh, Bohort, fair cousin, who, knowing my heart as well as I do, knows too that for nothing in the world would I play false to my lady, why did you not make my excuses to her?"

"I did all in my power, my lord," said Bohort, "but she did not ever consent to heed a word that I said."

"Advise me then," said Lancelot, "and tell me what I might do, for if I cannot be reconciled to her, I could not last long. But if she had pardoned me her ill will and her wrath, I would go away more joyously. But in such a state as I am now with her anger and ill will and no permission to speak to her, I do not think that I could live long, for grief and despondency would tear my heart apart. Therefore I ask you, fair good friend, to advise me, for I do not see what I can do with myself after what you have told me."

"My lord," said Bohort, "if you could get along without going where she is or looking upon her, I tell you truly that you would not see a month go by out of her sight and without hearing news of you before she would be thirsting more to have you beside her than you ever did for her at any time, and she would desire you more. And know for a truth that she would send for you if she knew you were near or far. Therefore, I advise formally that you go through this country amusing yourself and enjoying yourself and attending tournaments whenever they proclaim them. You have here with you your good and faithful household and a great part of your kindred, wherefore you ought to rejoice much, for they will bear you company, if such is your pleasure, in whatever place you may wish to go."

He answered that the advice was good, but he had no need of company, for he wanted to go away all alone except for the company of a squire that he would keep with him as long as he wanted him.

"But you, Bohort," he said, "will go on until you see me in person or my messenger who comes looking for you."

"My lord," said Bohort, "it would pain me much to have you leave us thus and go off with such poor company through this country, for if evil befell you in any way, how would we know it?"

"Do not fear," he said, "for He who has allowed me to have victory in all spots where I have been will not allow in His grace that misfortune befall me anywhere. And if it befalls me, you will know of it before any other, be sure."

Then Lancelot returned to his companions who were awaiting him in the middle of the field and said to them that he was obliged to go on business of his own where he could not take along a great company. So he selected a squire of his named Hanguis, and told him to follow him. The man said that he would do so gladly, for he was very happy at the choice. So Lancelot left his blood relatives and they said to him:

"Do not fail, my lord, to be at the tournament at Camelot in such a manner that we may recognize you."

He said he would be there unless a very great hindrance detained him. Then he called Bohort and said to him:

"If I am at the tournament, I will bear white arms without any markings; thereby you may recognize me."

So they parted and commended each other to God. But now the tale ceases to tell of them and returns to King Arthur.

VII
Poisoned Fruit and a Wound

Now the tale says that when the king had stayed with Morgan, his sister, as long as he liked, he left with a great company of people. When he was out of the wood, he journeyed on till he came to Camelot. When he arrived there and learned that Lancelot had been at court only one single day, his heart held many varied thoughts, for it seemed to him that if Lancelot loved the queen with a guilty love, as it had been claimed, he could not stay away from court so long nor turn his back on it as he was doing. This was something that put the king's heart at ease and made him disbelieve the words he had heard from Morgan, his sister. Still there was never an hour afterward in which he did not hold the queen more suspect than he had before the tidings that he had received.

The day after the king had come to Camelot, it happened that at dinner time Sir Gawain was eating at the queen's table with many other knights. In a room next to the hall there was a knight named Avarlan, who mortally hated Sir Gawain and had some poisoned fruit with which he thought to bring death to Sir Gawain. It was his idea that if he sent it in to the queen she would offer some to Sir Gawain before anyone else, and if he ate some, he would die forthwith. The queen, who suspected no treason, took the fruit and offered some to a knight of the Round Table named Gaheris of Karaheu. He, who held the offer very dear for love of the queen who had given it to him, ate some. As soon as it had passed his neck, he fell dead instantly before the eyes of the queen, and everyone at the table leaped up at once in astonishment at this marvel.

When the queen saw the knight dead before her, she was so grieved at this misadventure that she did not know what course to take concerning herself, for so many men of standing had seen what happened that she could not deny that it had taken place.

The news came to the king; a knight who had eaten with the queen told him.

"Sire," he said, "marvels have happened in there just now. My lady the queen has killed a knight by the greatest misadventure in the world. He was a knight of the Round Table and a brother of Mador de la Porte."

He told him what the adventure was. The king crossed himself at once in his surprise. He jumped up from the table to find out whether what had been told him was true or not; so did everyone else in the hall. When the king came to the chamber and found the knight dead, he said that here was a very great misfortune, and that the queen had done a very villainous deed, if she had done it knowingly.

"Certainly," said someone there, "for this act she deserves death if she truly knew that the fruit was poisoned, of which the knight died."

The queen did not know what to do, so very much astonished was she at this misfortune, except to say:

"So help me God in heaven, I am a hundred times sorrier than I could be glad. If I had thought that the fruit that I gave him was treacherously tainted, I would not have given it to him for half of the world."

"My lady," said the king, "under whatever conditions you gave it to him, the result is villainous and cowardly, and I greatly fear that you will be more vexed by it than you think."

Then the king said to all those who surrounded the body:

"My lords, this knight is dead, which is a pity; now think of doing the body as much honor as should be done the body of a valiant man. For certainly he was a man of merit and one of the good knights of my court. I never saw in my life a more loyal and just knight than he was. It grieves me more than many people can believe."

Then the king went out of the room and returned to the main hall and crossed himself more than a thousand times because of his wonder over a knight who died from such a mischance.

The queen left after the king and went out on a lawn with a great company of ladies and damsels. As soon as she was there, she began to lament much and said that God had indeed forgotten her when by such an accident she killed a man of as great merit as that one was.

"So help me God," she said, "I offered the fruit to him first only as a great kindness."

The queen lamented much the misfortune that had befallen her, and the ladies of the court shrouded the body as handsomely and richly as they could and did it as great honor as should be done the body of a man of merit. He was buried at the entrance to the church of My Lord St. Stephen of Camelot. And when the tombstone, as handsome and rich as could be found in the country, was placed above it, the knights of the Round Table by the common consent of all put an inscription which said: "Here lies Gaheris the White of Karaheu, the brother of Mador de la Porte, whom the queen caused to die from poison." Such were the words conveyed by the letters on the monumental slab of the dead knight. King Arthur mourned with all who were present at court. They suffered in such wise that little did they speak of the tournament until the time came for it.

But now the tale ceases to speak of King Arthur and his company and returns to Lancelot in order to relate the cause which kept him from going to the tournament which was held on the meadow at Camelot. At this point the tale tells that when Lancelot had left Bohort and Hector, his brother, he rode through the forest of Camelot, one hour forward, another back, and lay every night at the cell of a hermit to whom he had confessed once upon a time; the man did him all the honor that he could. Three days before the tournament, Lancelot called his squire and said to him:

"Go to Camelot, and bring me a white shield, three vermilion diagonal bands, and plain white horse-trappings. I have borne arms like that so many times that, if Bohort comes to the tournament, he may easily recognize me. I do it on his account more than for anyone else's, for I would in no wise like him to wound me, nor me him."

The squire left Lancelot to go to the city for arms that had been described to him, and Lancelot set off from the hermitage alone to go amuse himself in the forest, and he took along no arms except only his sword. That day it was very hot, and because of the discomfort that he experienced he alighted from his horse, took off its saddle and bridle and tied it to an oak tree close to him. When he had done this he went to lie down at the edge of a spring and straightway fell asleep because he found the spot cool and restful: before, he had been very hot. It happened that the king's huntsmen were on the track of a large stag and had pursued him into the forest; it came to the spring to quench its thirst, for it had been hunted this way and that. And when it had run into the spring waters, an archer who was mounted on a great war horse and was riding a long way ahead of the others turned in that direction to strike the animal in the chest. He happened to miss hitting the stag, because it leaped out a little before the shot. But the arrow did not go altogether without a hit, for it wounded Lancelot so severely in the left thigh that the head went through and a great part of the shaft.

When Lancelot felt himself wounded, he leaped up in great pain and distress, and saw the huntsman riding after the stag at as great speed as he could get out of the horse.

"Rascal, good-for-nothing," he cried, "what have I done to you that you should wound me while I slept? Know that you did it in an evil hour, and bad luck brought you here."

Then Lancelot drew his sword, and sought to run upon him, wounded as he was. When the man saw him coming and recognized that it was Lancelot, he turned around and fled as fast as he could. When he met his companions, he said:

"Do not go farther, boys, unless you want to die, for Sir Lancelot is at that spring, and I wounded him with an arrow when I thought to hit the stag. I am afraid that I have given him a mortal wound and that he is following me."

When the others heard these words, they said to their companion:

"You have come out very badly, for, if he is hurt at all and the king finds it out, we shall all be disgraced and destroyed because of it. If the king himself does not take a hand in it, no one save God could shield us from his kindred, provided they could learn that bad luck got him this way."

Then they turned and fled through the forest. Lancelot, who had remained by the spring very badly wounded, drew the arrow from his thigh in great pain and anguish. He saw that the wound was big and deep, for the arrowhead was very wide. He cut off at once a piece of his shirt to staunch the wound which was bleeding copiously.

When he had staunched it as well as he might, he came to his horse, saddled and bridled it, and mounted with great anguish. Then he rode off, whatever pain it cost, to the hermitage where he had stayed ever since he separated from Bohort. When the worthy man saw he was so wounded, he was much astounded; he asked who had done this to him.

"I do not know," said Lancelot, "what rascal put me into this shape, but I know they are of the household of my lord King Arthur."

Then he told how and wherefore he had been wounded.

"Certainly, sir," said the hermit, "that was an outright misfortune."

"It matters," said Lancelot, "not so much because of me as because of what I will lose by not going this time to the tournament at Camelot. I lost out also on another which took place not long ago at Tanebourc through a wound that I had at that time. That is the thing that most distresses and grieves me, for, because I had not been at the other, I would very gladly have been at this one."

"Since it has happened thus," said the hermit, "you will have to accept it, for, if you went there this time, you would do nothing that would bring you honor. Therefore you will stay here, if you believe me."

And the other said that truly he would stay, whether he liked it or not, for he had to. So Lancelot stayed because of that wound. He lamented much, for it seemed to him that he would die of vexation. In the evening when his squire came and found him so badly wounded, the lad was much taken aback. Lancelot told him to set down the shield that he had brought and the trappings and told him that he was now in a state that forced him to remain where he was. So he stayed there a whole fortnight, before he could ride as he liked.

Now the tale ceases to tell of him and returns to King Arthur. At this point the tale tells that King Arthur sojourned at Camelot after the death of Gaheris until time for the tournament. On the day set you could have seen on the meadow at Camelot some twenty thousand men on one side or the other, and there was not one whom people did not consider a valiant man and a good knight. And when they attacked each other, then you could have seen knights brought down thickly and often. Bohort of Gaunes carried off the prize that day, and all those who were on the field said that he had surpassed them all on either side. And the king who recognized him came to him and said:

"Bohort, I have caught you; you must come in. And you will stay with us, and be in our company as long as you like."

"I could not do so at all," said Bohort, "since my lord, my cousin, is not there. If he were, I would gladly remain and stay on as long as it pleased him to be with you. So help me God, if I had not thought to find him at this tournament, I should not have come. For he told me, when he left me recently, that he would come, that never for any reason would he fail to do so, if there were no hindrance that forcibly retained him."

"You will remain with me," said the king, "and will wait for him until he comes to court."

"Sire," said Bohort, "nothing can make me stay, for I do not believe that you will see him any more for a long time."

"Why," said the king, "will he not come? Has he become angry at us?"

"Sire," replied Bohort, "you will learn no more from me. Ask someone else, if you wish to know the truth."

"If I knew anybody in my court who could tell me, I would ask him," said the king. "But since I know no one, I shall have to accept the situation and wait until the coming of him concerning whom I ask you."

So Bohort left the king, and went away with his brother and Hector and his companions. Sir Gawain rode out a long way with them and said to Bohort:

"I greatly wonder why Sir Lancelot was not at this tournament."

"I am sure," said Bohort, "that I know for a fact that he is ill or in prison, wherever it may be, for if he were in full possession of his powers, I know well that he would have come."

Then they took leave of one another. Bohort rode off in the direction where he thought he might find the king of North Wales. He said to his brother and to Hector:

"I am only afraid that my lord is overwhelmed with grief because of the queen who has become angry at him. Cursed be the hour that ever love began, for I fear that it will still bring us something much worse."

"If I have ever known anything," said Hector, "you will certainly see, between our kindred and King Arthur, the greatest war that you have ever seen and all because of this thing."

Thus those who most loved Lancelot and were in great anxiety because of him began to speak of him.

Sir Gawain, after leaving them, rode till he came to Camelot. When he had alighted and gone up to the main hall, he said to the king:

"Sire, know truly that Sir Lancelot is ill, since he did not come to the tournament. There is nothing I should like to know better than the truth about his condition, to learn whether he is wounded, or absent because of some other illness."

"Certainly," said the king, "if he is ill, I am sorry he is not here, for with his presence and that of those with him my household is so much better that no one could counterbalance their presence."

Such words spoke King Arthur of Lancelot and of the kin of King Ban and he stayed on there with a great company of knights. On the third day after the tournament it happened that Mador de la Porte came to court. Nobody was bold enough to dare tell him news of his brother, for they knew he was a knight with such a great heart that they were certain that, as soon as he should know the truth, nothing would prevent him from taking vengeance to the extent of his power. On the next day he happened to go to the main church in Camelot. When he saw the tombstone newly placed he thought that it must be for one of the knights of the Round Table. He stepped over to find out who it was. When he saw the letters which said:

"Here lies Gaheris de Karaheu, the brother of Mador de la Porte, whom the queen caused to die from poison," then you would have seen a man astounded and in despair. He could not believe that it was true. Then he looked behind him and saw a Scottish knight who was a knight of the Round Table. He called to him at once and conjured him by the faith he owed him to tell him truly what he should ask him.

"Mador," said the knight, "I know what you wish to ask me. You want me to tell you if it is true that the queen killed your brother. Know that it is as the inscription testifies."

"Verily," said Mador, "this is certainly a pity, for my brother was most valiant, and I loved him sincerely as one brother should love another. I shall seek vengeance such as I may have."

Mador mourned greatly for his brother and stayed there till mass was over. When he knew that the king had sat down to eat, he left his brother's tomb, weeping, and went into the hall before the king, and spoke so loudly that all those in the room could hear, and he began thus his discourse:

"King Arthur, if you are as just as a king should be, give me a hearing in your court in such wise that, if anyone knows aught to ask of me, I shall give him justice according to your pleasure, and if I know aught to ask of anyone whatsoever, justice shall be done me as the court orders."

The king answered that he could not forbid that. Let him say what he wished, he would render justice according to his power.

"Sire," said Mador, "I have been your knight for fifteen years and have held land from you. Now I give you back land and homage, for now it does not please me to hold land from you in the future."

Then he stepped forward and divested himself of all the land that he held from the king. When he had done this, he said:

"Sire, I now require of you as a king that you do justice for me upon the queen who treacherously killed my brother. If she wishes to deny the act and not recognize that she has done treason and disloyalty, I shall be ready to prove it against the best knight that she may desire to put up."

After this speech a great hubbub arose in the court and many kept saying among themselves:

"Now the queen is bad off, for she will find nobody to go into battle

57

for her against Mador, since they all know for a certainty that she killed the knight concerning whom she is accused."

The king, who was grieved at this accusation, since he could not deny doing justice to the knight and justice clearly demanded the destruction of the queen, sent for her to come before him to answer what the knight asked. She came lamenting and vexed, for she knew well that she would find no knight who would go into the field for her, because they knew for a truth that she had killed the knight.

The tables had been removed and in the hall there was a great number of knights and noblemen. The queen came with bowed head; she seemed most evidently a perplexed and anxious woman. Sir Gawain accompanied her on one side and on the other Gaheriet, the most esteemed warrior of King Arthur's kindred except only Sir Gawain. When she stood before the king, he said to her:

"My lady, this knight accuses you of the death of his brother and says that you killed him treacherously."

She raised her head and said, "Where is the knight?"

Mador stepped forward and said, "Here I am."

"What!" she said, "Do you say that I killed your brother treacherously and knowingly?"

"I say," he said, "that you caused him to die disloyally and treacherously. If there were here any knight so bold that he wished to enter the field for you against me, I should be ready to fight him till he was dead or recreant this evening or tomorrow or on any day that those in this court shall choose."

When the queen saw that her accuser offered so boldly to prove her treason against the best knight there, she began to look about her to know if anyone would come forward to defend her from this accusation. When she saw that no one there moved, but that each lowered his eyes and listened, she was so astounded and dismayed that she did not know what would become of her, nor what to say or do, and nevertheless, amid all that anguish and that great fear that possessed her, she answered and said:

"Sire, I beg you to do me justice according to the opinion of your court."

"My lady," said the king, "the opinion of my court is such that if you acknowledge the act as Mador presents it against you, you are without recourse. But we cannot legally deny you a respite up to forty days to take counsel about this matter, to learn whether, within these limits, you can find some man of merit who will enter the field for you and defend you against this accusation."

"Sire," she said, "I claim the respite of forty days. Within that period, please God, I will find some valiant man who will enter the field for me, and if on the fortieth day I have not found him, do with me as you like."

The king granted her the respite. When Mador saw that the affair had turned out so, he said to the king:

"Sire, are you doing me justice in giving the queen such a long delay?"

"Yes," said the king, "you know that that is true."

"I shall go away then," he said, "and on that day I shall be here, if God keeps my body from death and imprisonment."

"I tell you, sir," said the king, "if you are not prepared then to do what you have offered, you will never after be listened to by me."

He said he would be there, if death did not detain him, for "no prison could hold me in view of this affair."

Then Mador left court and went off lamenting so loudly for his brother that no one saw him who did not consider it a marvel. The queen remained there weeping and dismayed, for she knew well she would never find a knight, not one, who would wish to enter the field for her, unless it were someone among the kin of King Ban. They would certainly not fail her if they were at hand. But she had so estranged and offended them that she might well consider herself shamed. Now she repented deeply, so that there was nothing in the world short of something shameful that she would not gladly do if only they were again there as they had been not long before.

VIII
Death, Rescue, and Reconciliation

The day after that accusation was made, it happened about noon that a boat covered with very rich cloths of silk came to shore below the tower at Camelot. The king had eaten with a great company of knights and was at the windows of the hall looking up the river and was very pensive and downcast because of the queen, for he knew well that she would have no succor from any knight there, since they had all seen clearly that she had given the knight the fruit of which he had died, and because they knew it for a fact, there was none who would dare risk himself with such stakes.

When the king, as he thought thus, saw the boat which was rich and beautiful come to shore, he showed it to Sir Gawain and said to him:

"There, nephew, is the most beautiful boat I have ever seen. Let us go see what there is within it."

"Let us go," said Sir Gawain.

Then they came down from the main hall, and when they were down, they saw the boat so artistically prepared that they all marveled.

"On my word," said Sir Gawain, "if this boat is as beautiful inside as out, it would be a miracle. I would almost say that adventures are beginning over again."

"I was about to say the same thing," said the king.

The boat was covered as with arches, and Sir Gawain lifted a corner of the cloth and said to the king:

"Sire, let us go aboard and see what there is there."

The king went aboard at once, and Sir Gawain after him. When they were within, they found in the middle of the vessel a very beautiful bed, prepared with all the best things with which a handsome bed can be prepared. On that bed lay a damsel newly dead, who had been very beautiful to judge by the look she still had. And then Sir Gawain said to the king:

"Ah, sire, does it not seem to you that Death was most ugly and villainous when it entered the body of such a beautiful damsel as this maid was so recently?"

"Indeed," said the king, "she seems to me to have been a most beautiful thing. It is a great pity that she died at such an age. Because of the great beauty in her, I would gladly know who she was and what her birth."

They looked long at her, and when Sir Gawain had examined her closely, he perceived that she was the fair damsel for whose love he had pleaded, she who had said that she would never love any other than Lancelot. Then he said to the king:

"Sire, I know well who this damsel was."

"Who was she?" said the king, "tell me."

"Sire," said Sir Gawain, "gladly. Do you perchance remember the beautiful maid, of whom I told you not long ago, the one whom I told you that Lancelot loved?"

"Yes," said the king, "I remember well. You gave me to understand you had asked for her love, but that she had rejected you outright."

"Sire," said Sir Gawain, "this is the maiden of whom we were speaking."

"Truly," said the king, "I am sorry. I should like to know the cause of her death, for I believe that she died of grief."

While they were speaking of these things, Sir Gawain looked beside

60

the damsel and saw a very rich little bag suspended at her belt, but it was not empty, so it seemed. He put his hand to it, opened it at once and drew out some writing. He handed the paper to the king who began at once to read and found that the letters said:

"To all the knights of the Round Table the damsel of Escalot sends greetings. I lay my complaint before you all, not so that you can ever right my wrong, but because I know you for the most noble men in the world, and the wisest. Know plainly that I have come to my end for having loved faithfully. And if you ask for the love of whom I have suffered the anguish of death, I answer that I have died because of the noblest and cruelest man in the world. He is Lancelot of the Lake, who is the cruelest that I know, for I could never beg him with flowing tears enough to make him willing to take pity on me. It has so weighed upon my heart that I have come to my end for having loved faithfully."

These were the words that the letters said. When the king had read them aloud to Sir Gawain, he said:

"Truly, fair maid, may you say that he for whom you died is the cruelest knight in the world and the noblest, for this cruel thing that he has done to you is so very great and so hateful that the whole world should blame him for it. Certainly I, who am a king, and who should not do so, would never have allowed you to die for the best cattle I have."

"Sire," said Sir Gawain, "now you can well perceive that I wrongly calumniated Lancelot when I said that he was sojourning with a lady or damsel with whom he was in love. You said truly that he would not deign to stoop to love a woman of such low degree."

"Now, tell me," said the king, "what shall we do with this damsel, for I cannot find good counsel within myself? She was a noble woman and one of the most beautiful damsels on earth. Let us have her buried with great honor in the main church at Camelot and let us place upon her tombstone an inscription which testifies to the true circumstances of her death; so that those who come hereafter may remember her."

Sir Gawain answered that he was in agreement with this proposal. While they were looking at the letters and the maiden and were lamenting her misfortune, the noblemen had come down from the main hall to the foot of the tower to see what there was in the boat. The king at once had the coverings taken off the boat and the damsel carried up to the hall. Many people assembled to see this marvel. And the king began to relate to Sir Gawain and to Gaheriet the truth about the damsel and how she had died because Lancelot would not grant her his love. These people told others who were very anxious to know the truth. The word went around from one to another until the queen heard the whole thing just as it had happened. Sir Gawain himself said to her:

"My lady, my lady, now I know that I lied about Sir Lancelot when I told you that he loved the damsel of Escalot and he was staying with her; for truly if he had loved with as great a love as I claimed, she would not yet have died; instead, Lancelot would have done all that she required of him."

"People calumniate many a man of merit, sir," she said. "It is a pity, for often they lose by it more than one suspects."

Then Sir Gawain left the queen. She remained much more sorrowful than she was before. She called herself a weary thing, of no account, poor in all her wits, and she said to herself:

"Unhappy wretch, how did you dare believe that Lancelot was inconstant, that he loved any woman but you? Why have you betrayed yourself and deceived yourself thus? Now you see that everybody in this court has failed you and left you in such great peril that you cannot come out of it without death, if you find no one to defend you against Mador. You have failed with all those here, for none will help you, for they are convinced that the wrong is yours and the right Mador's; wherefore they will all desert you and meanly allow you to be led to your death. Nevertheless, with all my appearance of guilt, if my beloved were here, the most faithful of all, he who once before delivered me from death, I know well that he would deliver me from this danger into which I have fallen. Oh, God, why does he not now know the great distress within my heart both for myself and for him? Oh, God, he will not learn of it in time! So I must die shamefully. And thereby he will lose so much that he will die of grief as soon as he hears that I have departed from this world, because never did a man love a woman so much as he has loved me, nor so faithfully."

Thus the queen wailed and grieved and blamed herself, and shamed herself for what she had done, because she ought to have loved and cherished above all men him whom she had spurned and driven away from her.

The king had the damsel buried in the main church of Camelot and had placed above her a very beautiful and rich tombstone and on it were letters that said:

"Here lies the damsel of Escalot who died for love of Lancelot." The letters were of gold and blue most richly executed. But now the tale ceases to speak of King Arthur and the queen and the damsel and returns to Lancelot.

Now the tale tells that Lancelot remained at the hermit's until he was somewhat recovered from the wound that the huntsman had made in him. One day after the third hour he mounted his horse, like one who wishes to go find amusement in the forest. Thus he left the hermitage and set about along a narrow path. He had ridden but a short time when he found a very beautiful spring beneath two trees. Beyond the spring a knight was lying completely disarmed; he had put his arms down beside him and tied his horse to a tree. When Lancelot saw the knight asleep, he thought he would not wake him, but let him rest. When he had awakened, then he could talk to him and ask who he was. So he alighted and hitched his horse rather near the other one and lay down on the other side of the spring. It was not long before the knight awoke because of the noise from the two horses that were fretting each other. When he saw Lancelot before him, he wondered greatly what adventure had brought him there. They greeted each other as they sat and asked after each other's state of being. Lancelot, who wished not to disclose who he was, answered when he saw that the stranger did not recognize him that he was a knight from the kingdom of Gaunes.

"I belong," said the other, "to the kingdom of Logres."

"Whence come you?" said Lancelot.

"From Camelot," was the answer, "where I left King Arthur with a great company of people, but I can tell you that there were more of them vexed than joyful on account of an adventure that happened there recently; it befell the queen herself."

"My lady, the queen?" said Lancelot, "for God's sake, tell me what it was, for I am anxious to know."

"I shall tell you," said the knight. "Not long ago the queen was dining in one of her rooms and with her a great company of ladies and knights. I myself ate with the queen that day. When we had had the first course, a servant lad came into the room and presented fruit to the queen. She gave some to a knight to eat. And he died just as soon as he had put the fruit in his mouth. A cry arose from around them and everybody rushed to see the marvel. When they saw the knight dead, there were a great many who blamed the queen. They laid the knight on the floor and ceased speaking, saying nothing more to the queen. A week or so ago it happened that Mador de la Porte, who was a brother to the dead knight, came to court. When he saw his brother's tomb and found out that the queen had caused his death, he went before the king and accused the queen of treason. The queen looked all round her to see if some knight there would come forward to defend her, but there was none so bold as to wish to accept a challenge for her. The king gave the queen forty days respite with the provision that if by the fortieth day the queen had found no knight who wished to enter the field against Mador, she should be destroyed and disgraced. That is the thing that has made people at court most downcast, for certainly she will never find a knight to venture on to the field for her."

"Now tell me," said Lancelot, "when my lady the queen was accused as you tell me, were there not there any of the valiant knights of the Round Table?"

"Yes, many," said the knight. "All five nephews of the king were there; Sir Gawain and Gaheriet and the other brothers, and Sir Yvain, King Urien's son, and Sagremor the Desreez, and many another good knight."

"How was it then," said Lancelot, "that they allowed my lady the queen to be shamed before them, and that there was nobody who defended her?"

"On my word," said the knight, "there was no one who ventured so much. And they were right, for they had no desire to be called disloyal on account of her, knowing quite certainly that she had killed the knight. They would have been disloyal, it seems to me, if they had deliberately become defenders of a false cause."

"Do you think," said Lancelot, "that this Mador will ever come to court again for this affair?"

"Yes, on my word," said the knight, "I am sure that he will come back on the fortieth day to follow up the accusation that he has made. And I firmly believe that the queen will be put to shame because she will never find a knight so good that he will dare take up his shield to defend her."

"I certainly believe," said Lancelot, "that there will be someone. Otherwise, she would have ill used the good things that she has done for knights from afar, if she found none who would undertake to defend her in this battle. I tell you that there are some in the world who would die rather than fail to save her from this danger. I beg you to tell me when the fortieth day will be."

The stranger told him.

"Now then know," said Lancelot, "that there is in this land a knight who for King Arthur's honor would not fail to be at court that day and defend my lady the queen against Mador."

"I tell you," said the knight, "that he who undertakes this adventure can win no honor in it, for if he should be victorious, all those at court would know that he had acted disloyally against right."

Then they abandoned the subject and said no more about it; instead, they remained together there till vespers. Then the knight went to his horse, mounted, and took leave of Lancelot, commending him to God.

When the knight was some distance off, Lancelot looked and saw an armed knight coming with his squire. He examined him until he saw clearly that it was Hector des Mares, his brother. He was glad of it and went to meet him on foot and shouted long enough for him to hear:

"Hector, welcome! What adventure brings you here?"

When Hector saw him, he alighted, took off his helmet at once and returned his greeting, as happy as a man could be, and he said to him:

"I was going to Camelot, my lord, to defend my lady the queen against Mador de la Porte, who has accused her of treason."

"You will stay now with me tonight," said Lancelot, "and after that till I am completely healed. When the day for battle is to be, we will go to court together. If the knight who made this accusation finds no one to defend the queen against him then, he will never find such a man."

On that, they were both agreed. Then Lancelot got on his horse, and Hector on his. They went straight to the hermitage where Lancelot had stayed so long. When the good man saw Hector, he showed great joy at his coming, both for love of Lancelot, and because he had known him of yore. That night Hector was anxious to know who had wounded Lancelot. Lancelot told him just how it had happened, and Hector wondered at the tale. They remained there a week until Lancelot was quite well from the huntsman's wound and was as healthy and in as good spirits as he had ever been at any time. Then he and Hector set off from the hermitage and began riding through the country with just their two squires, so secretly that it would have been hard to know that it was Lancelot.

One day they happened to meet Bohort, who was riding about in search of Lancelot to learn where he might find him. He had that week separated from Lionel, his brother, and left him with the king of North Wales, who had retained him to make one of his company. When they met, you would have seen wondrous joy between the cousins. Then Bohort drew Lancelot aside and said:

"Have you heard the news yet about the accusation brought against my lady the queen before the king?"

"Yes," he said, "I have been told."

"My lord," said Bohort, "know that I am not displeased about it, for, since she can find nobody to defend her, main force will oblige her to make her peace with you; one of us will have to fight Mador."

"Were she to hate me forever more, so that I would never find peace with her, I would not wish for her to be dishonored as long as I live, that much is sure, for she is the most noble lady who has brought me the greatest honor since I first bore arms. So I will venture to defend her, not so confidently as I have in other battles, for I know quite well, from what I have heard, that the wrong will be mine and the right Mador's."

That night the cousins lay at a castle called Alfain. From then until the end of the respite only four days remained. Then Lancelot said to Hector and Bohort:

"You will go to Camelot and stay there till Tuesday, for that is the day for my lady, and between now and then inquire of my lady if I may ever have peace with her. Then you will come to me when I have won my battle, if it pleases Our Lord that I have the honor of doing so, and at that time you will tell me what you have found out from her."

They said that they would gladly do so. In the morning they left Lancelot, and he forbade them to tell a living being that he was to come to court.

"But so that you may know me when I come, I tell you that I will bear white arms and a shield with an oblique band. By that means you may know when others do not know who I am."

Then both took leave of Lancelot, and he remained in the castle in the company of a single squire and had arms prepared as he had described them. But now the tale ceases to tell of him and returns to Bohort his cousin.

At this point the tale tells that when the two cousins had left Lancelot, they rode till they came to Camelot at the ninth hour. This they could easily do, for Alfain was only four English leagues from Camelot. When they had alighted and disarmed, the king went out to welcome them, for they were two of the knights he esteemed most on earth. Sir Gawain and all the men of most merit there did likewise. They received them with honor as great as is due such knights. Now, when the queen heard that they had come, there was never again such great joy as she felt because of their arrival. She said to a damsel who was with her:

"Since those two have come, my girl, I am sure as sure that I shall never die alone, for they are such valiant men that they will venture body and soul before I receive death at any place where they are. Praise be to God, who has brought them at such a moment, for otherwise it would have gone very ill with me."

While she was speaking thus, Bohort appeared, for he was very desirous of speech with the queen. As soon as she saw him come in, she rose to meet him and told him that he was welcome. He answered with a wish that God grant her joy.

"Indeed," she said, "I cannot fail to be joyous, since you have come.

I thought that I was far from any joy. But now I really believe that I shall recover it presently through God's help and yours."

He answered as if he knew nothing of this affair:

"My lady, how does it happen that you have lost all joy if you do not recover it through God's help and mine?"

"What, sir!" she said. "Do you not know what has happened to me since you saw me?"

He said, "No."

"No?" she said. "I shall tell you in such wise that I shall never lie to you, not by a single word."

Then she told him the truth of what had befallen her so that there was nothing lacking.

"Now Mador accuses me of treason, and there is no knight here so valiant that he dares defend me against him."

"The truth is, my lady," said Bohort, "that if knights are failing you, it is no great wonder, for you failed the best knight in the world. It will not be too unreasonable, it seems to me, if you come to harm, for you caused the death of the best knight known; wherefore I am now happier at this mischance that has befallen you than I have been in a long time at anything I have seen, for now you will know and recognize what a loss has she who loses a valiant man. If he were here now, he would not fail for the whole world to fight this battle against Mador, even though he knew for certain that the wrong was his. But you are brought to such a pass, thank God, that you will never find anyone who will meddle with this for your sake. Thus you may well be in danger of suffering every shame, it is my opinion."

"Bohort!" said the queen, "whoever might fail to succor me, I know well you will not fail me."

"My lady," he said, "may God never help me if you ever find succor in me, for you have taken from me him whom I loved above all men. I should not help you, but harm you with all my might."

"What?" said the queen. "Have I taken him from you?"

"Yes," he said, "so that I do not know what has become of him, nor ever, since I told him news of you, have I known where he went, no more than if he were dead."

Then the queen was distressed; she began to weep bitter tears and was so downcast that she did not know what was to become of her.

When she spoke, she said loud enough for Bohort to hear her:

"Oh God, why was I ever born, when I have to end my life in such pain and grief?"

Then Bohort went away; he was taking vengeance on the queen with words. When he was out of the room and she saw that she would find no comfort, she began a lamentation as marvelous and as great as if she saw dead before her the thing she loved most in the world. She said almost in a whisper:

"Fair sweet friend, now I know well that the kindred of Ban loved me only because of you, for they have failed me when they thought you failed me. Now I may well say that in this hour of need I shall have no resource in you."

The queen wailed and wept night and day. Her grief never ended, rather it became greater from day to day. The king was greatly distressed, for he could not find a knight who would enter the field for him to take up the cause against Mador. Everybody refused to have aught to do with it, for they knew that the queen was wrong and Mador right. The king himself spoke of it to Sir Gawain and said to him:

"I beg you, nephew, for God's sake and for love of me to enter this battle against Mador to defend the queen against the accusation."

"Sire," he answered, "I am ready to do your will, providing you swear to me as a king that you are counseling me loyally as one should a loyal knight. For we know well that the queen killed the knight, as she is accused of doing. I and many another saw it. Now see if I can defend her loyally, for if I can do so, I am ready to go into the field for her. If I cannot, I tell you that even if she were my mother, I would not enter it, for he is not yet born for whom I should wish to become disloyal."

The king could find naught else in Sir Gawain nor in any other of the valiant men there, for they were all stubborn in not wishing to become disloyal for the king or for anyone else. The king was in great dismay and anxiety. The evening before the battle was to take place the next day, you could have seen in the great hall of Camelot all the noblest men of the kingdom of Logres, for they were assembled to see what end the queen would arrive at in her battle. That evening the king said to the queen:

"Truly, my lady, I know not what to say about you. All the best knights in my court have failed me, wherefore you may say that tomorrow you will receive a shameful and villainous death. I would rather have lost all my lands than have had this happen during my lifetime, for I never loved anything on earth as much as I have loved and still love you."

When the queen heard these words, she began to weep copiously, and so did the king, and when they had grieved thus for a long time, the king said to the queen:

"Did you ever ask Bohort or Hector to undertake this battle for you?"

"No, my lord," said the queen, "for I do not believe that they would do so much for me, since they hold no lands from you, but are from a foreign country."

"Nevertheless, I advise you," said the king, "to ask them both. When those two have failed you, afterward I would not know what to say nor any counsel to give."

She said that she would ask them to learn what she could find by doing so.

Then the king left the chamber, lamenting beyond all measure. The queen sent word at once for Bohort and Hector to come speak to her; they came at once. When the queen saw them coming, she fell at their feet and said as she wept:

"Ah! Noble men, famous for your great hearts and your high lineage, if you ever loved him whom men call Lancelot, succor me and help me in my need, not for love of me but for love of him. If you will not do this, know that I shall be shamed before evening tomorrow and villainously dishonored, for in fine all those who belong to this court have failed me in my great need."

When Bohort saw the queen so tormented and in such distress, he took pity on her, raised her from the floor, and said weeping:

"My lady, be not so dismayed. If before the third hour tomorrow you have no better aid than mine would be for you, I will go to battle against Mador."

"Better aid?" said the queen. "Whence could it come?"

"My lady," said Bohort, "that I cannot tell you, but I will hold to what I have said."

When the queen heard these words, she became very happy, for she thought immediately that he was speaking of Lancelot who was to come to her aid. Bohort left the queen at once and Hector with him. They went into a large chamber where they usually lay when they came to court.

The next day at the hour of prime the great hall was filled with barons and knights awaiting the arrival of Mador. There were some who were in great fear for the queen, for they believed that she would find no knight to defend her. A little after the hour of prime Mador came to court and with him a great company of knights who were all relatives of his. He dismounted and then went up to the hall, armed except for his helmet, shield, and lance. He was a very tall knight, full of such great might that in Arthur's court hardly any other knight was known to be as strong as he. When he came before the king, he made the offer of battle just as he had done before. The king said in answer:

"Mador, the queen's quarrel is to be brought to an end in such a fashion that, if she on this day finds no one who will defend her, her body is to be treated as the court determines. Now stay here till the hour of vespers. If by then no one comes forward to undertake battle for her, you shall be justified in your accusation and she shall be found guilty."

Mador said that, since so it was, he would wait. Then he sat down in the middle of the hall with all knights of his kin about him. The room was so crowded that it was a marvel, but all remained so quiet that you could not have heard a living thing. They stood thus till long after the hour of prime.

A little before the third hour, behold Lancelot entered armed so that he lacked nothing that a knight should have. But he came in such wise that he brought with him neither knight nor servant. There he was, armed in white armor with a diagonal band of red on his shield.

When he arrived at court he alighted and tied his horse to an elm tree which was there and hung his shield upon it. When he had done this, he went up to the great hall and without removing his helmet came thus before the king and his barons so that not a soul there knew him save only Hector and Bohort. When he stood before the king, he spoke so loudly that all there could hear him well, and he said to the king:

"Sire, I have come to court because of a marvel that I have heard about in this country, for some people have given me to understand that on this day a knight was to come who accused the queen of treason. If this is true, I have never heard of such a mad knight. For this we all know, whether acquaintances or strangers, that nowhere on earth is there a woman as virtuous as she. And because of the virtue that I know lies within her, I have come here, prepared to defend her if there should be any knight here who accused her of treason."

At these words Mador stepped forward and said:

"Sir knight, I am ready to prove that disloyally and treacherously she killed my brother."

"And I am ready," said Lancelot, "to defend her against the accusation of disloyalty and treason."

Mador was not deterred by these words and held out his pledge token to the king, and Lancelot did likewise. The king accepted them both. Then Sir Gawain said to the king:

"Now I would indeed believe that Mador makes an unjust accusation, for however his brother died, I would swear on saints' relics that to my knowledge the queen thought of no disloyalty or treason. All sorts of evil might befall, if this knight had in him no prowess or might."

"Truly," said the king, "I know not who this knight is, but I believe that he will gain honor thus, and I consent to it."

70

Then the hall began to empty out the people. Great and small came down from it and went to the meadow outside the city where the battles usually took place in a very fair spot. Sir Gawain took the knight's lance and said he would carry it to the field for him, and Bohort took the shield. Lancelot mounted at once, and rode off to the field. The king sent for the queen and said to her:

"My lady, here is a knight who risks death for you. Know that if he is conquered, you will be destroyed and he will come to a bad end."

"Sire," she said, "may God be on the side of right just as truly as it is that I thought no disloyalty or treason."

Then the queen took her knight, sent him into the field and said to him:

"Fair sweet sir, go forward in God's name; may Our Lord help you today."

Then the knights drew up opposite each other, spurred their steeds and came together at as great speed as they could get from the horses, and they struck each other so hard that neither shield nor hauberk saved them from giving each other great deep wounds. Mador was carried from his horse to the ground so roughly that he was stunned by his fall, since he was big and heavy. But he got up forthwith, like a man who was not at all sure of himself, for he had found his enemy strong and hard in the joust. When Lancelot saw him on foot, it seemed to him that, if he pursued him on horseback, he would be blamed for it. So he alighted and let his horse go where it might. Then he drew his sword, put his shield before his head and went to attack Mador where he was and gave him such a great blow on his helmet that the man was dizzy from it. Nevertheless, he defended himself the best he could, and gave Lancelot great blows over and over again. But all that was of no use to him, for before noon was past Lancelot had him in such shape that he had made blood flow from his body in more than ten places.

He drove him around so much and belabored him so that all those on the grounds saw clearly that Mador was defeated and that he would be killed, if his adversary so willed. All those around the field praised him who was fighting Mador, for it seemed to them that they had not seen for a very long time such a valiant man as he. And Lancelot, who was well acquainted with Mador and did not wish his death, because sometimes they had been companions in arms, saw that he had brought him to the point where he could kill him, if he wished. He took pity on him and said:

"Mador, you are conquered and brought to shame, if I like; you can see that you will fall if the battle lasts longer. Therefore I would advise you to renounce your accusation, before you suffer evil because of it. And

I will bring it about that my lady the queen will forgive you for this suffering that you have laid upon her and the king will declare you quit of all pursuit."

When Mador heard the kindness and the generosity of the offer, he knew at once that it was Lancelot. So he knelt before him, took his sword, held it out to him, and said:

"My lord, here is my sword, I place myself completely at your mercy. Know that I hold it to be no shame, for certainly I could not hold out against as doughty a knight as you are, and you have proved it here and elsewhere."

When the king heard that it was Lancelot, he did not wait for him to come out of the field, but rushed out and ran to Lancelot and embraced him, armed as he was. Sir Gawain came forward and unlaced his helmet for him. Then you could have seen such great joy around him that you have never heard of greater. The queen was declared free of the accusation that Mador had made against her, and if she had been angry at Lancelot, she now considered herself mad and stupid.

IX
Adultery and Rescue

One day it happened that the queen was alone with Lancelot. They began to speak of many things, until the queen said:

"My lord, I wrongly believed you guilty with the damsel of Escalot, for I know truly now that if you had loved her with so great a love as many people gave me to understand, she would not yet be dead."

"What, my lady," said Lancelot, "is that young lady really dead?"

"Yes, indeed," said the queen. "She lies yonder in St. Stephen's Church."

"By God," he said, "it is a pity, for she was very beautiful. I am sorry, so help me God."

Such words and very many others they said together.

If Lancelot had loved the queen before, now he loved her more than he had ever done at any time, and she loved him as much. They behaved so foolishly that many people there learned the truth. Sir Gawain himself knew it as quite evident, and so did his four brothers. It happened one day that they were all five in the great hall speaking on this subject in a close group. Agravain was much more agitated about it than any of the others. While they were speaking of this matter, by chance the king came out of the queen's chamber. When Sir Gawain saw him, he said to his brothers:

"Be quiet, here is our lord the king."

And Agravain answered that he would never be silent on that account. The king heard that speech, and said to Agravain:

"Tell me, nephew, of what you are speaking so loudly."

"Ah," said Sir Gawain, "for God's sake, let the matter be. Agravain is more bothersome than he should be. Do not concern yourself with this subject. No good could come of it either to you or to any worthy man."

"In God's name," said the king, "I want to know it."

"Oh, please, sire, the whole thing is impossible, for in what he says there is nothing but gossip and lies, the meanest ones on earth. Therefore I would counsel you as my liege lord that you give up questioning at once."

"By my head," said the king, "I shan't do that; rather I charge you now by the oath you have made me to tell me what you were quarreling over just now."

"It is a wonder about you," said Sir Gawain. "You have such a burning desire and are so curious to learn news. Certainly, even if you were to become wroth with me and drive me poor and ruined from your land, I would not tell you, for if you believed it, even though it be the greatest lie on earth, such evil could come of it that never in your times has so great befallen."

Then the king was more astonished than before. He said he would find out or have them all destroyed.

"On my word," said Sir Gawain, "God willing, you will never find out from me, for at the last I would have your hatred because of it. There would be nobody, not I nor any other, who would not repent your knowing."

He left the room at once and so did Gaheriet. The king kept calling after them, but they would not return. Instead, they went away as melancholy as could be, and they told each other that unhappy was the hour when that subject came up, for if the king found out the facts and took issue with Lancelot, the court would be destroyed and put to shame, because Lancelot would have as a help the full power of Gaul and of many another country.

So the two brothers went away so laden with grief that they did not know what they should do. The king, who was left with his other nephews, took them into a room opening on a garden. When they were inside, he closed the door behind them. Then he conjured them by the faith they owed him to tell him what he required of them. First he asked

73

Agravain, and he said that he would not tell; let him ask the others. And they said that they would never speak on the subject.

"When you refuse to tell me," said the king, "either you will kill me or I will kill you."

He ran to a sword lying on a bed, drew it from its scabbard, advanced on Agravain and shouted that without fail he would kill him if he did not tell what he was so desirous of hearing. He raised the sword to strike him in the middle of his head. When Agravain saw him so hot with anger, he cried:

"Ah, sire, do not kill me! I will tell you. I was saying to Sir Gawain, my brother, and to Gaheriet and to my other brothers here present that they were disloyal and traitorous in suffering for so long the shame and dishonor that Sir Lancelot of the Lake brings upon you."

"What!" said the king. "Is Lancelot shaming me? What is this about? Tell me, for I never suspected him of bringing about my shame, for I have always so honored him and held him so dear that he ought in no way to bring shame upon me."

"Sire," said Agravain, "he is so loyal to you that he dishonors you through the queen your wife, and he has known her carnally."

When the king heard these words, he changed color and grew pale, and he said:

"All this is a wonder."

Then he began to think and was silent for a long time.

"Sire," said Mordred, "we kept it from you as long as we could, but now the truth must out and we must tell you. Insofar as we have concealed it from you, we have been perjured and disloyal toward you. Now we acquit ourselves of our duty. We tell you with certainty that such is the truth. Now consider how this shame is to be avenged."

At this news the king was downcast and grieved and in such pain that he did not know what he should do. Nevertheless, when he spoke, he said:

"If you ever loved me, bring it about that you catch them in the act. If I do not then take such vengeance as one should on a traitor, I never wish to wear a crown again."

"Sire," said Guerrehet, "give us counsel, will you? It is a fearsome thing to bring to his death so valiant a man as Lancelot, for he is strong and bold and his kin are powerful in every manner; thus it will happen, you well know, that if Lancelot dies the kindred of King Ban will begin a war against you so great and wondrous that the most powerful men in all your realm will have much to do to hold out. You yourself, if God takes no hand, may be killed, because they will be more eager to avenge Lancelot than to preserve themselves."

"Have no cares about me, but do what I tell you, so as to catch them together, if you can; I require it of you on the oath you gave me when you became knights of the Round Table."

And they gave their word to do so, since he was in such anguish. All three swore to it. Then they went out of the room and off to the main hall.

That day the king was in deeper thought than usual; it was clear that he was angry. Sir Gawain and Gaheriet came at the ninth hour. When they saw the king, they knew well from his look that he had been told news of Lancelot. For that reason they never approached him but went over to the windows of the great hall. The room was quiet and serious. There was no one there who dared say a word, because they saw that the king was in a bad mood. While things stood thus, an armed knight came in and said to the king:

"Sire, I can tell you news of the tournament at Karahais; the people from the kingdom of Sorelois and from the Waste Land have lost everything."

"Were there any knights there from here?" said the king.

"Yes, sire. Lancelot was there and he carried off the prize on every side."

The king's brow clouded when he heard this news and he began to think. When he had thought a long time, he arose and said so loudly that many could hear him:

"Oh, God! What pain and what a pity when treason ever found shelter in so valiant a man!"

The king went into his chamber and lay down on a bed wrapped in thought, for he knew well that if Lancelot were caught in this affair, and came to his death in it, never would so great a torment have taken place in that country for the death of a single knight. And still he would rather die than leave his shame unavenged before him. Then he sent for his three nephews. When they came, he said to them:

"Gentlemen, Lancelot will soon come in from the tournament; now instruct me how he may be surprised in this affair that you have unveiled to me."

"On my word," said Guerrehet, "I do not know."

"In God's name," said Agravain, "I will show you how. Send out word to all your servants that you will go hunting in the morning. Then he will come lie with the queen; we will stay behind to let you know the truth. And we will be posted here in a room, so that we will take him prisoner and keep him until you come back."

The king gladly agreed to this proposal.

75

"But take care," he said, "that not a soul knows about it until the thing is done as you have described it."

At this point Sir Gawain appeared. When he saw them talking so close together, he said to the king:

"Sire, God grant that nothing but good comes of this council; for I am expecting more harm to you than to anyone else. Agravain, fair brother, I beg you not to begin a thing you cannot finish. Say nothing about Lancelot unless you know it for a certainty, for he is the best knight you ever saw."

"Gawain," said the king, "flee from here, for you are a man in whom I will never have faith, for you conducted yourself badly toward me when you knew my shame and suffered it and did not let me know of it."

"Truly," said Sir Gawain, "no treason of mine ever did you harm." Then he came out of the room, saw Gaheriet, and said to him:

"In spite of everything, Agravain has told the king what we did not dare tell him; know for sure that evil will come of it."

"You may be sure," said Gaheriet, "that I will never take a hand in it. Never will a man of such merit as Lancelot be accused by me of this villainous act. Now let us leave Agravain to do what he has undertaken. And if good comes of it, let him profit by it, and if evil comes, he cannot say that it was through us."

They left court and went to Gaheriet's quarters. As they were going down through the city, they met Lancelot and his companions. When they came upon each other, from as far off as they could see one another, they gave demonstrations of great joy.

"Sir Lancelot," said Gaheriet, "I ask a boon of you." Lancelot granted it gladly, provided it was something he could do.

"Many thanks," said Gaheriet. "Now I wish you and your company to come lodge with me. Know that I ask you more for your good than for your harm."

When Lancelot heard these words, he said "yes" gladly. They turned around and went to Gaheriet's place just as they were. Then squires and servants came up to disarm Lancelot and the others who had come from the tournament. When it was supper time, they went to court all together, for they greatly loved Lancelot.

Lancelot marveled, when he had arrived there, that the king who usually welcomed him warmly, said not a word to him that time, but turned away his face as soon as he saw him coming. He did not perceive that the king was angry with him, for he did not believe that the king had heard such news as had been told him. Then he sat down with the knights, and began to talk cheerily, but not as customarily because he saw the king preoccupied. After supper, when the tablecloths had been removed, the king summoned his knights to go hunting in Camelot Forest the next morning. Then Lancelot said to the king:

"Sire, you will have me for a companion on the way."

"My lord," said the king to Lancelot, "you may stay behind this time, for I have so many other knights that I will not suffer for lack of your company."

Then Lancelot perceived that the king was angry at him, but he had no suspicion as to the cause; he was very sorry about it.

In the evening when it was time to go to bed, Lancelot left court with a great company of knights. When they were at their lodgings, Lancelot said to Bohort:

"Did you see the mien that King Arthur showed me? I believe that he is angry at me about something."

"My lord," said Bohort, "know that he has bad news of you and the queen. Now watch what you do, for we are coming to the war that will never end."

"Ha," said Lancelot, "who was the man who dared tell news of it?"

"My lord," said Bohort, "if it was a knight, it was Agravain, and if it was a woman, it was Morgan, King Arthur's sister."

The two cousins talked long that night about the matter. The next day, when it grew light, Sir Gawain said to Lancelot:

"Gaheriet and I will go into the forest. Will you come with us?"

"No," said Lancelot, "I shall stay here, for now I am in no mood to go where my will takes me."

Sir Gawain and Gaheriet rode after the king into the forest. As soon as the king had set out, the queen called a messenger and sent him to Lancelot, who was still abed. She told him that for no reason should he fail to come to her. When Sir Lancelot saw the messenger, he was glad, and told him that he would go, for he would follow him. Then he dressed and got ready and pondered as to how he might go most secretly so that nobody would know of it. He took counsel with Bohort, who begged him in God's name not to go.

"If you go, you will reap evil from it, for my heart, that never till now was afraid for you, keeps telling me so."

Lancelot answered that for no reason would he fail to go.

"My lord," said Bohort, "since your mind is set on going, I will give you directions for the way to go. There is a garden which stretches from here to the queen's chamber. Enter it. Thus you will find the quietest path most nearly free of people that I know. I beg you in God's name not to fail for any reason to carry your sword with you."

When Lancelot approached the tower, Agravain, who had his spies placed on every side, learned that he was coming, for a boy said to him:

"My lord, Sir Lancelot is coming this way."

Agravain told him to keep still. He himself went straight to a window which opened on the garden and watched Lancelot coming swiftly toward the tower. Agravain, who had a great company of knights with him, led them to a window, pointed out Lancelot to them, and said:

"There he is. Now take care, when he is inside the room, that he does not escape."

They said that he would have no chance to escape, for they would catch him naked. Lancelot, who did not suspect that he was watched, came to the door that gave out on the garden from near the chamber, opened it, entered, and went from room to room till he came to the one where the queen awaited him.

When Lancelot was inside, he locked the door behind him so that, as luck had it, he was not to be killed. He took off his garments and got into bed with the queen. But he had not been there long when those who were on the watch to catch him came to the chamber door. When they found it locked, there was not one of them who was not taken aback; then they knew that they had failed in what they wanted to do. They asked Agravain how they would get in. He instructed them to break down the door, for otherwise they would not enter. They struck at it and pried until the queen heard them. She said to Lancelot:

"Fair sweet friend, we are betrayed!"

"What, my lady, how so?"

Then he listened and heard at the door a great noise from people trying to break in, but without success.

"Ah, fair sweet friend," said the queen, "now we are put to shame and we shall die; now the king will know about you and me. Agravain has worked up all this snare."

"As for that, my lady," said Lancelot, "have no care. He has brought about his own death, for he will be the first to die."

Then they both got out of bed and dressed as best they might.

"My lady," said Lancelot, "have you a hauberk here or any other armor with which I can arm my body?"

"Alas, no," said the queen. "Rather our misfortune is so great that we shall have to die, you and I. I regret it, so help me God, more for you than for me, for your death would be a much greater loss than mine. Yet, if God willed that you should escape from here safe and sound, I know that the man is not yet born who would dare procure my death for this misdeed, as long as he knew you were alive."

When Lancelot heard these words, he advanced toward the door like a fearless man, shouting at those who were beating at it:

"You evil, cowardly knights, wait for me, for I am going to open the door to see who will come forward."

Then he drew his sword, opened the door, and said, "Come on!" A knight named Tanaquin, who hated Lancelot mortally, stepped out before the others. Lancelot, who had his sword raised, struck him so hard, since he put his full strength into it, that neither helmet nor iron hood prevented the man's being split to the shoulders. Lancelot pulled back his sword, and his opponent fell dead on the floor. When the others saw him in this shape, there was not one who did not draw back so that the doorway was left empty. When Lancelot saw this, he cried to the queen:

"My lady, this war is over. When you like, I will depart, for I shall not fail to at all because of any man here."

The queen said she would that he were safe, no matter what might happen to her. Then Lancelot looked at the knight whom he had killed, who had fallen half within the chamber. He drew him in and closed the door, then he disarmed him and armed himself as best he could. Then he said to the queen:

"My lady, since I am armed, I should now be able to leave in safety, God willing."

And she told him that he should leave if he could. He went to the door, opened it, crying that they would keep him no longer that day. Then he leaped out among them all, sword drawn, and struck the first man he met so that he stretched him on the floor in such wise that the stricken man had no power to rise. When the others saw that blow, they retreated and the boldest made way for him. When he saw that they had let him alone, he got into the garden, went off to his quarters and found Bohort, who had greatly feared that he would not come back when he liked. For he was sure in his heart that the kinsmen of King Arthur had spied on Lancelot in some way so as to catch him. When Bohort saw his lord who had left unarmed, coming dressed in armor, he perceived that there had been a fight. He went to meet him and asked:

"My lord, what turn of fortune gave you armor?"

Lancelot told how Agravain and his two brothers had spied upon him, tried to catch him in the act with the queen and how they had brought along a large company of knights.

"They would have captured me, too, because I was not on the watch, but I put up a stiff fight, and did so well that with God's help, I escaped."

"Ah, my lord," said Bohort, "now matters are worse than before, for now what we concealed so long has been discovered. Now you will see the war begin that never will come to an end in our lifetime. For if the king has till now loved you more than any man, he will hate you so much the more as soon as he knows that you acted against him to the point of shaming him with his wife. Now you must consider how we shall act together, for I know well that the king will be my mortal enemy. But, so help me God, I am distressed for my lady, the queen, who will be sentenced to death on your account. If it were possible, I should like for us to plan in counsel how she may be delivered from this affair safe in body."

At this point Hector came in. When he learned that things had come to such a pass, he was most grieved and said:

"The best I see is for us to leave and go into that forest out there, so the king who is in it now will not find us. When it is time for my lady the queen to be sentenced, I know that it is certain that she will be brought outside of town to be destroyed. Then we will rescue her whether they like it or not, those people who will think they have brought her out to her death. When we have her with us, we may get out of the country, and go off to the kingdom of Benwick or to that of Gaunes. If we can succeed in conducting her to safety there, we need have no fear of King Arthur and all his might."

Lancelot and Bohort accepted this proposal. They had knights and servants mount at once, thirty-eight of them by head count, and they rode out of the city and took their station on the edge of the forest where they knew it to be the thickest, so that they might be less noticed till evening. Then Lancelot called a squire of his and said to him:

"Go straight to Camelot and inquire about till you have news about my lady the queen and what they wish to do with her. If they have sentenced her to death, come tell us as fast as you can, for no matter how great the pain and travail that we must have to rescue her, nothing can prevent our might from saving her from death."

Then Lancelot's young man went off on his horse by the straightest road possible to Camelot, and went on till he came to King Arthur's court.

But now the tale ceases to speak of him and returns to Sir Gawain's three brothers at the moment when Lancelot had left them, when they had found him in the queen's room.

Now the tale tells that at the time that Lancelot had left the queen and escaped from those who thought to take him, that is, those who were at the chamber door, they entered the room, seized the queen, and heaped shame and ugly words upon her much more than they should have and said now the thing was proved and that she could not escape from death. She listened to their shaming most sorrowfully and wept so piteously that the felon knights should have taken pity on her.

80

At the ninth hour the king came from the woods. When he had alighted down in the courtyard, immediately the news that the queen had been caught with Lancelot reached him. The king was very much grieved, and asked if Lancelot had been taken prisoner.

"No, sire," they said, "for he defended himself so vigorously that no other man could have done what he did."

"Since he is not here," said King Arthur, "we will find him at his lodgings. Now have a great many men armed, and go take him prisoner, and when you have taken him, come to me. I shall do justice to him and the queen together."

Then as many as forty knights went armed from there, not willingly, but because it had to be done, for the king had given the order with his own mouth. When they had come to Lancelot's quarters, they did not find him there. There was not a knight among them who was not very glad of it, for they knew well that if he had been found and they had tried to take him by force, they would have been in for a great, cruel fight. Then they returned to the king, and told him that they had missed Lancelot, for he had gone off hours before and taken with him all his knights. When the king heard this, he said that he thought it a bad thing. Since it turned out that he could not take vengeance on Lancelot, he would avenge himself on the queen in such a manner that people would talk of it forever after.

"Your Majesty," said King Yon, "what do you wish to do?"

"I wish the strictest justice to be done her for the crime she has done. And I command you, first of all, because you are a king, and then afterward the other barons who are here present, and I require you on the oath you have made me to examine among you by what death she should die, for she cannot escape without sentence of death. If you yourself behave in such a manner toward her that you say she should not die, die she will."

"Sire," said King Yon, "it is not according to custom or usage in this country that any man or woman shall be sentenced to death after the ninth hour, but in the morning, if we are brought to the point where we have to give judgment, we will do so."

Then King Arthur said no more and was so sorrowful that all night long he would never drink or eat, nor did he ever wish that the queen be brought before him. In the morning at the hour of prime, when the barons were assembled in the great hall, the king said:

"My lords, what should be done with the queen by just judgment?"

The barons gathered in counsel and asked Agravain what should be done, asked him and the other two brothers. They said that they con-

81

sidered that justice required that she should die a shameful death, for she had been unforgivably disloyal when she had let another knight lie with her instead of the king, who was a man of such high qualities.

"We say by just judgment that for that thing alone she has deserved death."

The others of necessity agreed, for they saw that it was the king's will. When Sir Gawain saw that the trial had come out so that the death of the queen was announced, then he said that, God willing, he would not accept the pain of seeing the execution of the one woman who had exalted him to very great honor. Then he went to the king and said:

"Sire, I yield back to you all that I hold from you, and never again in my lifetime will I serve you, if you allow this disloyalty."

The king made no answer to this speech, for he had another matter on his mind. Sir Gawain left court at once and went straight to his lodgings, lamenting as if he had seen the whole world dead before him. The king commanded his servants to make on the meadow at Camelot a great and marvelous fire into which the queen was to be put, for by no other method should a queen die who has been guilty of disloyalty, since she is a consecrated being. Now cries and uproar shook the city of Camelot, and people gave voice to lamentations as great as if the queen were their mother. Those whom he had ordered to make the fire made it so great and marvelous that everybody in the city could see it.

The king commanded that the queen should be brought before him. She came weeping bitterly, dressed in a vermilion garment of light silk, a gown, and a mantle. She was so beautiful and so attractive a woman that nowhere on earth could one be found as beautiful and attractive for her age. When the king saw her, such great pity seized him that he could not look at her but ordered her to be taken from before him and that there should be done what the court required by its judgment. They led her at once from the great hall and out through the streets. When the queen had come out of the court and the people in the city saw her approach, then you could have heard people crying from all sides:

"Ah, lady, gracious above all other ladies, more courteous than any other, where will the poor ever again find pity? Ah, King Arthur, who have brought her to her death by your disloyalty, may you yet repent, and may the traitors who have accomplished this die a shameful death!"

Thus spoke the people of the city and followed after the queen, weeping and crying as if out of their minds. The king ordered Agravain to take forty knights and go guard the field where the fire had been lighted, so that, if Lancelot should come, he would be powerless before them.

"Sire, is it your desire that I go?"

"Yes," said the king.

"Then command my brother, Gaheriet, to come with us."

The king gave the order, and Gaheriet said that he would have naught to do with it. Nevertheless, the king threatened him until he promised to go. He went to put on his armor and so did the others. When they were armed and were out of the city, they perceived that they numbered a good eighty men.

"Now, Agravain," said Gaheriet, "do you think that I have come to struggle against Lancelot if he should wish to rescue the queen? Know for a certainty that I will not attack him; instead I would rather he kept her forever than that she should die thus!"

Agravain and Gaheriet rode along debating until they neared the fire.

Lancelot, who was ambushed at the edge of the forest with all his people, as soon as he saw his messenger returning, asked what news he brought from King Arthur's court.

"My lord," the man answered, "bad, for our lady the queen is sentenced to death, and there is the fire in which they are preparing to burn her."

"Gentlemen," cried Lancelot, "to horse! There is a man who thinks that he will cause death and who will die himself. Now God grant that, if He ever heard a sinner's prayer, I come first upon Agravain who planned this affair for me."

They examined to see how many knights they were; they found on counting that they numbered thirty-two. Each man mounted his horse, and they took their shields and lances; then they rode off toward the place where they saw the fire. When those on the meadow saw them coming they cried all together:

"Here is Lancelot! Flee! Flee!"

And Lancelot, who rode in front of all the others, headed toward Agravain and cried:

"Villain, traitor, you have come to your end."

Then Lancelot struck him so hard no armor could prevent his putting his spear through his body. The blow was true, sent home by a man of courage and strength. He brought him to earth and the lance broke with the fall. Bohort, who was coming on as fast as his horse could gallop, shouted to Guerrehet to be on guard; he defied him to mortal combat. He headed his horse toward him and struck him so hard that no armor stopped his putting the spear into his chest. He carried him from his horse to the ground in such shape that he needed no physician. The others put their hands to their swords, and close combat began. Now, when Gaheriet

83

saw that his two brothers had fallen, do not ask whether he was angry, because he thought they were dead. Then he headed toward Meliadus the Black, who was laboring hard to help Lancelot avenge the queen's shame. He struck him so hard that he knocked him into the fire, and then put his hand to his sword like a man of great courage, and he struck another knight, bringing him to earth at Lancelot's feet. Hector, who was on the watch, saw Gaheriet, and said to himself:

"If that man lives long, he may do us much harm. It is best for me to kill him before he does worse to us than he has done."

Then Hector spurred his horse and came toward Gaheriet with sword drawn, and struck him so hard that he made his helmet fly off his head. When Gaheriet found his head unprotected, he was amazed. Lancelot, who was riding about dealing blows here and there, did not recognize him. So he struck him so hard on his head that he split it down to his teeth.

At that blow, as soon as they saw Gaheriet fall, King Arthur's men gave way, but those who were pursuing them kept after them so that out of the whole eighty only three were left; Mordred was one, and the other two were knights of the Round Table. When Lancelot saw there was no longer anyone from the king's household who was resisting him, he came to the queen and said to her:

"My lady, what shall we do with you?"

She answered like a woman glad of this adventure that God had sent her:

"My lord, I should like you to put me in safety some place where King Arthur would have no power."

"You will mount a palfrey," said Lancelot, "and will come with us into that forest, there we will take counsel as to what is best."

She agreed to his proposal.

Then they put her on a palfrey and rode into the forest where they saw that it was thickest. When they were well within it, they examined to see if they were all there; they saw that they had lost three of their companions. Then they asked each other what deeds they had performed.

"On my word," said Hector, "I saw three die that Gaheriet killed by himself."

"What!" said Lancelot. "Was Gaheriet at this affair?"

"My lord," said Bohort, "what are you asking? You killed him yourself."

"Yes, God is my witness," said Hector, "you killed him."

"Now may we well say," said Lancelot, "that never again will we have peace with King Arthur or with Sir Gawain because of their love for Gaheriet. Now the war will begin which will never have an end."

Lancelot was much troubled by the death of Gaheriet, for he was among the knights whom he loved most in the world. Bohort said to Lancelot:

"My lord, it would be well for us to consider how my lady the queen may be put in safety."

"If we could succeed," said Lancelot, "in taking her to a castle that I conquered long ago, I think she would have little to fear from King Arthur. The castle is wonderfully strong, and is situated at a spot where it cannot be taken by siege. If we were there and had stocked it well, I would summon from near and far knights whom I have served many times. There are many who are mine by their oath, and they will all come to my aid."

"Where," said Bohort, "is this castle of which you speak, and what is its name?"

"Its name," said Lancelot, "is the Castle of Joyous Guard, but when I conquered it in the days when I was a knight newly made, it was called Dolorous Guard."

"Ah, God," said the queen, "when shall we be there?"

They all accepted this proposal, and they set out along the great forest road, saying that never could so many from King Arthur's household come after them but that they would kill them. They rode on thus till they reached a castle called Kalec that was within the forest. Its lord was a count who was a good knight of great power who loved Lancelot above all men. When he learned of Lancelot's coming, he was much rejoiced and received him with great honor, displayed all the respect that he ever could, and promised to help him against all men, even against King Arthur, and he said to him:

"My lord, if it pleased you, I would turn this castle over to you and to my lady the queen. You should accept my offer, it seems to me, for the place is very strong, and if you wish to stay here, you need not fear anybody nor all King Arthur's power."

Lancelot thanked him warmly and said that he would not stay there for any reason. So they left that castle and rode for days till they came to a place four leagues from Joyous Guard. Then Lancelot sent a messenger to say that he was coming. When the people in the castle learned this, they came to meet him, displaying as much joy as if he were God himself. They received him much more royally than they would have received King Arthur. When they learned that he wished to stay there and why he had come, they swore on saints' relics that they would stand by him until death. Then Lancelot sent for the knights of the county and they came in great plenty.

But now the tale ceases to speak of them and returns to speak of King Arthur.

X
Preparations for War

Now the tale tells that when King Arthur saw Mordred come flee-ing with such a small company he wondered greatly how that could be. He asked those who came first why they were fleeing.

"Sire," a youth said, "I must tell you bad news, you and all those here. Sire, know that of all the knights who took the queen out to the fire only three have escaped. Mordred is one, and I do not know who the other two are. I believe all the rest are dead."

"Ha!" said King Arthur, "was Lancelot there then?"

"Yes, sire," the youth said, "and he has done more yet, for he is carry-ing the queen off with him. He rescued her from death and with her has plunged into the forest of Camelot."

The king was so grieved at this news that he knew not what to do. At this point Mordred arrived and said to the king:

"Sire, it went badly for us. Lancelot has gone off after defeating us all, and he is taking the queen with him."

"After them!" said the king. "They will never go off in this way, if I can stop it."

Then he had knights and servants armed and all those who were with him. They mounted as fast as they could, and issued from the city covered with iron and went on till they came to the forest and rode up and down to learn whether they could find what they were seeking. But it turned out that they found nobody. The king was of the opinion that they should separate along several roads and that they would find them more easily.

"In God's name," said King Karados, "such is not my advice, for if they separate and Lancelot finds them, because he has a great company of strong bold knights with him, those whom he encounters are finished, for he will kill them."

"Whatever shall we do?" said King Arthur.

"Send your messengers to all the sailors in the ports of this country to say that nobody shall be so daring as to give passage to Lancelot. Then he will have to stay, like it or not, in this country, and since he will be still here and we can easily find out where he is, we may easily take him prisoner and then you can take vengeance on him. Such is my advice."

Then King Arthur called his messengers and sent them to all the ports in the land and forbade anyone to be so bold as to give Lancelot passage. When he had sent his messengers, he turned back toward the city, and when he came to the spot where his knights lay dead, he looked to the right and saw lying there Agravain, his nephew whom Lancelot had slain. The dead man was pierced through the body with a spear so that the spearhead showed on the other side. As soon as the king saw him, he recognized him; then he had such great grief that he could not hold himself in his saddle, but fell to the ground in a faint over the body. When he finally recovered his breath and could speak, he said:

"Ah, fair nephew, he who struck you hated you so much. Surely, people understand that he who cut from my family such a knight as you were has put great grief into my heart."

Then he removed the helmet from Agravain's head and looked at him; afterward he kissed his eyes and mouth, which was quite cold, and so he had him borne into the city.

The king lamented beyond all measure and went weeping from one spot to another. He searched until he found Guerrehet, whom Bohort had killed. Then you would have seen the king in great lamentations, striking his hands together in their gauntlets, for except for his helmet he was still armed. In his grief he said that he had lived too long when he saw dead in such pain those whom he had reared pleasantly. While he was lamenting thus, after causing Guerrehet to be placed on his shield and carried into the city, he still went examining the field. Then he looked on the left and saw the body of Gaheriet, whom Lancelot had killed. He was the nephew whom he loved most, save only Gawain. When the king saw the body of him whom he was so accustomed to love, there was no sort of mourning that a man can exhibit for another that he did not show. Then he hastened to him at a run and embraced his body tightly. He swooned so that there was no baron who did not fear he would die before them. He remained thus longer than it would take a man to walk half a league. When he recovered his senses he said aloud so that all could hear:

"Ah, God! now have I lived too long! Ah, Death! if you tarry longer, I will hold you to be too slow. Ah, Gaheriet! if I must die of grief, I shall die because of you. Fair nephew, in an evil hour was ever the sword forged with which you were felled, and cursed be he who struck you, for he has destroyed me and my kindred."

The king kissed Gaheriet's eyes and mouth, bloody as they were, and mourned so loudly that those who saw him marveled. Nevertheless, there was no one present who was not lamenting, for they loved Gaheriet with a mighty love.

With all these cries and wailings Sir Gawain came out of his quarters, thinking that the queen was certainly dead and that this great mourning was for her. When he had come out into the streets and the people saw him, those who first caught sight of him said to him:

"Sir Gawain, if you wish to see the source of your great grief and the destruction of your flesh, go up into the main hall, and there you will find the greatest grief you ever saw."

Then Sir Gawain was greatly perplexed by this news. He did not answer, but went along the streets, head bowed. He did not believe that this great mourning was for his brothers, for he knew nothing of it yet; instead, he thought it was for the queen. As he went through the streets, he looked to right and left and saw old and young weeping together. Each said as he came near:

"Go, Sir Gawain, go see what grief awaits you."

When Sir Gawain heard what everybody was saying, he was more dismayed than before, but he dared make no outer show of it. When he came into the great hall, he saw all those there mourning as loudly as if they saw all the princes on earth dead. When the king saw Sir Gawain arrive, he said:

"Gawain, Gawain, here is surpassing grief for you and for me, for here lies dead your brother Gaheriet, the most valiant in our family."

He showed him the body, bloody as it was, clasped between his arms against his breast. When Sir Gawain heard these words, he had no power to answer nor to stand erect. Instead, his heart failed him, and he fell to the floor in a faint.

Then the barons were so troubled and so grief-stricken that they thought never again to be joyful. When they saw Gawain fall, they took him up in their arms and wept sorely over him, and said:

"Ah, God, here on every hand there is great evil wrought."

When Sir Gawain recovered from his swoon, he arose and ran where he saw Gaheriet lying dead. He took him from the king and clasped him to his bosom and began to kiss him. And as he kissed his heart failed him. He fell to the floor and was longer in a faint than he had been before. When he came to his senses, he sat down beside Gaheriet and gazed upon him. When he saw him wounded so unmercifully, he said:

"Ah, fair brother, may the arm that struck you be cursed. Fair sweet brother, he who struck you thus hated you greatly. Brother, how had he the heart to deliver you to Death? Fair sweet brother, how can Fortune, who had furnished you with all good qualities, allow your destruction, so ugly and so villainous? She used to be so sweet and loving toward you and had raised you up on her master wheel. Fair brother, she did this to kill me so that I might die from grief for you. Indeed, I have every right to die, and it would suit me well, for since I see your death befall, I am a man who would no longer live, except until the hour when I have avenged you upon the disloyal wretch who did this to you."

Sir Gawain began with words like these, and he would have pronounced yet more, but his heart so choked him that he could not utter a word. When he had long been silent, grieved above all others, he looked to the right and saw Guerrehet and Agravain, lying before the king dead on their shields on which they had been brought in. When he saw them, he recognized them, and he said so loudly that all could hear:

"Ah, God! truly I have lived too long when I see my flesh slain so grievously!"

Then he cast himself upon them over and over again, and by his lamentations made the barons present fear that he would die on their hands. The king asked his barons what he should do with Gawain, "for if he is here long, I think he will die of grief."

"Sire," said the barons, "it is our opinion that he should be carried from here and laid in a chamber, and have guards about him until his brothers shall be buried."

"Thus shall it be done," said the king.

Then they took Sir Gawain, who was still in his swoon, and carried him into a chamber. Sir Gawain lay there silent, so that no one drew a word from him either good or bad.

That night in the city of Camelot the sorrowing was such that there was no one who did not weep. The slain knights were disarmed, and each was shrouded as his lineage required. Coffins and tombstones were made for them all. For Guerrehet and for Agravain two coffins were made so handsome and so rich as should be prepared for the sons of kings, and their bodies were placed beside each other in St. Stephen's Church, which was then the main church in Camelot. Between the two tombs the king had a tombstone placed fairer and richer than any of the others and there they laid the body of Gaheriet raised higher than his two brothers. At the entombment you could have seen much weeping. All the bishops and archbishops in the country came and all the nobles in the land. They did such honor to the bodies of the slain knights as was within their power, especially to the body of Gaheriet, because he had been a man of such high merit and such a good knight. They had inscribed upon his tombstone letters which said:

"Here lies Gaheriet, the nephew of King Arthur, killed by Lancelot of the Lake."

And the names of those who had killed them were put upon the other two tombs.

When all the clergy who had come had performed the service as they should, King Arthur returned to his great hall and sat among his barons most sorrowful and pensive. He would not have been so wroth if he had lost half his kingdom. All the other barons were in a similar state. The hall was completely filled with high barons. They were as silent as if not a soul were there. When he saw them settled in peace, the king spoke so loudly that all could hear:

"Ah, God, you have upheld me in great honor, and now I am in a little time plunged down into great misfortune, for no man has lost so much as I have lost. When lands happen to be lost through violence or treason, they are something that can sometimes be recovered, but when through mischance one loses his close kinsman who cannot be recovered, no matter what befalls, then the loss is final, then the harm is so great that in no way can it be amended. This loss has not been visited upon me by the judgment of Our Lord God, but through the pride of Lancelot. If this grievous loss had befallen us by the vengeance of Our Lord, then we would have had some honor left, and we should have suffered it without complaint, but it has been put upon us by a man whom we had many times raised high and enriched in our land as if he were begotten from our own flesh. This is the man who has laid this hurt and this shame upon us. And you are all my sworn vassals and hold lands from me. Therefore I require you, by the oath that you gave me, to counsel me, as one should counsel his liege lord, so that my shame may be avenged."

Then the king ceased speaking and remained quiet, waiting for his barons' answer. They began to look at each other and urge each other to speak first. After they had been long silent, King Yon stood up and said to the king:

"Sire, I am your man; I must then counsel you for our honor and yours. Your honor, without a doubt, is to avenge your shame. But anyone who wished to look to the welfare of the king would not, I believe, begin a war against the kindred of King Ban, for we clearly see that Our Lord has raised them above all other families, so that now there is not to my knowledge a man so valiant that, if he wished to wage war against them, he would not have the worst of it, except you alone. Therefore, sire, I beg you for God's sake not to begin war against them, for I believe that you are not at all the stronger; certainly to my knowledge they will be very hard to defeat."

At these words a clamor arose in the hall, for they greatly blamed and scoffed at King Yon for what he had said, and all said publicly that he had spoken these words from cowardice.

"Certainly," King Yon answered, "I did not say what I did because I was any more afraid than the rest of you; but I am sure that, since war will be begun, if they can succeed in reaching their own country safe and sound, they will fear your efforts much less than you think."

"Really, Sir Yon," said Mordred, "I have never heard a man of such merit as you seem to be give such evil counsel as this is. If the king believes me, he will go and take you along, whether it is your will or not."

"Mordred," said King Yon, "I will go more willingly than you; let the king set out when he likes."

"You are squabbling over a strange thing now," said Mador de la Porte. "If you wish to begin a war, you will not have to go far to find it, for they tell me that Lancelot is on this side of the sea at a castle that he conquered long ago when he began to go seeking adventures; it is called Joyous Guard. I know this castle well, for I was in prison there once, and was in fear of death, when Lancelot freed me and my companions."

"On my word," said the king, "I know that castle very well; now I ask you whether you think he took the queen there with him."

"Sire," said Mador, "know that the queen is there, but I do not advise you to go there, for the castle is so strong that they fear no siege from any side. And those who have taken their stand inside are such valiant men that they would have little fear of your efforts. Whenever they saw a chance to do you a bad turn, they could do so at will."

When the king heard this, he said:

"Mador, you are telling the truth about the strength of the castle, and you are not lying about the pride of those within. But you know well, as does everybody here, that since I first wore my crown, I have not undertaken a war which I did not end to the honor of me and my kingdom. Therefore, I tell you that in no way will I hold back from making war on those who have taken from me my dearest kindred. So I now give a summons to all here, and I will send out near and far for all those holding lands from me. When they are assembled, we will set out two weeks from today from the city of Camelot. And because I do not want any of you to lag behind in this enterprise, I require you to swear on saints' relics that you will go on with this war till this shame upon our honor is avenged."

The relics were brought at once, and those within the hall swore that oath, the poor as well as the rich. When they had all sworn that oath to maintain this war, the king sent word near and far by his messengers for all those holding land from him to be on the day named at Camelot, for then he would wish to move with all his power upon the Castle of Joyous Guard. Everyone agreed and prepared to go to the land which is close by the Humber. Thus was the war undertaken that later brought woe to King Arthur. Though he and his forces had the upper hand at first, in the end they were defeated.

Now news spreads quickly through the world: the very next day after this thing was debated, the news of it was on the way to Joyous Guard, carried by a youth who set out from court at once; he was a servant of Hector des Mares. When he came where he was expected by those who eagerly desired news from court, he said that war was so firmly decided upon that it could not fail to come about, for the most powerful men of the court had sworn this thing. And also all the others who held lands from King Arthur had been summoned.

"Really," said Bohort, "has the thing gone so far?"

"Yes, my lord," said the messenger. "You may soon see King Arthur with his forces."

"By God," said Hector, "it will be an evil hour for them if they come, for they will repent it."

When Lancelot heard this news, he called a messenger and sent him to the kingdoms of Benwick and Gaunes, and warned his barons to stock their fortresses, so that if by chance he should happen to leave Great Britain and had to come to the kingdom of Gaunes, he might find the castles strong and defensible so as to hold out against King Arthur, if need were. Then he sent to Sorelois and the kingdom of the Strange Land for all the knights whom he had served so that they might aid him against King Arthur. Because he was everywhere so beloved, so many came that if Lancelot had been a king holding lands, many people think he would not have assembled such a great body of knights as he assembled then.

But the tale ceases to tell of him and returns to King Arthur.

XI

Joyous Guard

Now the tale tells that on the day fixed by King Arthur for the assembling of his men at Camelot, they came and they were so many on foot and on horseback that nobody had ever seen such a show of knighthood. Sir Gawain, who had been ill, had regained his health. On the day when they were assembled, he said to the king:

"Sire, before you depart from here, I would advise you to select from the barony here present as many good knights as were killed recently in the rescue of the queen, and that you give them places at the Round Table to replace those who have died, so that we may have the same number of knights as before, that is, so that we shall be one hundred and fifty. I tell you that, if you do this, your company will be of greater worth in every respect, and will be more dreaded."

The king agreed to this proposal and commanded that it should be carried out, saying that it was good in every way. He immediately called together the high barons and commanded them on their oaths to elect among the best knights as many as were lacking at the Round Table and to leave none aside because of poverty. They said that they would gladly do so. They drew aside and took seats at the head end of the hall. They examined to see how many they lacked at the Round Table; they found that by count they needed seventy-two. They straightway selected as many and seated them in the seats of those who had died or were with Lancelot. But there was none so bold as to dare sit in the Perilous Seat. A knight named Eliant sat in Lancelot's seat. He was the best knight in all Ireland and was a king's son. In Bohort's seat sat a knight named Balynor. He was the son of the king of the Strange Isles and was a very good knight. In Hector's place sat a knight from Scotland, powerful in arms and in the number of friends. A knight who was a nephew of the king of North Wales was seated in Gaheriet's seat. When they had done this on the advice of Sir Gawain, the tables were set and everyone sat down. That day at the Round Table and at King Arthur's table seven kings served. They held their lands from Arthur and were his liege men. That day the knights who were to go to war prepared for their journey and worked late into the night before they were all ready.

In the morning, before the sun had risen, thousands set out thirsting to harm Lancelot. King Arthur, as soon as he had heard mass at the main church at Camelot, got to horse with his barons. They rode to a castle named Lamborc. The next day they rode as far as they had the preceding day. So they journeyed on, day by day, till they came within half a league of Joyous Guard. Because they saw that it was so strong that it feared no attack from many people, they lodged in pavilions beside the River Humber, but quite far from the castle. All day they spent setting up camp. They kept before them their knights in armor so that if it happened that the people in the castle sallied out to fight, they might be well received as one should receive one's enemy. So they made camp.

But the forces in the castle, who were keen and on the watch and who had sent a large detachment the night before into a wood near there to surprise the hostile army when the fitting time should come, so that they would be assailed from both wood and castle—those within the castle did not become at all dismayed at that investment when they saw it, but said among themselves that they would let the besiegers sleep in peace the first night, but would attack them the next day, if they saw an opportune moment. The body of men who had been sent into the wood numbered forty knights, led by Bohort and Hector. Their comrades in the castle told them that when they saw a vermilion pennon flying above the main fortress they should stride along a broad front against King Arthur's people. At the same moment those left in the castle would come out so that the army would be assailed on two sides. The men in the wood watched the castle all day to know if they should see the vermilion pennon which was to be their signal to come forth. But they saw nothing, for Lancelot would not even allow the army to be attacked the first day. Instead, he let them rest all that day and all night, for not a bow was drawn nor a stone hurled from a machine. Thus the enemy were more confident than they were before and said to one another that if Lancelot had large forces he would certainly not have failed to sally out with his whole garrison to fight them, for he who willingly submits to damage from his enemy is not a knight. When Lancelot saw that the castle was besieged in this fashion by King Arthur, the man on earth whom he had loved the most, then he recognized him as his mortal enemy and was so afflicted that he knew not what to do, not because he was afraid for himself, but because he loved the king. He took a maiden, led her into a room, and said to her privately:

"You will go to King Arthur, young lady, and tell him in my name that I wonder greatly why he has thus begun war against me, for I did not think I had done him wrong so much as that. If he says that it is because of my lady the queen for whose sake he has been given to understand that I brought shame upon him, tell him that I am ready to defend the claim that I am not truly guilty against one of the best knights in his court. For love of him and to recover his good will, that I have lost for evil reasons, I will place myself at the disposal of his court. And if the war has been begun because of the death of his nephews, tell him that I am not guilty of these deaths to the point that he should have such mortal hatred of me, for those who were killed were the cause of their own deaths. If he does not wish to grant these two things, tell him that I will take account of his strength, grieving more than anyone else at this quarrel between him and me, grieving so much that nobody could believe it. And let the king know that, since war has been begun, I shall defend myself as best I can. As for his own body, truly, because I consider him

94

my lord and my friend, though he has not come to see himself as my lord but as my mortal enemy, I assure him that he need not fear me; rather, I will protect his person forever to the extent of my power against all those who wish to harm him. Tell him, young lady, these things from me."

The damsel replied that she would carry out the message. Then she went to the castle gate and passed through it quietly. It was the hour of vespers, and King Arthur was seated at his meat. When she came to his army, she found no one to hinder her, for they saw that she was a damsel bearing a message. Therefore, they led her to King Arthur's tent. She, recognizing the king among his barons, approached him and told him what Lancelot had bidden her to say, just as he had communicated it to her. Sir Gawain, who was near King Arthur and had heard this message, spoke before any of the other courtiers had voiced a word of this matter, and said while all the barons listened:

"Sire, you are close to vengeance for your shame and the hurt that Lancelot did your friends. When you left Camelot, you swore to wipe out the kindred of King Ban. I tell you these things, sire, because you are in a good position to avenge this shame. You would be disgraced and your family brought low, so that you would never again have honor, if you made peace with Lancelot."

"Gawain," said the king, "the thing has gone so far that never as long as I live, whatever Lancelot may say or do, will he ever have peace from me. He is, I must say, the man whom I should most easily forgive a great injury, for, it is certain, he has done more for me than any other knight. But in the end he has sold it to me too dearly, for he has bereft me of my close relatives and those whom I loved most, except you alone. On this account there can be no peace between him and me, nor will there be; this I pledge you as a king."

Then the king turned to the damsel and said:

"Damsel, you may tell your lord that unconditionally I will do nothing that he requests, but I assure him of mortal war."

"I am sorry, sire," said the damsel. "It is a greater pity for you than for anyone else. And you, who are one of the most powerful kings on earth and the most famous, you will be destroyed and brought to death, or else wise men have been many times deceived. And you, Sir Gawain, who should be the wisest, are the most foolish of all, much more so than I thought, for you are procuring your death, and you can see it quite openly. Now, think. Do you not remember what you saw long ago in the Adventurous Hall in the Castle of the Rich Fisher King, when you saw the battle of the leopard and the serpent? If you recalled the marvels that you saw there and the interpretation that the hermit gave you, never would this war have come to pass, so long as you could turn it aside. But your evil heart and your great misfortune drive you into this enterprise. You will repent of it when you cannot mend calamity." Then she turned again to the king and said, "Sire, since I can find naught but war in you, I shall go back to my lord and tell him your message."

"Damsel," said the king, "go."

Then the damsel left the army and went to the castle, where she was expected. There she entered. When she was before her lord and she had told him that in no way could he find peace with King Arthur, Lancelot was greatly troubled, not because of fear, but because he loved the king with a great love. Then he went off to a room and began to think intently. As he thought, he sighed very deeply, so that the tears came to his eyes and ran down his face. When he had been thus a long time, it came about that my lady the queen entered and found him so wrapped in thought that she was with him a long while before he saw her. When she saw that he was so deep in thought, she spoke to him and asked why he was so downcast. He said that he was thinking with sorrow that he could find no peace with or forgiveness from King Arthur.

"My lady," he explained, "I do not say this because we should fear that he could do us great harm, but I say it because he gave me so many honors and did so many kindnesses that it would bring me great sorrow if harm befell him."

"Sire," the queen said, "you must take his might into consideration, but anyhow tell me what you wish to do about it."

"I intend," he said, "that we shall go into combat tomorrow, and may God help him, to whom He will give the honor, for the host which besieges this castle will soon be driven from it, if my efforts are to any avail, and since so it must stand that I can find neither peace nor love among its knights. I am a man who will never again spare any of them, save only the person of King Arthur."

So their conversation ended, and Lancelot went out to the main hall and sat among his knights and feigned greater joy than his heart held. He ordered the tables to be set and that they should be as richly served as if they were at King Arthur's court. When those present had eaten, those most in his confidence asked:

"What shall we do tomorrow? Do you not intend to attack those in the army?"

"Yes," he said, "before the third hour."

"Good," they said. "If we are shut in here longer, those fellows will consider us cowards."

"Be not dismayed," said Lancelot. "Because we have not moved, they are now more sure of themselves than they were and fear us less. They think, because we have not come out, that we have not a soul among us. But, if it pleases God, before the hour of vespers tomorrow they will know whether I am alone in here, and if I can bring it about they will repent what they have undertaken, for without fail we will make a sally tomorrow and charge against them. Therefore, I beg you to be all armed so that we can move out at whatever hour we perceive is to our advantage."

Everybody held this proposal to be good, for they were pleased and eager to be able to attack King Arthur's people. It gave them great courage to have on their side Lancelot and Bohort, who were the most renowned for prowess and knightly acts. That evening they worked diligently at preparing their equipment and seeing that nothing was lacking. They kept so quiet that night that the people in the host spoke much of it, and told the king that he should be certain that there were so few people inside that he could easily take the castle. The king said that he could not believe that there was not a plentiful stock of men within.

"Certainly, sire," said Mador, "there are men in great plenty in there; I tell you truly, and good, excellently trained knights."

"How do you know?" said Sir Gawain.

"I know it well, my lord," said Mador, "and I will give you my head to cut off, if you do not see them come out before tomorrow evening."

In such a manner they talked in the host about the people in the castle, and when it was bedtime, they had guards posted on every side so awake and close together that it would have been hard to do them harm.

The next day, as soon as those in the castle had made ready and arranged themselves in six divisions, they raised the vermilion pennon on the main tower. The moment the watchmen saw it, they pointed it out to Bohort. He said to them:

"Now there is naught to do but move forward, for my lord is on his horse, and his company too, and will come out without delay. So we have only to strike into the host, so that as we go nothing be left standing but all knocked to the ground."

His men answered that they would do their best. Then they sallied from the grove where they had set up their ambush and came out into the open. They caused their horses to advance together as quietly as possible, but they could not prevent the enemy from perceiving the clumping of their horses as they heard them approach. Those who first saw them shouted: "To arms, to arms!"

The cries were so loud that the people in the castle could hear them. They said that the watch had run back among the hostile forces, and they had only to attack on their side. And so they did. Then Lancelot ordered the gate to be opened and for them to march out in as great order as they should. They did so at once, for they had a great desire to sally forth.

Bohort, who had come out of the ambuscade, met King Yon's son on a great war-horse as soon as he came near the host. On sight they set their horses to running at each other. King Yon's son broke his spear, and Bohort struck him so hard that neither shield nor hauberk saved him from having the spearhead and the wood behind it thrust through his body; he was borne to earth, done unto death. The others who came after began to knock over pavilions and tents, and kill people, and lay low everybody they overtook. Then the hue and cry began in the camp so loud that you could not have heard even the thunder of God. Sir Gawain, seeing how things had gone, ordered his arms brought in all haste, and those commanded brought them. The king himself put on his armor to meet the need; so did all the barons because of the uproar that they heard all around them. As soon as the king and those around him had mounted, he saw his pavilion fallen to the ground, and the dragon that was on the globe above it, and the other pavilions too. Bohort and Hector were doing all this; they wanted to capture the king. When Sir Gawain saw the marvel that they were accomplishing, he showed them to the king and said:

"Sire, there are Bohort and Hector doing all this damage to you."

Then Sir Gawain spurred against Hector. He struck him so hard on the helmet that it quite stunned him, and if he had not quickly grasped his horse's neck he would have fallen to the ground. Sir Gawain, who mortally hated him, when he saw him stunned thus, did not wish to leave him then, and like one who knew much about war, he struck him again, so that he made him lean forward against his saddle bow. When Bohort saw Sir Gawain pressing Hector so fiercely that he was almost bringing him to earth, he could not hold back from helping him, for he loved Hector very much. Then he advanced on Sir Gawain, his sword upraised, and struck him so hard that he put the sword two inches into his helmet. Sir Gawain was so stunned that he rode on at once, leaving Hector, and quitted Bohort; he was so giddy that he did not know which way his horse was taking him.

Thus the struggle before the king's tent began, but those in Bohort's company would have been killed if it had not been for Lancelot and the people from the castle who charged when they had all arrived at the camp, and both sides were mingled together. Then you would have seen blows dealt and received, and men dying in great pain. They showed each other quickly that they mortally hated one another, for there were so many killed and wounded that day that there could not be a heart so hard as not to be moved by pity. But above all those bearing arms in that day's battle,

Sir Gawain and Lancelot did the best. The tale tells that Sir Gawain, who was still mourning for the death of Gaheriet, killed more than thirty knights that day. Without fail that day he could never give up doing great deeds until the hour of vespers.

When night had come, King Arthur's knights returned to their quarters as fast as ever they could, like people who had suffered great travail. So did the other party, which withdrew into the castle. When they were inside, they looked to see how many of their people they had lost. They found that they lacked a good hundred knights without counting slain servants of whom the tale makes no mention, and they had naught to show for it but ten prisoners whom they had brought to the castle by force.

At the castle, when they had disarmed, they all went to eat in the main hall, the wounded as well as those who were whole, just as it chanced with each. That night after supper they spoke much of Sir Gawain, and said no one had done so well that day save Lancelot and Bohort.

And those in the host, when they were in their tents and had looked to see how many of their knights they had lost, they found that there were two hundred missing, whereat they were greatly wroth. When they had eaten that evening, they began to talk about the party in the castle and said that clearly they were not without many people and they were valiant and vigorous men. They accorded the prize for that day to Sir Gawain and Lancelot, and said that they were the two knights who had done the best in the battle.

When it was bedtime, because they were weary and worn, some went to bed. The others kept watch over their forces all night, for they feared that the people in the castle might come to the tents, and they did not mean that they should find them unarmed, but ready to welcome them.

That night after supper Lancelot spoke to his comrades and said:

"Gentlemen, you have now learned that the enemy knows how to strike with swords, for today we tried them out close at hand, and they us. But they cannot greatly rejoice in the gains they made, though they have more people than we do. It came out well for us, thank God, for we held out against their efforts with few people. Now examine what we shall do tomorrow and how we will contend with them from now on, for I should like, if it might be and God willed to allow it, for us to bring this war to so honorable an end that our honor should be upheld as it has been in this beginning. Now tell me what you would have me do, for nothing shall be done against your advice."

They said that they wished to return to battle on the morrow.

"Gentlemen," said Lancelot, "since it is your will to fight with them, consider now who will go out first." Bohort said that nobody should go ahead of him, for just as soon as it was light he would issue forth with his armor on to fight those in the host. Hector said that he would be next after him with the second division. Eliezier, King Pelles' son, a good knight and bold, said that he would lead the third division and be in charge of those from his country. Another, a knight from Sorelois, the Duke of Aroel, who was a most excellent knight, requested the conduct of the fourth division, because he was a valiant man who knew a great deal about war. Afterward there were so many people of the castle that they established eight divisions, each containing one hundred armed knights; in the last, wherein lay their greatest power and reliance, they placed and established by the common will Lancelot. So they settled all their divisions on the evening before the battle and set good leaders over each. That night they tended the wounded. When Bohort saw that Hector was wounded and learned that Sir Gawain had wounded him, he was not a little angered. He said in the hearing of all that he would avenge him if he had the chance. The people in the castle who were wounded rested that night, for they were very weary.

The next day, before the sun had risen, as soon as it was light and they had dressed and shod themselves, they ran to arms; then they marched out of the castle one after the other in proper order. When the enemy saw them coming down they leaped to their arms and came out of the pavilions all prepared. Sir Gawain was leading the first division and Bohort the first of his party. Of this Sir Gawain was not regretful, for this was the man on earth that he hated most with a mortal hatred. When they approached each other, they charged at one and the same time, spears leveled, horses running as hard as they could, and they struck each other so hard that no armor saved them from both being borne to the ground so smitten that neither had power to rise. It was no wonder, for in both the spearhead passed out behind. After that blow the two first divisions came on apace. They charged each other and struck back and forth so wondrously, because they hated each other mortally, that you would soon have seen a hundred no longer able to rise, for many were killed and many wounded. At this time defeat and misfortune were the lot of those from the host, for in that first of Lancelot's divisions there was a knight from the Strange Land who did such marvels with his arms at that clashing together that King Arthur's people were defeated by him. When they had somewhat cleared the place, the men from the castle ran where Sir Gawain and Bohort lay wounded. They took them up and would have carried off Sir Gawain, because they found in him no ability to defend himself, if the men from the host had not rushed that way to rescue him. They made such successful efforts, that he had to be left to his friends whether the men from the castle liked it or not. Nevertheless, amidst that distress and that great anguish Bohort's men labored so hard that they carried him off on his shield up to the castle, wounded as he was. You never saw a man or woman display such grief as the queen did when she saw him wounded and bloody as he was. The surgeons were called and they drew out the spear stump with its head. When they had examined the wound insofar as they could see it, they said that it would be very dangerous in the healing.

The forces which were assembled on the meadows above the River Humber began with the morning the battle which lasted till the vespers of that summer day. You never saw, neither you nor any other, such a cruel combat nor so treacherous a one as that was through the day, for there were many killed and wounded on both sides. That day King Arthur bore arms and did so well that no man on earth of his age could have done as well. History affirms that in his forces no knight, young or old, did as well as he did. With the example that he gave, his men did so well that the men from the castle would have been defeated, had it not been for Lancelot. When the king, who recognized him by his arms, saw what he was doing, he said to himself:

"If that fellow lives long, he will put my men to shame."

Then the king ran at him, sword drawn, like a man of great boldness. When Lancelot saw him coming, he did not get ready to put up a defense except by covering himself, for he loved the king too mightily. The king struck him so hard that he cut into his horse's neck, so that he brought down Lancelot. When Hector, who was near Lancelot, saw this blow, he was very angry, for he feared that Lancelot had been wounded. He charged the king and struck him so hard on the helmet that King Arthur was so stunned that he did not know whether it was night or day. And Hector, who knew well that it was the king, dealt another blow so that the king could not hold his seat in the saddle, and rolled to the earth beside Lancelot. Then Hector said to Lancelot:

"Cut off his head, my lord; our war will be over then."

"Ah, Hector," said Lancelot, "what are you saying to me? Do not say it again; it would be pains wasted."

With these words, Lancelot rescued King Arthur from death, for Hector would have killed him. When Lancelot himself had put King Arthur back on his horse, they left the battle. The king went to his army and said so that all about him might hear:

"Did you see what Lancelot did for me today when he was in a position to kill me and would not lay a hand on me? On my word, he has now surpassed in goodness and courtesy all the knights that I ever saw.

101

Now I would that this war had never been begun, for he has today won my heart with kindness better than the whole world could have done by force."

The king said these words in his privy council, upon which Sir Gawain, wounded as he was, was very angry when he heard them.

When Lancelot had returned to the castle, the men who disarmed him found that he had many wounds, of which the least would have made many another knight consider himself greatly hampered. When they had disarmed him and Hector, he and his brother went to see Bohort. They asked his surgeon whether he was badly wounded. The man replied that the wound was wondrous large, but that it would heal quickly, he thought.

XII
Parting

The king continued to lay siege to Joyous Guard for two months and more. Those inside came out repeatedly and fought those outside so many times that they lost a great many knights, because they did not have as many people as the enemy had. Within that period it befell that the Pope in Rome learned that King Arthur had put aside his wife and that he was threatening to kill her, if he could lay hands on her. When the Pope heard that she had not been caught in the act of the misdeed of which she was accused, he sent word to the archbishops and bishops of the country that all land held by King Arthur should be placed under interdict and excommunication unless he took back his wife in peace and honor, as a king should hold a queen. When the king heard this order, he was greatly wroth; nevertheless, he loved the queen with such great love, though he believed firmly that she had betrayed him, that he was easily conquered. He said, however, that the war between him and Lancelot would never end, even if the queen returned, since he had undertaken it.

Then the Bishop of Rochester came to the queen and said to her:

"My lady, you must go back to King Arthur, your lord, for so the Pope commands. He will swear to you before all his barons that he will consider you henceforth as a king should consider a queen, nor will he ever again take account of words that have been spoken concerning you and Lancelot, nor will any man in his court no matter where you are."

"I will take counsel, my lord," she said, "and I will tell you soon what I am advised to do."

Then the queen asked Lancelot, Bohort, Hector, and Lionel to come to her in a chamber. When they were before her, she said:

"My lords, you are the men of this world in whom I have the greatest trust. Now I beg you to counsel me to my advantage and my honor, according to what you think is best for me. News has come to me which should please both you and me much, for the king, who is the noblest man in the world, as you say yourselves every day, has requested me to go to him, and he will hold me as dear as he ever did before. He does me great honor by making the request of me and by overlooking my misdeeds toward him. And you will profit by this, for certainly I shall never leave here if he does not forgive you his ill will, at least so that he will permit you to leave the country, and guarantee against your losing anything, not even the worth of a spur, as long as you are in this country. Now give me what advice you wish, for if you prefer that I should remain here with you, I will stay, and if you wish me to go away, I will go."

"My lady," said Lancelot, "if you did what my heart desires, you would stay, but nevertheless, since I wish that this affair should turn out to your honor rather than according to my desire, you will go to your lord, King Arthur. If you did not go now after this offer that he has made you, there is no one who will not openly know your shame and my great disloyalty. Therefore, I wish you to send word to the king that you will go to him tomorrow. And I tell you, when you leave me, you will be so richly accompanied according to our powers that never was noble lady better honored. I do not tell you this because I love you less than ever a knight loved a lady in our lifetime, but I say it for your honor."

Then his eyes filled with tears, and the queen too began to weep. When Bohort heard that Lancelot had granted the queen his consent for her to go to King Arthur, he said:

"My lord, you have given your permission very lightly; God grant that good may come of it for you. But I am sure you never did anything of which you will repent as much. You will go to Gaul and my lady the queen will be in this country, that is, you will not see her soon or late, not at one time nor yet at another. I know your heart and the great longing you will have for her, so that I know truly that it will not have been a month until you would like to have given the whole world, if it were yours, on condition that you had not done this generous act. I fear that you will suffer from it much more than you think."

When Bohort had said these words, the other two spoke in agreement and began to blame Lancelot; they said:

"My lord, why do you fear the king so that you give up my lady?"

He said that he would give her up, whatever might come of it, even

103

if he were to die for want of her. So the conference ended, when they heard Lancelot say that for no reason would he fail to give her up. The queen went back to the bishop who was waiting in the great hall and said:

"My lord, now you may go to my lord the king. Greet him in my name and tell him that under no conditions would I leave here, unless he let Lancelot depart without losing so much as the value of a spur, nor a soul from his household."

When the bishop heard these words, he thanked God sincerely, for now he saw that the war was over. He commended the queen to God and all the others in the hall, too. Then he went down from the castle and rode on until he came to the king's tent and told him the news that he had heard in the castle. When the king heard that they were willing to give up the queen, he said so that all present might hear:

"By God, if the queen meant as much to Lancelot as I have been given to understand, he is not at all so near defeat in this war that he would give her up for months—not if he loves her with mad love. Because he has done my will in the matter of this request so readily, I will do unconditionally what the queen has set as her conditions. I will let him go out of this country, and he will find no one who will take from him the worth of a spur but that I will give twice the value in return."

Then the king commanded the bishop to go back to the castle and tell the queen in the king's name that Lancelot could leave the country without loss of property, and that the king himself, because Lancelot had so readily granted his request, would provide him with ships from his own fleet to pass over to Gaul.

The bishop mounted forthwith and went back to the castle and gave the queen the king's message. So the matter was arranged on both sides for the queen to be given over to her lord the next day, and for Lancelot to leave the kingdom of Logres. He and his company would go to the kingdom of Gaunes where they were the rightful lords and rightful heirs. That night the people in the host were glad and joyous when they saw that the war was over, for the greater part of them were much afraid that they would have the worst of it if the affair lasted long.

If they were much happier and more joyous than they had been, the people in the castle were shedding tears and lamenting, the poor as well as the rich. Do you know why they were so downcast? Because they saw that Lancelot, and Bohort, and Hector, and Lionel were as dejected as if they saw the whole world slain. That night the mourning was great at Joyous Guard. When day had dawned, Lancelot said to the queen:

"My lady, this is the day that you will leave me and when I must depart from this country. I do not know if I shall ever see you again.

Here is a ring that you gave me long ago when I first came to know you. I have kept it since then till now for love of you. Now I pray you to wear it henceforth for love of me and I will have the one that you are wearing on your finger."

She gave it to him gladly. Thus their speech together ended and they retired to dress as handsomely as they might. That day the four cousins were richly equipped. When they had got to horse with all the others in the castle, they rode out to the royal army with more than five-hundred horses all with trappings of silk, and came on as though to a tourney, showing the greatest joy you ever saw. The king came to meet them with a great company of knights. When Lancelot saw the king come close to him, he alighted and took the queen's horse by the bridle and said to the king:

"Sire, here is the queen whom I return to you. She would have been dead long since by the disloyalty of men in your household if I had not ventured to rescue her. I did not behave so because of any kindness she ever did me, but only because I knew her for the lady of greatest worth in the world. The loss of her would have been too grievous and too great a pity, if the traitors in your household who had sentenced her to death had accomplished what they wished to do. It is better that they should die in their villainy than that she should be killed."

Then the king received her silently and thoughtfully, because of the words that he had heard.

"Sire," continued Lancelot, "if I had loved the queen with a guilty love, as they have given you to understand, I would not have yielded her to you for a long time; you would not have had her by force."

"Lancelot," said the king, "you have done so much that I am grateful to you. What you have done may sometime have its recompense."

Then Sir Gawain came forward and said to Lancelot:

"You have done so much for my lord the king that he is grateful to you. But he still requires one thing from you."

"What, my lord?" said Lancelot. "Tell me and I will do it if I can."

"He requires you," said Sir Gawain, "to quit his land and never again to be found upon it."

"Sire," said Lancelot to the king, "is it your will that so it should be?"

"Since Gawain wishes it," said the king, "it is my pleasure. Leave my lands on this side of the sea and go into your own beyond it, which are beautiful and rich."

"Good, my lord," said Lancelot, "when I am in my lands, will I be sure of peace with you?"

"You may be sure," said Sir Gawain, "that you will not fail to have

105

war, and fiercer than you have had up till now, and it will last until Gaheriet, my brother, whom you killed in cowardly fashion, is avenged upon your own body. I would not take the whole world in exchange for your severed head."

"Sir Gawain," said Bohort, "leave off your threats, for I tell you truly that my lord fears you little. If you ventured to come after us into the kingdom of Gaunes or of Benwick, be sure that you would be in greater danger of losing your head than my lord would be. You said that my lord killed your brother in cowardly fashion. If you wished to prove that like a loyal knight, I would defend my lord against you so that, if I were conquered on the field, Sir Lancelot would be shamed, and, if I could make a recreant of you, you would be sentenced as a false accuser. The war would stop at once. Certainly, if you were willing, it would be a very proper thing that this quarrel should be settled by you and me rather than by forty thousand men."

Sir Gawain held out his gauntlet and said to the king:

"Sire, since he makes this offer of himself, he will go no farther ever, for I am ready to prove against his body that Lancelot killed Gaheriet my brother by treason."

Bohort leaped forward and said he was ready to defend his cause. The battle would have been set if the king had so willed, for Sir Gawain asked nothing better, and Bohort would have liked to be body to body against him. But the king refused both gauntlets and said that under no conditions would this battle be allowed, but that when they had left that spot, each should do the best he could, and that Lancelot might be sure that as soon as he was in his country he would find war greater than he could believe.

"Truly, sire," said Lancelot, "you would not be able to carry on this war as easily as you are today, if I had been as much of a harm to you as I was a help on the day when Galehaut, the lord of the Distant Isles, became your liege man at the very moment when he had the power to take your land and honor from you, when you were about to have shame heaped upon you, lose your crown, and be disinherited. If you had remembered that day as you should have done, you would not have undertaken to build this war against me. I do not say these things, sire, for fear of you, but because of the love that you should have for me if you rewarded acts of kindness as a king should. Certainly, when we arrive among our liege men and summon together our forces and our friends, and have our castles and fortresses stocked, I assure you that, if you come and we wish to harm you with all our power, you have never done anything of which you have repented as much as you will this enterprise, for know truly that you would find in it neither profit nor honor. And you, Sir Gawain, who are so cruel as to embitter the king against us, should certainly not have done so, for, if you remember how I rescued you long ago from the Dolorous Tower, the day that I delivered you from the prison of Karados the Great, whom I killed and who had so to speak put you to death, you would never have had any hatred for me."

"Lancelot," said Sir Gawain, "you have never done anything for me that in the end you did not sell me very dearly, for you have so grievously bereft me of those I loved most, that our family has been brought very low, and I am suffering shame because of it. Therefore, there can never be peace between you and me, nor will there ever be again as long as I live."

Then Lancelot said to the king:

"Sire, I shall quit your land tomorrow in such a manner that for all the services I have rendered you since I was first a knight, I shall not carry away the worth of a spur."

Thus ended the parley. The king returned to his tents and took along the queen. Then began among them rejoicing as great as if our Lord God had come down to earth. But while those in the king's host were joyous and happy, the people from the castle went away so sorrowful, for they were most uneasy at seeing their lord more thoughtful than was usual. When Lancelot had dismounted, he ordered his whole household to make ready their furnishings, for on the morrow he would set out, as he planned, to ride to the sea and take passage for the land of Gaunes. That day Lancelot called a squire named Kanahin and said to him:

"Take my shield from that room and go straight to Camelot, and carry it to the main Church of St. Stephen and leave it where it may remain in the sight of all, so that all who see it hereafter may remember the wonders that I have accomplished in this land. Do you know why I do that place this honor? Because there I first received the order of knighthood. That is why I love that city above all others and why I wish my shield to be there in my stead, for I do not know whether adventure will ever again bring me there, after I shall have left this country."

The young man took the shield, and Lancelot put in his charge four beasts of burden laden with riches, so that the priests in the church might pray for him forever more and exalt their church. When the bearers of these presents had come there, they were received with great joy. When they saw Lancelot's shield they were no less happy to have it than the other gifts. They had it hung at once in the middle of the church to a silver chain richly, as if it had been the body of a saint. And when the people in the country heard of it, they came to see it in great numbers

107

and solemnly, and many wept when they saw the shield, because Lancelot had gone away.

But now the tale ceases to speak of them and returns to Lancelot and his company.

At this point the tale tells that after the queen was surrendered to the king, Lancelot left Joyous Guard. With the king's own permission he gave the castle to a knight of his who had long served him, with the condition that, wherever the knight might be, he would receive the income from the castle during his lifetime. When Lancelot issued from the castle, one could see that there might well be four hundred knights, not counting the squires and the others who, afoot or on horseback, followed the company. When Lancelot came to the sea and boarded a vessel he looked back at the land and the country where he had had so many good things and where he had received so many honors. He grew pale and began to sigh deeply, and his eyes filled with tears that overflowed. When he had stood long in this state, he said in such a low voice that nobody on the ship heard him, save only Bohort:

"Ah, sweet land, filled with happy things in which my spirit and my life remain completely, may you be blessed by the mouth of him whom they call Jesus Christ, and blessed be all who remain within you, be they my friends or my enemies. May they have peace! May they have rest! May God give them greater joy than I feel! May God give them victory and honor over all those who wish to do them any harm! Truly, they will have such good fortune, for nobody could be in such a pleasant country as this is who would not be more blessed by fortune than any others. I say so who have experienced it, for as long as I stayed there good luck was poured out upon me more abundantly than it would have been if I had been in any other land."

Thus spoke Lancelot when he departed from the kingdom of Logres. As long as he could see the shore he looked back toward it, and when he had lost it from sight, he lay down upon a bed. He began to lament so wondrously that not one could have seen him who was not seized by pity because of it; and his mourning lasted till they came to shore.

XIII

Invasion

When Lancelot and his company had landed, they mounted, and rode till they came near a wood. In that wood Lancelot alighted and ordered his tents to be pitched there, for he wished to stay the night. His orders were carried out by those assigned to the duty. That night Lancelot lodged there and left the next morning and journeyed till he reached his lands. When the people of the country knew that he was coming, they went to meet him and received him with great joy, as was fitting for their lord.

The day after he had come, having heard mass, he came to Bohort and Lionel and said to them:

"Give me a boon, I pray you."

"My lord," they said, "it is not proper that you should pray us, but command, for we shall not fail, at risk of life or limb, to do your will at once."

"Bohort, I require you to become lord of Benwick, and you Lionel shall have Gaunes, which belonged to your father. Concerning Gaul, which King Arthur gave me, I shall never speak to you, for if he had given me the whole world, I would turn it back to him now."

And they said, since such was his will, they would accept it. Lancelot said that he desired them to be crowned on All Saints' Day. So both went on foot and received their fiefs from him, and from the day that they became seized of them it was only a month and two days till All Saints' Day. When the people of the country learned that on that day they were to be crowned and installed, the one with the kingdom of Benwick and the other with that of Gaunes, you could have witnessed great rejoicing throughout the land and ploughmen more than usually merry. Those people might well have said that the most melancholy and despondent of all was Lancelot, for hardly could one draw a smile from him, and still he showed greater joy and a greater semblance of happiness than his heart provided.

On the day of the feast of All Saints, all the noble barons of the land assembled at Benwick. On the very day that the two brothers were crowned, Lancelot received news that King Arthur wished to come with an army against him, and would come without fail as soon as winter was over, for he had already gathered part of his equipment. All this was being done at the instigation of Sir Gawain.

When Lancelot heard the news, he answered him who brought it thus:

"Let the king come and be welcome! We shall surely receive him well, please God, for our castles have strong walls and are strong otherwise, and our land is well stocked with food and knights. Let the king come in safety, for he need not fear death wherever I am as long as I can recognize him. But as for Sir Gawain, who is so hostile to us and should not be so, and who pursues our ruin so hard, I tell you that, if he comes, he will never depart safe and sound, if I can ever do aught about it. He never in his life undertook a war of which he repented as much as he will repent of this one—if he comes."

Thus spoke Lancelot to him who had brought this news, and he assured him that King Arthur would be better received than he thought. And the man told him that the king would not have undertaken the expedition if Sir Gawain had not made him do it.

But now the tale ceases to tell of Lancelot and returns to King Arthur and Sir Gawain.

Now the tale tells that all that winter King Arthur dwelt in the kingdom of Logres most comfortably, for he saw naught that displeased him. While he rode through his cities, stopping from day to day at his castles where he knew them best stocked, Sir Gawain urged him so much to recommence the war against Lancelot that he gave his word as a king that as soon as ever Easter should be past, he would go against Lancelot with an army assembled by proclamation, and would make such efforts, even if he were to die doing so, that he would raze the fortresses of Benwick and Gaunes till he left no stone resting on another. King Arthur made this promise to Sir Gawain; he made a promise that he could not carry out.

After Easter in the spring when the cold had abated, the king summoned his barons and made ready his ships to pass the sea; the rendezvous was at the city of London. When they were to set out, Sir Gawain asked his uncle:

"Sire, under whose guard will you leave my lady the queen?"

The king began at once to think about in whose charge he might leave her. Mordred came forward and said to the king:

"Sire, if it pleased you, I would stay to guard her. She will be in safer hands and you should be more tranquil than if she were in the keeping of any other."

And the king said that it was his will that Mordred should remain and guard her as he would himself.

"Sire," said his nephew, "I swear to you that I will guard her as dearly as my own body."

The king took her by the hand, gave her to him, and told him to guard her as loyally as a liege man should guard the wife of his lord. Mordred received her thus. The queen was greatly vexed at being given to him to guard, for she knew of so much evil and disloyalty in him that she thought that trouble and vexation would certainly come of it. Much worse came than she had thought. The king put in Mordred's hands the keys to his treasury so that, if he should need silver or gold when he had crossed to the kingdom of Gaunes, Mordred could send it to him when he asked for it. The king ordered those in the country to do in every respect what Mordred wished, and he made them swear on saints' relics that they would not neglect anything he ordered. They took the oath of which the king repented with such dolor that he was to be conquered in pitched battle on Salisbury Plain, where the mortal battle was, as this very story will relate in detail.

After this step, King Arthur set out from the city of London with a great company of stalwart men, and traveled till he came to the sea. The queen journeyed with him to that point, whether he liked it or not. When the king was about to go aboard the ship, the queen mourned greatly and said as she kissed him in tears:

"Sire, may Our Lord watch over you where you must go and bring you back safe and sound, for I have surely never had till now such great fear for you as I have now. However your return may come out, my heart tells me that I shall never see you again, nor you me."

"My lady," said the king, "yes, you will, God willing; do not fear or tremble, for you could gain nothing by fear."

Then the king went aboard the ship, the sails were hoisted to catch the wind, and the sailors stood prepared to do what they should. It was not long before the wind had carried them so far from shore that the voyagers saw themselves on the high sea. Their wind was favorable, and they soon came to shore. They praised Our Lord greatly. When they had landed, the king ordered their furnishings to be taken from the ships and their pavilions set up on the shore, because he wished to rest. The men carried out his commands exactly. That night the king lay in a meadow not far from the seashore. On the morning when he started off from there, he looked to see how many men he might have; they found that there were more than forty thousand. Then they traveled on till they were in the kingdom of Benwick. And when they entered it, they did not find ruinous castles, for there was none that Lancelot had not had repaired or

111

newly rebuilt. When they were there, the king asked his men which way he should go.

"Sire," said Sir Gawain, "we will go straight to the city of Gaunes where King Bohort and King Lionel and Lancelot and Hector are lodged with all their forces. If by any chance we could surprise them, we would easily bring our war to an end."

"By God," said Sir Yvain, "it is folly to go straight to that city, for there all the resources of this land are gathered; therefore, we should do better first to go destroy the castles and towns around that city, so that we would not have to watch around us when we had laid siege to the garrison within it."

"Ha!" said Sir Gawain. "Do not be dismayed, for there will be nobody so bold as to dare venture out of a castle as long as they know that we are in the land."

"Gawain," said the king, "let us go besiege Gaunes, since that is your will."

So King Arthur and his army went straight to Gaunes. As he drew near, he met a very old woman riding a white palfrey and richly appareled. When she recognized King Arthur, she said to him:

"King Arthur, behold the city you have come to attack. Know truly that to do so is madness and you are following foolish counsel. Out of this enterprise that you have begun you will gain no honor, for you will never take the city, but will abandon it without having aught accomplished; that will be the honor that you will gain. And you, Sir Gawain, who have advised the king to proceed thus and by whose counsel this war has been begun, know that you are pursuing your own ruin so hard that you will never see the kingdom of Logres again safe and sound. You may truly say that now the time draws near that long ago was promised you when you left the castle of the Rich Fisher King, where you endured much shame and ugly treatment."

When she had spoken thus, she rode off at a great pace, for she wished to hear no words that Sir Gawain or King Arthur might say to her. She went straight to the city of Gaunes, rode in, and came to the palace, where she found Lancelot and the two kings who had with them a great company of knights. When she had reached the main hall, she came to the two kings. She told them that King Arthur was half a league away and that at that moment one might see ten thousand men. They said that it was no matter of concern to them; they were not afraid. Then they asked Lancelot:

"My lord, what shall we do? King Arthur is causing his men to set up camp out there. We ought to attack them before they are well settled."

Lancelot said that they would attack them on the morrow. King Bohort and all the others agreed. Lancelot had it cried through the city that they should be on horseback before the hour of prime. A great many people were merry and joyous, for they liked war better than peace. That night those in the host were tranquil, and those in the city were at peace. The next morning, as soon as it was light, the people in the city arose and put on their armor as fast as they could, for they greatly desired to see the hour when they could fight those outside. When they were all ready, they came before the palace and stopped in the street all on horseback until they could ride out. That day Lancelot and Hector set up their divisions and gave each a good leader. The army outside established twenty divisions. In the first division were Sir Gawain and Sir Yvain, because they had heard that Lancelot and Bohort were in the first division on the other side.

When these two divisions met, Sir Gawain and Lancelot fought each other, and Yvain fought Bohort. All four were brought to earth, and Yvain almost broke an arm. Then the divisions came out on either side. Then the combat began so great and so general that you could see a great many knights fall. But Lancelot got astride his horse again, and put his hand to his sword, and began to deal out great blows around him. King Arthur's people put Sir Gawain back on his mount, whether the forces from the city liked it or not. So all the divisions were engaged before the third hour was past and began the struggle in which many a valiant man died and many a good knight. But when King Lionel came to the battle, you could have seen King Arthur's men much dismayed by the wonders that they saw King Lionel do. The besieging army would that day have lost a great many if it were not for King Arthur, who did excellently in that battle. He himself wounded King Lionel in the head. The people from the city were so frightened when they saw him so badly wounded that the battle ended before vespers, and the defenders of the city withdrew into it.

Thus the armies from within and without fought four times in a week. On either side many knights died a violent death but, nevertheless, those outside lost more men than those inside, for Lancelot, and Bohort, and Hector, who were ready for any need and were always prepared to harm their enemies, did very, very well. The people of the town were confident because of the three cousins, for it seemed that the besiegers were much frightened only by them. But the tale tells no more of them now but returns to Mordred.

113

XIV
Treason

Now the tale tells that when King Arthur had confided the queen to Mordred's guard and had left the kingdom of Logres to attack Lancelot, as the tale has already related, and Mordred had remained seized of all the king's land, then he called in all the high barons of the country and began to hold sumptuous courts and give great gifts very, very often, till he conquered the hearts of all the noble men who were left in King Arthur's land so entirely that he could command nothing in the country that was not done just as if King Arthur were there.

Mordred frequented the queen so much that he fell in love with her so deeply that he did not see how he could keep from dying if he did not have his will of her. He did not dare tell her in any fashion; still he loved her so very intensely that no man could love more without dying of love. Then Mordred thought of the great act of treason which has been talked of ever since, for he caused letters to be written which were sealed with a false seal counterfeited from King Arthur's seal. They were delivered to the queen and read before the high barons. A bishop from Ireland read them. The letters ran thus:

"I greet you as a man who has been wounded unto death by the hand of Lancelot, and all my men have been killed and cut to pieces; I am seized by pity for you more than for any other people because of the great loyalty that I have found in you, and to have peace I beg you to make Mordred, whom I held as my nephew—but he is not—king of the kingdom of Logres, for without fail you will never see me again, for Lancelot has wounded me mortally and has killed Gawain. And furthermore I require you by the oath you made me to give the queen as a wife to Mordred. If you do not do so, great evil might befall you, for if Lancelot knew that she was not married, he would attack you and take her for a wife, and that would be a thing by which my soul would be most doleful."

All these words were written in the false letter and, without any changes, were read before the queen. Mordred had done this treacherous thing so that nobody knew a word about it except him and the man who had brought the letter. When he heard it read, he pretended to be overwhelmed, so that he dropped among his barons as though in a faint. But it can truly be said of the queen that she began to lament in such trouble that no one could have seen her without being touched with pity. The lamentations began through the hall so that one could not have heard the thunder of God. When the news spread through the city and people learned that King Arthur was killed and all those who had gone with him, the poor and the rich mourned for King Arthur. He was the most loved prince in the world, for he had always been mild and gentle with his people. Mourning for this news lasted a week so continuously great that there was nobody who rested except a very little.

When the mourning had somewhat subsided, Mordred came to the barons, to those who were most powerful and asked them what they would do about what the king had ordered. They decided in counsel that they would make Mordred king and would give him the queen for a wife and would become his liege men. They had to do it for two reasons, one, because the king had required it of them; the other, because they saw no man among them who was as worthy of such an honor as he was.

When they told Mordred that they would carry out completely what the king had required of them, Mordred gave them great thanks:

"Since it is your pleasure that these arrangements be accomplished as the king requested, we need only send for the queen. The archbishop here will give her to me for a wife." They said that they would have her come before them. They went to seek her in a chamber where she was and said:

"My lady, the noble men of your land await you in the hall and beg you to come to them. Thus you will hear what they wish to say. If you do not wish to come, they will come to you."

She said she would go, since they requested it. She rose and went to the hall. When the barons saw her coming, they rose to meet her and received her with great respect. One of them who was the best speaker spoke these words to her:

"My lady, we have asked you to come to us for a single reason. God grant that good may come of it for you and for us, because we certainly would like it; and this is what it is. Death, we know, has taken King Arthur, your lord, who was so noble a man and held us so well at peace. Now that he has quitted this world, we grieve deeply. Because this kingdom, where the power of the lord is spread over all lands, has been left without a governor, it has been necessary for us to consider what man might be worthy to hold an empire as rich as this one to which you were brought as its mistress, for without fail he to whom God gives the honor of this kingdom can only be he who has you for a wife. Concerning this matter we have decided, since decide we must, that we should seek for you a man of great worth and a good knight who will know how to govern the kingdom well. So we have looked among us for someone to have you as a wife, and we will do homage to him. My lady, what do you say to that?"

115

The queen, who was surprised and abashed, said, weeping to him who spoke to her, that she had no desire to take a husband.

"My lady," he said, "such cannot be the case. No one can uphold your stand, for we shall certainly not leave this kingdom without a lord. Otherwise we should certainly suffer if war welled up against us from somewhere. That is why you must, as though by force, do our will in this matter."

She said that she would give up the throne and go out of the country, like one lost, rather than ever take a lord. "And do you know," she said, "why I say this? I say it because I could never have a husband of such high merit as him whom I have had. Therefore I pray you to reason no more with me on this subject, for I would do nothing of the kind, and I should hold it against you."

Then others spoke up and said:

"My lady, your refusal is of no use to you. You must do what you must do."

When she heard them, she was a hundred times more dismayed than before. She asked those who were pressing her:

"Now tell me who it is that you wish to give me for my lord."

"Mordred," they said. "We know no knight among us who is so worthy to hold an empire or a kingdom as he is. He is certainly a valiant man and a good knight and bold."

When the queen heard these words, it seemed to her as if her heart had failed her, but she dared give no show of it so that those who stood before her might perceive it, for she was hoping to free herself by efforts much different from what they thought. When she had thought long over what they had said, she answered:

"As to Mordred, I certainly do not say that he is not a valiant man and a good knight, nor do I go against your proposal, nor do I accept it yet. But allow me a delay to think it over and tomorrow at the hour of prime I will answer you."

Mordred stepped forward and said:

"My lady, you shall have a yet longer respite than you have requested; they will give you a week's delay, provided that at the end of the time fixed you will do everything they require of you."

She gladly consented to that, like a woman who wished nothing but to be rid of them.

Then the discussion ended. The queen went off to her room, and shut herself up with only a maiden for company. When she saw herself without other witnesses, she began to lament as though the whole world lay dead before her. She cried, "Alas, I am a wretched creature," and beat

116

her face and wrung her hands. After she had lamented thus a long time, she said to the damsel who was with her:

"Go look for Labor and tell him to come to me."

The maiden said that she would do so gladly.

This Labor was a wonderful knight of the greatest merit and cousin-german to the queen. He was the one man upon whom the queen could rely in great need, excepting Lancelot. When he had come before her, she bade the damsel to go elsewhere, and the order was obeyed. The queen herself closed the door after her. When she saw herself all alone with the man in whom she had such confidence, she gave way to her sorrow, and then she said to the knight through her tears:

"For God's sake, give me counsel, cousin mine."

When Labor saw her weeping so bitterly, he too began to feel sad and said:

"My lady, why are you tormenting yourself so? Tell me what troubles you, and if I can help you in your sorrow, by whatever means I can, I will free you from it; I give you my word as a loyal knight."

"Fair cousin," said the queen, still weeping, "I am in as desperate case as a woman can be because the nobles of this kingdom wish to give me in marriage to that disloyal traitor, who is, I tell you truly, the son of King Arthur, my lord. Even if he were not, he is so disloyal that I would not take him, no matter what they might do. I would rather have them burn me alive. I will tell you what I have thought of doing. Give me advice according to what you are about to hear. I want to have the tower of this city filled with soldiers and crossbowmen and provisions. I want you yourself to seek out the soldiers and make then swear on saints' relics one by one that they will reveal to nobody why they are stationed there, and if someone asked, within the period before I am to answer them, why I am having the tower stocked, I would respond that it was against my marriage festival."

"My lady," said Labor, "there is nothing that I would not do to protect you. I will find knights and soldiers to keep the tower; meanwhile you will have provisions brought in. When you have stocked the tower well, if you take my advice, you will send a message to Lancelot. You will send him word that he must succor you. I tell you, when he knows your need, he will not fail to come to your aid with forces so great that by their efforts he can easily deliver you from this vexed trouble you are in despite all those of this country. Mordred, I know well, will never be so bold as to await him for a pitched battle. If the fact is that the king is alive—for I do not believe that he is dead—the messenger will find him wherever he is in Gaul. As soon as ever he heard the news, he would come to this country with all the army that he led from it. And thus you would be rid of Mordred."

When the queen heard this advice, she said that it greatly pleased her, for in such a manner she thought that she would be free of this danger where the nobles of the land had put her. So their counsel ended.

Labor sought out knights and soldiers among those in whom he had the most confidence, so that, before the week was over, he had assembled some two-hundred soldiers and knights who had all sworn on saints' relics that they would go into the tower of London and would defend the queen against Mordred as long as they could hold out up to death. The thing was done so secretly that none knew it save only those who took part in it. Within that limit the queen had the tower stocked with everything that may help or be of value to a man's body and that could be found in the country.

When the day came that the queen was to give the answer, as she had given her word, the high barons of the kingdom, who had been summoned for this affair, came together and assembled and were in the hall. The queen, who had not forgotten anything, had already caused to enter the tower those who were to bear her company and were so well provided with arms that they could not be better equipped. When they were all within, the queen entered too and immediately had the drawbridge raised. She went up on the battlements of the tower and said to Mordred who was below and who had well perceived that the queen had outwitted him:

"Mordred, Mordred, in evil fashion have you shown that my lord was akin to you, you who sought to take me for your wife, whether I desired it or not. Certainly you thought to do so in an evil hour for you, for I must tell you that this thing will put you to death."

Then she descended from the battlements and came to a room in the tower and asked those with her what she might do.

"My lady," they said, "be never dismayed; know that we shall defend this tower well against Mordred, if he is of a mind to assail it, for we fear his power but little, and he will have no power to set foot in it nor will any of his company, as long as we have food in here."

The queen was much comforted by these words. When Mordred, who was outside with his company, perceived that he had thus been deceived and had missed getting the queen, he asked the barons what he could do about it.

"For the tower is strong and defensible and surprisingly well stocked with food. Those who have gone inside are valiant men and bold. My lords, what counsel do you give me?"

"Sire," they said, "the tower must be attacked from every side over

118

and over again. Know that it is not of such great strength that it can hold out long against us, because no aid from anywhere will reach them, except as they have it from themselves."

"On my word," said Mordred, "I am not of a mind to besiege it unless I am surer of you than I yet am."

They said that they would give him all the assurance that he could require of them.

"Then I beg you," he said, "to give me your word loyally and swear to me on saints' relics that you will help me to the death against my mortal enemies, even against King Arthur, if fate should ever bring him this way."

"This we will gladly do for you," they said.

Then they knelt before him and all became his liege men and swore on saints' relics that they would aid him against all men even unto death. When they had given this oath, he said to them:

"My lords, I thank you. You have done much for me by electing me to be lord over you and doing me homage. Indeed, I am so sure of you that there is no nobleman on earth whom I would not dare await on the battlefield if only I had your forces in my company. It only remains now to have me seized of your castles and fortresses."

Each gave him a pledge as guarantee of possession, and he accepted it from each.

Then he ordered that the tower should at once be besieged on all sides, and he had his men armed and siege engines set up and ladders brought to climb up on the battlements. Now those within the tower ran to arms. You could have seen a great and wondrous assault, for those outside wanted to mount by force because there were many of them, but those within would not suffer it, but killed them and beat them down into the ditches and defended themselves so well that before the assault ceased, you could have seen more than two hundred men lying in the ditches.

When those outside saw that those within were doing them so much damage, they drew back and ordered that the assault be halted; the men who were carrying on the assault did as they were commanded, for they were much dismayed to find their enemies defending themselves so well. Thus the queen was besieged and assailed over and over again in the tower of London, but always she had people with her who defended her well at every point.

One day the queen called a messenger of hers in whom she had much confidence, and said to him:

"You will go to Gaul to learn news of my lord the king, whether he is alive or dead. If he is living, you will tell him in what state I am and

119

beg him in God's name not to fail to come succor me as soon as ever he can. Otherwise I should be brought to shame, for this tower cannot hold out forever against Mordred and those helping him. If my lord is dead and you learn the facts concerning him and Sir Gawain, you will go straight to Gaunes or Benwick where you will find Lancelot. When you have found him, tell him that I send friendly greetings and that he should come to my rescue with the power he has in Gaunes and Benwick. You may tell him that if succor fails me, I am brought to shame and dishonored, for I could not last long against Mordred, since he has all those of this land as counselors and helpers."

"My lady," said the young man, "I will do all this, if I can reach the land of Gaunes safe and sound, but I am discouraged as to how I can slip out of this tower, for it is surrounded by our enemies on every side and I do not know how to go about it."

"You must find a way to get out and carry your message as I have stated it to you. Otherwise, I shall never be free of these traitors."

In the evening, after nightfall, the youth took leave of his lady, went to the gate, and succeeded in passing through it and through all Mordred's men. He was so fortunate that he was not stopped anywhere by anybody, for those who saw him thought him to be one of their party. As soon as he was beyond them, he went to find quarters in the city and before bedtime was successful in obtaining a good, strong mount. He set out on his road at once, journeyed on to the sea, and crossed it. He then heard that King Arthur was not dead, but had laid siege to the city of Gaunes. The young man rejoiced at this news.

But now the tale ceases to speak of the messenger and returns to King Arthur and his company.

XV
Gaunes

Now the tale tells that when King Arthur had sat before the city of Gaunes about two months, he understood that he would draw no honor from the siege, for those within defended themselves so wondrously that they damaged their enemies every day. One day King Arthur said privately to Sir Gawain:

"Gawain, you have made me undertake an enterprise in which we shall never gain honor; it is this war that you have begun against the kindred of King Ban, for they are so good at fighting that nowhere on earth are men as good. Now think what we can do about it. I tell you that we can very well lose more than we can gain, because they are at home among their friends and have with them knights in great plenty. Know truly, nephew, if they hated us as much as we do them, we would have lost everything because of their great power and their efforts. Think what we can do about it."

"Sire," said Sir Gawain, "I will take counsel with myself, and I shall be able to give you an answer tonight or tomorrow morning."

That day Sir Gawain was more thoughtful than usual. When he had thought as long as he liked, he called a servant of his and said:

"Go into the city of Gaunes and tell Lancelot of the Lake that, if he has the courage to dare defend himself from the accusation that he treacherously slew my brother, I am ready to prove against his body that he killed him disloyally by treason, and if he can conquer in such a trial as I propose, my uncle will go back with all his host into the kingdom of Logres and never again will demand from the people of Benwick anything that has arisen between us. If I can conquer on the field, I ask nothing more; the war will at once be ended, if the two kings will hold their lands from King Arthur. If they will not, we will never leave here before they are humbled and killed."

When the young man heard the words, he began to weep tenderly and said to Sir Gawain:

"My lord, what do you wish to do? Have you such a great desire to undergo shame and go to your death? For Sir Lancelot is a good knight and a seasoned one. If you were killed in such a combat we should all be abased and brought to shame, since you are the best knight in this host and its greatest man. I will never carry this message, please God, when I see your death so plainly there, for I would be very bad and disloyal if by my means or my words a man as noble as you should be brought to death."

"All you tell me," said Sir Gawain, "is of no use; you must carry this message, or else this war will never end. And it is proper that it should be ended by him and me, for he began it and I pursued it. When it had been abandoned, I made my uncle, King Arthur, revive it. Therefore it is proper that I should have the first joy or the first grief. I can tell you that, if I did not see my cause was just, I would not now go to battle with him for the best city in the world, since I perceive and recognize that he is, by himself, the best knight I ever met. But it is general knowledge that wrong and disloyalty would make a coward of the best knight in the world, and a just cause and loyalty would make the most cowardly a brave man and a valiant one. That is why I should fear Lancelot less, for I know that he is in the wrong and I in the right. For that reason neither you nor any other person should fear me, for in all places Our Lord aids the just. That is my faith and my belief."

Sir Gawain spoke so warmly to the youth that he gave his word to go into the city of Gaunes, and tell Lancelot all that Sir Gawain required.

"Now, be sure," said Sir Gawain, "to go there before tomorrow at the hour of prime."

The young man promised to do so.

That night they let the matter rest and spoke no further about it. The combatants had arranged a truce a week before which was to end three days later. The next day before the hour of prime the young man went to the city of Gaunes, and waited until Lancelot was up and had heard mass, and the two kings also. When they had come to the palace and seated themselves in the seats of honor there, the young man came to Lancelot and said:

"My lord, Sir Gawain, whose man I am, sends me to you and tells you through me that if your people and ours fight together at all as they have begun, there must be too grievous hurt to both our parties. But heed this well: Sir Gawain sends word, that, if you dare accept this challenge, he is ready to prove before everyone in this country that you killed his brothers disloyally. If he wins in this trial and makes you recreant, you cannot escape without death, for he declares that he would not take, as ransom for your head, anything at all. If you can defend your cause and make him recreant, the king, his uncle, will go back to the kingdom of Logres and will keep the peace with you the rest of his life and never speak of this thing. If you refuse this challenge and do not dare go out against him, the whole world should shame you, for then one could see and know openly that you are guilty of the accusation. Now choose what you will do, concerning the challenge given through me."

When Lancelot heard what the messenger said, he answered the proposal, much troubled, for certainly he would never have sought to fight Sir Gawain.

"Certainly, fair friend, this message is strong and vexatious for me, because for my part I would never in my life have sought for any reason on earth to fight Sir Gawain, because he is a man of merit and because of our comradeship since I was first a knight. But an accusation as grave as that of treason would bring me such shame, if I did not defend myself against it, that I would never again have honor, for he who does not defend himself against an accusation of treason is viler and more worthy of shame than for any other reason. Therefore tell him from me that, if he wishes to give caution for keeping this agreement, he will find me in my armor on the field of battle at whatever hour he likes. Now you may leave; tell him just what I have said. I speak this not because I fear him but because I loved him so much that I would never have sought to fight him in single combat."

The young man said that he would deliver the message and he departed. King Bohort said to Lancelot:

"Such a wise man as Sir Gawain should never set his hand to such a mad accusation, for everybody knows that you killed his brothers by no treachery at all, but in the open field, in a spot where there were more than a hundred knights."

"I will tell you," said King Lionel, "why he behaves thus. He is so grieved over his brothers' deaths that he would rather die than live. He would avenge himself upon Sir Lancelot more gladly than upon anybody else. That is why he has made such a felonious accusation; it matters not to him whether he lives or dies."

"I think," said Lancelot, "that we shall very soon be on the field of battle. I do not know how it will end, but this much I know; if I had the upper hand and could cut off his head, I would not kill him for the whole world, for he seems to me a man of too much worth and he is the man, in spite of everything, whom I have most loved and still love, excepting the king alone."

"On my word," said King Bohort, "you are a wonder, loving him so entirely while he hates you mortally."

"On my word," replied Lancelot, "you can behold this marvel. He can never hate me so much that I do not love him. I should not have said it so frankly except that I am about to live or die, since I have come to the battle."

Lancelot uttered such words concerning Sir Gawain, at which all those who heard him marveled much and held him in even higher regard than they did before.

The youth who had come from Sir Gawain and heard Lancelot's answer, left the city of Gaunes and rode until he came to Sir Gawain. He told him forthwith what he had found in the city and concluded:

"My lord, you will certainly have battle if you give caution to Sir Lancelot that the king will go back to his country if he can defeat you on the field."

"On my word," said Sir Gawain, "if I do not bring it about that the king himself shall make the necessary oath, I never wish to bear arms again. Now be silent, say no more about this matter, for I believe I will succeed in the arrangement."

Then Sir Gawain went to the king, and knelt before him, and said:

"Sire, I pray you and require you to give me a boon."

The king granted his desire very readily since he did not know what he wanted to request. He took him by the hand, and made him rise.

"Sire, do you know what the boon is that you have granted me? You have agreed that you will be my pledge to Lancelot, if he can defeat me on the field, that you will lift the siege and go back to the kingdom of Logres in such wise that never as long as you live will you commence a war against this country."

When the king heard this news, he was astounded and said to Sir Gawain:

"Have you undertaken a battle with Lancelot? By counsel with whom did you do that?"

"Sire," said Sir Gawain, "that is how it is. The arrangement cannot be stopped now till one of us lies dead or recreant."

"Fair nephew," said the king, "I am really so regretful over this undertaking in which you have engaged yourself that I have not been as much troubled by anything that happened to me as I am by this. I know of no knight anywhere with whom I should not rather see you engaged in battle than with this one, for we know him as the most valiant man of proved power in the world; anywhere you look he is best among the best. Therefore I am so fearful for you that, believe me, I would rather have lost the best city I have than have you ever speak of such a thing."

"Sire," said Sir Gawain, "the thing has gone so far that it can no longer be halted, and if it could be halted, I would not abandon it under any conditions, for I hate him so mortally that I should rather die than not venture on the field to kill him. If God were so kind as to allow me to be able to bring him to death and avenge my brothers, I should never again be pained by anything that happened to me. And if he happens to kill me, at least then the grieving that torments me day and night will be ended. Know that in some way to gain relief, whether alive or dead, I have undertaken this battle."

"Fair nephew," said the king, "now may God help you, for you certainly never undertook anything which dismayed me as much as this, and rightfully, for Lancelot is too good a knight and too hardened in combats. You have found it out by your own experience. At certain times, I have heard you tell this yourself."

Then Sir Gawain said to the youth who had carried the message:

"Go tell Lancelot to come speak to my uncle and me between our army and the city. Let him come unarmed, for my lord the king and all those with him will be unarmed."

The youth left his master and went to the city and found Lancelot and Bohort and his brother, who were still speaking privately together by a window concerning what Sir Gawain had proposed. Lancelot was saying that he greatly regretted the battle and that there were no two knights in the king's host against whom he would not more gladly fight than against Sir Gawain, because of the love he had for him.

The messenger came straight to where he saw them, knelt before Lancelot, and said to him:

"My lord, Sir Gawain and the king send me and they request you to go out there with your two companions to parley with them. You will be all unarmed, for they will come in like manner. There, oaths will be exchanged so that nobody can withdraw from the agreements."

Lancelot said that he would gladly go and would take with him King Bohort and his brother, Hector. The messenger left at once and returned to the camp and reported to the king and Sir Gawain what he had done. Then King Arthur got on his horse and chose King Karados to go with him; the third person was Sir Gawain. They mounted on war-horses and unarmed advanced toward the city gate. They were wearing light silken clothing because it was very hot. When they came near the city, they saw King Bohort and Lancelot and Hector issuing from the gate. As soon as they had approached one another so close that they could speak together, Lancelot said to Bohort:

"Let us dismount before my lord the king who is coming there; he is the most praiseworthy man now on earth."

They said they would never, please God, alight from their horses before their mortal enemy. Lancelot said that although he was his enemy he would alight for love of him. He at once dismounted and his companions did so also. The king said to those with him:

"By God, there is in those three men good reason for everybody to praise them, for there is more courtesy and kindness than in any other folk, and they are so well furnished with chivalry that there is not their like in the whole world. Would to God that there were between us as great love as I ever saw earlier. May God never help me if I would not be happier about that than if someone gave me the best city that there is in the world."

XVI

The Duel

Then Lancelot got off his horse and so did his companions. Lancelot, as soon as he was near the king, greeted him with great humility, but the king did not return his greeting, because he saw that Sir Gawain would be too hurt if he did.

"Sire," Lancelot said to him, "you sent for me to come speak with you, and I have come to hear whatever you wish to say."

Sir Gawain advanced and answered for the king:

"Lancelot, my lord the king has come here to do what you required of me. You know well that you and I have undertaken a battle on the ground of mortal treason because of my brothers' deaths, whom you killed treacherously, disloyally, as we all know. I am the plaintiff and you the defendant. But because it is your desire that after this battle no other should be begun, you wish, as I understand, that my lord the king pledge himself if you win the battle and get the better of me that neither he nor any of his men will harm you ever again as long as he lives, but completely abandon the siege and go back into their own country."

"Sir Gawain," said Lancelot, "if it were your pleasure, I would leave this battle unfought. As it now stands, I could not break it off without the shame's being mine and without my being accused of cowardice. But you have done so much for me, as has also my lord the king here present, that with difficulty can I find the will to come bear arms against you, especially in mortal battle. Know that I do not speak out of cowardice nor because I fear you, but out of good will, for as soon as I am armed and mounted on my war-horse, with God's help, I shall be able to defend myself against you; nor do I speak boastfully nor because you are not the best knight in the world, but because, if it were your pleasure, I would have peace between you and me. To gain peace, I would do, as God permitted, all that you might dare demand, even to becoming with my brother Hector your liege man. All my kindred will do homage to you, except only the two kings, for I should not wish them to place themselves in servitude to others. All this I will do—and yet more; for I will now swear to you on saints' relics, if you wish, that I will leave Gaunes tomorrow before the hour of prime and go away into exile barefooted and in rags, all alone without company for as much as ten years. If I die within that period, I forgive you my death, and I will cause all my kindred to declare you guiltless of it. If I return at the end of ten years, and you are then living and my lord the king here present is also, I wish to

126

have the company of you two as closely as I have ever had it yet. And further I will give you an oath, different from what you believe, so that there may be no cause for accusations of felony. I will swear to you on saints' relics that never to my knowledge did I kill Gaheriet, your brother, and that his death made me more sorrowful than it did glad. All this I will do, not for any fear I have of you, except within reason, but because it seems to me that it would be a pity if one of us should kill the other."

When the king heard the generous offer that Lancelot made to have peace, he was astonished, for he would not have believed at all that Lancelot would make it. He said to Sir Gawain, with tears in his eyes:

"Fair nephew, for God's sake, do what Lancelot requests, for certainly he offers you all the amends that a knight can offer to atone for killing a kinsman. Certainly, no man as valiant as he ever said more than he has said."

"No," said Sir Gawain, "there is no use begging me. I would rather be stuck with a spear through my chest and have my heart drawn from within me than not to do what I have promised you, whether I live or die."

Then he held out his gauntlet and said to the king:

"Sire, here I am ready to prove that Lancelot disloyally killed my brothers, and let the combat be fixed at whatever day you will."

Lancelot, weeping, went forward and said to the king:

"Sire, since I see that the battle cannot be avoided, if I did not defend myself, I should not be considered a knight. Here is my pledge to defend myself. I regret that I must do so. Let the battle be tomorrow, if that pleases Sir Gawain."

Sir Gawain at once assented, and the king accepted the pledges. Then Lancelot said to the king:

"Sire, I request that you give me your word as a king that, if God gives me the honor of victory, you will lift the siege before this city and return to the kingdom of Logres with all your men in such wise that never again as long as you live neither you nor anyone among your kindred will do us harm, unless we harm you first."

King Arthur gave his royal word. Then they separated, and as they did so Hector said to Sir Gawain:

"Sir Gawain, you have refused the handsomest offer and the most generous amends that ever so noble a man as Sir Lancelot offered a knight; certainly, for my part I hope it goes badly with you, and I believe it will."

Lancelot told Hector to be silent after that, for he had said enough, and he did so. They walked away from each other at once and returned to their horses and got on them. Then they rode, the ones, into the city, and the others, into the camp.

But you never saw such great lamentations nor such a great outcry as Sir Ywain began to make, when he learned for a fact that the battle was sworn on both sides between Sir Gawain and Lancelot, and that it could not be canceled. He came to Sir Gawain and reproached him harshly and said to him:

"My lord, why did you do this? Do you hate your own life so much that you have undertaken a battle against the best knight in the world, before whom no man could ever endure in battle without in the end being put to shame? My lord, why have you undertaken this battle, wrongfully besides, for he will defend himself with right on his side? Truly never before did you do such wonders."

"Do not be dismayed, Sir Ywain," said Sir Gawain, "for I know as a certainty that I am in the right and he in the wrong. Therefore, I will fight more sure of myself against him were he double the best knight that he is."

"It is certain, Ywain," said King Arthur, "that I should prefer to have lost half of my kingdom than that this thing should have come to where it is, but since it cannot be halted, we shall see how it comes out and await the mercy of Our Lord. And there are still greater marvels, for Lancelot offered him, so as to have peace, to become his liege man with all his companions except the two kings, and if that offer did not please Gawain, he would go into exile for ten years, and on his return he would ask nothing else than to be in our company."

"On my word," said Sir Ywain, "that was such a great offer that after it I can see on our side only unreasoning behavior. Now may God grant that it does not fall out ill for us, for certainly I have never had such great fear of misfortune as I have now, because I see right on that side and wrong on this."

There were great lamentations in the host from King Arthur and his people; the boldest wept and mourned so deeply that tongue could not dare tell what heart contained. But the people in the city were not truly sorry, for when they heard a description of the great offer that Lancelot made Sir Gawain, they said that God would send shame upon Gawain, for he was too proud and overweening.

That night Lancelot did a watch in the main church of the city with a great company of people and during it confessed to the archbishop all the sins against Our Lord of which he felt guilty, for he greatly feared that it would go ill with him in the combat with Sir Gawain on account of the death of his brothers whom he had killed. When dawn broke he slept till the hour of prime, as did all the others who had watched with him. When the hour of prime came, Lancelot, who was very loath to see what he had to do, rose and dressed and saw the noble men who were waiting on him. He asked for his arms at once, and they were brought to him, good and beautiful and strong and tough and light. His friends armed him the best they could. You could have seen at the arming a great number of barons, each carefully bent on serving him and examining to see that nothing was lacking. When they had prepared him as best they could, they came down from the great hall into the court below. Lancelot bestrode a strong, swift war-horse covered with iron down to its hoofs. When he was on his horse, the others mounted afterward to accompany him. He rode out of the city so that in his party you could have seen ten thousand men, among whom there was not one who, for love of him, would not have handed his body over to death, if need were.

They rode on till they came to a meadow outside the walls, where the battle was to take place. They had come in such wise that there was not one who bore arms, except only Lancelot, nor was there one who went out on the field; instead they stopped around it on the sides toward the city.

When the people in the host saw them outside of the city, they brought Sir Gawain his war-horse; the noble men of the army had already armed him. They came on to the field just as those from the city had done. The king took Sir Gawain by the right hand and took him to the field of battle, but he was weeping as bitterly as if he had seen the whole world dead before him. Bohort took his lord by the right hand, led him to the field of battle and said to him:

"My lord, proceed. May God give you honor in this battle."

Lancelot crossed himself on entering the field and fervently commended himself to God.

The day was bright and clear, the sun was up and beginning to shine on the armor. The knights, who were valiant and sure, spurred forward against each other, lowered their lances, and struck each other so hard on their bodies and shields that both were unhorsed, so stunned that they did not know how to direct their minds, just as if they were dead. The horses that felt free of their load, ran off, one this way, the other that, but found no one to come near them, for everybody had his attention fixed elsewhere. At the moment of the fall of the two knights, you could have seen many a valiant man dismayed and many a tear falling. But after a pause Lancelot rose first and put his hand to his sword, still stunned, though, by his fall. Sir Gawain was hardly slower; he ran to his shield that had been carried off from his neck and set his hand to Excalibur, King Arthur's good sword. He rushed against Lancelot and gave him such a heavy blow on his helmet that he dented it and knocked it awry. Lancelot, who had given and received many a blow, in no wise spared his opponent; instead, he gave him such a blow on his helmet that Sir Gawain had difficulty standing up under it.

Then the fight between them became so furious that never had such a cruel one between two knights been seen. Anyone who saw blows given and received by the mighty men must have remembered them. So the fight went on for a long time, and they hacked at each other with the sharp swords so often and so hard that the coats of mail were cut to pieces on their arms and hips, and the shields were so maltreated that you could have put your fists through them, and pieces were lopped off at the top and bottom, and the helmets which good laces held on them were of little use to them, because they were so dented and cut up by the swords that nearly half of them lay on their shoulders. If the knights had not been of the great strength that they were at the start they could not have been long alive. But they were so weary and exhausted that many a time it happened that their swords turned in their hands when they thought to strike each other. Each of them had a good seven wounds of which the least could have sent another man to his death, and still amidst the travail that they suffered from blood lost they kept up the assault till nearly the third hour. But then they had to rest, unable to endure longer. Sir Gawain drew back first and leaned upon his shield to catch his breath; then Lancelot did likewise.

When Bohort saw Lancelot draw back after the first bout, he said to Hector:

"Now for the first time I fear for my lord, when he has to stop to rest before bringing a knight to defeat. He is resting now in the middle of his battle; that is certainly something that greatly dismays me."

"Know, sir," said Hector, "that, if it were not for love of Sir Gawain, he would not be doing so, for he had no great need of it."

"I do not know," said King Bohort, "what he wants to do, but for my part, I would have given anything in the world, if it belonged to me, to be facing Sir Gawain now. The field would surely soon be empty."

Thus the two knights were in their battle, and one had gained the upper hand, but when Sir Gawain saw clearly that it was noon, he called Lancelot back to the fight as fresh as if he had not yet dealt a blow. He assailed Lancelot so wondrously that the latter was astounded, wherefore he said to himself:

"On my word, I could believe that this man is a devil or an evil spirit, for I was telling myself just now when I left him in peace, that he was worn out with fighting; now he is as fresh as if he had not struck a blow in battle."

Lancelot spoke thus of Sir Gawain, who regained strength and speed at noon; he said the truth. The marvel had not begun there. Wherever Sir Gawain had fought, his strength had been seen to increase about noon. Because some people consider it a fable, I will tell you how it happened.

The truth is that when Sir Gawain was born, his birth took place in Orkney, in a city called Nordelone. After he had been born, King Lot, his father, who was very joyful about it, had him carried into a forest to a hermit who dwelt in the forest. He was a worthy man of such holy life that Our Lord did miracles for him, like straightening cripples or making blind men see. Our Lord did many other miracles for love of that holy man. The king sent the child to him because he did not wish him to receive baptism from any hand but his. When the holy man saw the child and learned who he was, he gladly baptized him and called him Gawain, for that was the holy man's own name. When the child was baptized, one of the knights who had brought the child said to the holy man:

"Do something, sir, so that the kingdom will praise you and so that the child, when he reaches the age to bear arms, shall be more blessed than others."

"Remember, sir knight," the holy man said, "that grace does not come from me, but from Jesus Christ. Without him there comes no grace worth anything. Nevertheless, if by my prayer this infant might receive a greater measure of grace than any other knight, he shall have it. Stay here tonight, and tomorrow I will let you know what kind of man he will be and how good a knight."

That night the king's messengers stayed there till morning. When the holy man had said mass, he came to them and said:

"Gentlemen, concerning this child, I can tell you that he will certainly be praised for prowess above his companions, and never in his life will he be conquered near midday, for through my prayers he is so endowed that every day at noon his strength and his might will increase wherever he is, and whatever pain and travail he has suffered before then will not prevent his feeling at that hour completely fresh and agile." It turned out just as the holy man had said, for every day his strength and might increased about noon wherever he might be. By this means he killed many a valiant man and won many a battle as long as he bore arms. When it occurred that he fought against some knight of great power, he assailed him and pressed him as best he could till noon, so that at that hour his opponent was so weary that he could do no more. When he thought he might rest, then Sir Gawain assailed him mightily, like one who at that hour was

131

strong and swift. Thus he soon brought him to defeat; that is why many knights feared to enter the lists with him unless it was after noon.

That measure of grace and that might of his he had by the prayer of the holy man, and well was it shown that day when he fought the son of King Ban of Benwick. One could see quite clearly that before that hour Sir Gawain was hard pressed and near defeat, so that he had to rest. But when his strength had returned, as it always did, he leaped upon Lancelot so swiftly that no one could have seen him who would not have said that he seemed not to have dealt a blow that day, he was so quick and light. He began at that time to press Lancelot so continuously that he brought blood from his body in more than ten places; he pressed him so hard because he thought to bring him to defeat, and thought that if he failed to conquer him about noon, he would never succeed in doing so. Therefore he struck and flailed Lancelot with his sharp sword; Lancelot was bewildered but still held up. When King Bohort saw that Lancelot was so nearly down that he could do scarcely more than hold out, he said so loud that many could hear:

"Ah, God, what do I see? Ah, prowess, what has become of you? Ah, my lord, are you under enchantment who are thus being overwhelmed by a single knight? I have always seen you do greater deeds of arms by yourself than two of the best knights in the world could do. And now you are so hard pressed by the prowess of a single knight!"

So the battle went on until after noon while Lancelot did little but withstand Sir Gawain's attack and cover himself. But meantime he grew somewhat rested and regained his strength and breath. He rushed upon Sir Gawain swiftly and gave him such a great blow on the helmet that he made him stagger. He was so borne down by that blow that he was forced to draw back. Then Lancelot began to beat at him and deal him great blows with his sharp sword, and force him to yield ground. Sir Gawain, who now was the most afraid that he had ever been and who saw himself about to suffer complete shame unless he could defend himself, plucked up his strength for fear of death and assembled all his prowess. He defended himself in such anguish that in his great distress, blood sprang from his nose and mouth, besides from the other wounds he had, which were bleeding more than was good for him. So the battle of the two knights went on till the ninth hour; then both knights were in such bad shape that the need of both was quite apparent. The place where they fought was littered with links from their coats of mail and with fragments from their shields. But Sir Gawain was so exhausted with the wounds that he had that he expected naught but death, nor did Lancelot remain so whole but that he had greater need of rest than of combat, for

Sir Gawain had pressed him hard and kept him so busy that blood flowed from his body in more than thirteen places. If these men had been other knights, they would have been dead long since from the travail which they had suffered, for each had a heart within him which seemed to have done little unless he brought the other to death or to defeat so that it might be seen which was the better.

The struggle went on thus till vespers; then Sir Gawain was so exhausted that he could scarcely hold his sword. Lancelot, who was not overly weary and who could still endure, rained blows on him and pushed him first this way, then that; Sir Gawain, however, still held out and persisted, covering himself with as much of his shield as he had left. When Lancelot saw that he had him down, and that everybody on the spot saw it clearly, and that there was no longer any defense worth consideration, he drew close to Sir Gawain and said to him:

"Ah, Sir Gawain, it would be very reasonable that I should be called quits of this accusation that you have made against me, for I have defended myself against you till nearly vespers, and by vespers a man who accuses another of treason should have fought out his quarrel and won his battle or he should rightfully have lost his case. Sir Gawain, I am telling you this so that you may have mercy upon yourself, for if you maintain this battle longer, someone must die in vile fashion and our kinsmen will be blamed. So that I may do what you would not dare request, my prayer is that we should cease fighting."

Gawain said that he wished no help from God if he granted such a thing willingly, and he said to Lancelot:

"Be sure that one of us must die on this field; it cannot be otherwise."

Lancelot was in great sorrow at this reply, for he would not have liked at all that Sir Gawain should die by his hand. He had tested him so much that he had not thought in the morning that there was so much prowess in him as he had found that day. Lancelot was the one man on earth who most loved good knights. Then he went over where he saw the king, and said to him:

"Sire, I was begging Sir Gawain to give up this battle, for it is certain that if we do more, one of us two must suffer for it; it cannot be otherwise."

When the king, who recognized that Sir Gawain was being defeated, heard Lancelot's kindly words, he answered:

"Lancelot, Gawain will not leave the battle, if it is not his pleasure, but you can leave it, if you wish, for it is already past the hour. You have done what you should."

"Sire," said Lancelot, "if I thought that you would not reproach me with cowardice, I would go away and leave Sir Gawain on the field."

"It is certain," said the king, "that you never did anything that I was as grateful for as I would be for this."

"So, by your leave, I will go away," said Lancelot.

"God keep you," said the king, "and bring you to salvation as the best knight that I ever saw and the most courteous."

Then Lancelot went off toward his own people. When Hector saw him coming, he said to him:

"My lord, what have you done? You were conquering your mortal enemy, and still you cannot take vengeance, but let him escape after he has accused you of treason?"

"Oh, brother," said Lancelot, "what are you saying? So help me God, I would rather have a spear run through my body than kill such a valiant man."

"He would have killed you," said Hector, "if he had been able. Why did you not do as much for him?"

"I would not do it," said Lancelot, "for my heart within me could not consent to it."

"I am certainly sorry for that," said King Bohort. "I think that it is something you will yet repent for."

Then Lancelot mounted a horse that had been readied for him and rode into the city. When he had reached the big courtyard and was disarmed, the physicians saw that he was badly wounded and had lost so much blood that another man would have died of it. When Hector saw the wounds, he was much dismayed, and when the physicians had examined them, he asked whether they could be healed.

"Indeed, yes," said the physicians. "However, he has lost so much blood and the wounds are so deep that we are much concerned; still, we know that he will recover from them."

Then they dressed Lancelot's wounds and put on them what they thought was good. When they had done their best for him, they asked how he was. "Very well," said Lancelot. Then he said to King Lionel and King Bohort who had come to see him:

"Good, my lords, I tell you that since I first bore arms, I have no reason to fear any man till today, but today I had without a doubt the greatest fear I ever had, for when noon came and I had pushed Sir Gawain till he was so exhausted that he could no longer do more than defend himself weakly, then I found him so vigorous and swift that if he had held out long with such prowess, I could not have escaped death. I marvel much how that could happen, for earlier I know that he was recreant and hard pushed; in a very short time such strength had come to him that he was more vigorous and swifter than he had been in the beginning."

"You are certainly right," said Bohort. "In that hour I was so afraid for you that I never before was as much so, and if he had held out as he began that time, you would not have escaped death, since he would not have been as generous as you have been. I have seen enough of you two to know that you are the two best knights in the world."

Thus the men in Gaunes spoke of the battle, and greatly wondered how Sir Gawain had lasted so long against Lancelot, for they all knew that Lancelot was the best knight in the world and about twenty-one years younger than Sir Gawain. At that time Sir Gawain could well have been seventy-six years old and King Arthur ninety-two.

XVII
From War to War

When the men in Arthur's army saw that Lancelot had entered the city, they went to Sir Gawain, who was leaning on his shield in such shape that he could not hold himself up. They put him on a horse and led him straight to the king, then disarmed him, and found him so badly hurt that he swooned in their hands. The physician was called. When he had seen the wounds, he said that he would heal him rather soon except for a deep wound in his head. The king said to him:

"Fair nephew, your mad hatred has killed you. It is a pity, for never again will there come from your line as good a knight as you are and have been."

Sir Gawain was unable to answer to anything the king said, for he was so ill that he did not think he would see the next day. Great and small wept there, when they saw Sir Gawain in such unexampled distress. The rich wept and the poor, for they all loved him with a great love. They remained close to him all night to see how he would fare, for at any moment he might die in their hands. Sir Gawain did not open his eyes all night long nor say a word nor move at all, any more than if he were dead, except that after a long time he moaned in anguish.

As soon as it was quite light, the king ordered his tents and pavilions to be struck, for he would stay there no longer, but he would move into Gaul and sojourn there until he knew whether Sir Gawain would recover. In the morning, as soon as light permitted, the king left Gaunes, lamenting much, and had Sir Gawain borne in a litter, so sick that the physician himself expected naught but death.

The king went to lodge in a city called Meaux and stayed there till Sir Gawain was on the way to recovery. When the king had spent a long time in that city, he said that he would soon go to the kingdom of Logres. Then news came to him which much displeased him, for a young man said one morning as he rose:

"Sire, I bring you very vexing news."

"What is it?" said the king. "Tell me."

"Sire, the Romans have invaded your land. They have already burned and laid waste all Burgundy, and killed and wounded the men, and pillaged the country. I know for a truth that this week they will advance on you with their army to fight you in a pitched battle. You never saw so many people as they have."

When King Arthur heard this news he told the youth not to talk about it, for if his men heard it related as he told it, there would be some more dismayed than they should be. The youth said that he would say no more about it. The king went to Sir Gawain, who was somewhat recovered, except for the wound in his head, from which he was to die. The king asked how he felt.

"Well, sire, thank God," said Sir Gawain, "I am well enough to bear arms."

"It is necessary that you should be," said the king, "for very bad news has come."

"What is it?" said Sir Gawain, "please tell me."

"On my word," said the king, "a boy has told me that forces from Rome have invaded this land, and this week are to come upon us and fight a pitched battle. Consider what we should do."

"Well, the best thing I see," said Sir Gawain, "is to set out tomorrow to meet them and to join battle with them. I think the Romans are so faint-hearted and so weak that they can never last against us."

The king said that so it should be.

Then he asked Sir Gawain again how he felt, and the answer was that he was as light on his feet as he ever was and felt as powerful, except for the wound in his head "which is not completely healed, I am sorry to say. Nevertheless, I will not fail to take up my arms as soon as need be."

The king departed the next day from the castle where he had been sojourning, and traveled on with his people till he met on the border of Burgundy and Champagne the emperor of Rome with a very large army. But they were not as good knights as the men from Great Britain. King Arthur, before he attacked, sent an embassy of knights to the Roman host to ask the emperor for what reason he had entered his land without his leave. The emperor answered and said:

"I have not entered his land, but our own, for there is no land that he should not hold from us, and I have come here to avenge one of our princes, Frolle of Germany, whom he killed some time ago with his own hand. Because of the treason he did then, he will never have peace from us until he does us homage and holds his land from us in such manner that he and those who succeed him send us tribute every year."

The king's ambassadors answered thus:

"Since we can find nothing else in you, we defy you in the name of King Arthur, and know that you have come to the battle in which you will be put to shame on the field and all your men killed."

"I do not know," said the emperor, "what the outcome will be, but we came here to do battle, and by battle we will gain or lose this land."

The messengers then left the emperor, and when they had come to the king, they told him what had happened.

"It only remains, then," said the king, "to march on them, for I would rather die than hold land from the Romans."

In the morning the men of Logres got under arms, and the king set up ten divisions. When he had done so, the first ones went to strike the Romans so wondrously that they were all taken aback. Then you could have seen on the battlefield knights falling on both sides, until the ground was covered with them. The Romans were not so adept with, or used to, bearing arms as the men from the kingdom of Logres. Therefore, you could have seen them stumbling about as if they were dumb animals. When King Arthur, who was leading the last division, had come into the fighting, then you could have seen him killing Romans and doing great wonders with his body, for in his time there was no man of his age who could do as much. Sir Gawain, in another part of the field, with Kay, the seneschal, and Girflet began again to do such deeds that no one should blame him. As he rode fighting amidst the battle, which was a very great one, he came upon the emperor and a nephew of his. Those two had greatly hurt the men from Logres, for they went about killing and felling whomever they encountered. When Sir Gawain saw the marvel of their strength, he said to himself:

"If those two live long, it might be bad for us, for they are good knights."

Then he charged upon the nephew of the emperor and dealt him such a hard blow with his sword that he cut off his left shoulder. The prince felt mortally wounded, and dropped from his horse to the ground. At that blow the Romans rushed up and attacked Sir Gawain from every side. They smote him with swords and spears up, down, and sideways, and made large, wondrous wounds in his body, but nothing hurt him so much as the blows on his helmet, for thus the wound in his head was opened, from which he was to die. When the emperor saw his nephew so stricken, he charged upon Kay, the seneschal, and struck him so hard that he ran his spear into his body. Kay fell so badly wounded that he lived only three days afterward. The emperor drew his sword and spurred toward Girflet and dealt him such a mighty blow on his helmet that he was stunned, so that he could not hold his seat in the saddle, but plunged down from his horse. King Arthur saw those two blows and understood that it was the emperor; then he galloped in that direction and struck the emperor on his helmet with all the might of his bright sharp sword so hard that nothing could stop his making the emperor feel the blade of his sword right down to his teeth. He drew out his sword, and the emperor fell to earth, which was a great pity, for he was an excellent knight and a young man.

When the Romans saw their lord lying dead, they at once were thrown into a panic and turned to flee wherever they could. The Britons pursued them, killing and cutting them down so cruelly that there were only a hundred left. These were taken prisoner and were brought before King Arthur, and he said to them:

"You shall die unless you swear to do my will."

They gave their oaths. He had the emperor's body taken up and put on a bier, and then said to the Romans:

"You will carry your emperor back to Rome, and will tell those whom you find that in lieu of the tribute which they are demanding, I send them the body of their emperor; no other tribute will King Arthur ever pay them."

The prisoners said that they would deliver the message. They left the king, and he remained on the battlefield, for he did not want to move that night.

The tale tells no more of him and his men, and returns to the youth whom Queen Guenevere had sent to King Arthur to tell him of Mordred's treason and relate how she was besieged in the tower of London.

Now the tale tells that the very day the Romans were vanquished, as the tale has related, the youth whom the queen had sent to Gaunes from the kingdom of Logres to bring the news about Mordred came before the king who was glad and joyful at the adventure which God had sent him, beautiful except that Sir Gawain was so badly wounded that he understood he would never escape. Sir Gawain complained of no wound so much as he did of the one in his head that he had got from Lancelot; the

Romans had renewed his pain that day by the great blows that they had rained upon his helmet. He was bleeding so freely because he had done mighty deeds that day in the battle. If he had not been so doughty, the Romans would not have been conquered by the people who were there against them.

Then the queen's messenger came before the king, and said:

"Sire, Queen Guenevere, your wife, sends me to you. Her message is that you have been betrayed and deceived, and it is no act of yours that has kept her from being shamed with all her kinsmen." Then he told how Mordred had behaved, and how he had been crowned lord of the kingdom of Logres, and how all the high barons who held lands from King Arthur had done him homage, in such wise that, if King Arthur came there, he would not be received as a lord, but as a mortal enemy. Afterward, he told how Mordred had laid siege against the queen in the tower of London and was having it assaulted every day. "Because my lady fears lest he will destroy her, she bids you for God's sake to bring her succor as fast as you can, for certainly, if you delay, she will soon be captured. He hates her so mortally that he will do shame upon her body, and great shame will be yours."

When the king heard these words, he was so overwhelmed that he could not say a word. At last he told the youth that he would right matters, if it pleased God. He began to weep bitterly. When at length he spoke, he said:

"Ah, Mordred, now you make me know that you are the serpent that long ago I saw come out of my belly to burn my lands and attack me. But a father never did to a son what I shall do to you, for I will kill you with my two hands; let the whole world know it. May God never will that you die by other hands than mine."

Many high men heard these words. They marveled much, for they learned for a fact by these words the king had said that Mordred was his son. The wonder of those there was very great. The king ordered those about him to make known throughout the host that night that they should be ready to mount their horses the next morning, for the king would go to the sea to pass over into the kingdom of Logres. When this news was known in the host, you would have seen tents and pavilions coming down on the heights and in the low places. The king commanded his people to make a litter whereon Sir Gawain should be carried, for the king would not leave him far from himself, for if he died, he wished to see him die, and if he lived, he would be the more joyous. The men did just what the king had ordered.

In the morning at break of day the host got into motion, and when

139

they were on their road, they marched till they came to the sea. Then Sir Gawain spoke clearly to those about him, and said:

"Ah, God, where am I?"

"My lord," said one of the knights, "we are on the seashore."

"And which way do you wish to go?" he asked.

"My lord, we wish to pass over into the kingdom of Logres."

"Ah, God," said Sir Gawain, "may you be praised when it pleases you that I should die in my own land, for which I have longed so much."

"My lord," said the knight to whom he was speaking, "do you then believe you will die thus?"

"Yes, truly," he said, "I know that I will not live a fortnight. I regret more not to be able to see Lancelot before I die than I regret my death, for, if I saw him whom I know to be the best knight in the world and the most courteous, I could plead for his forgiveness for having been so villainous toward him at the last. It is my opinion that then my soul would be more tranquil after my death."

The king came up at these words and heard what Sir Gawain was saying.

"Fair nephew," he said, "your felony has done me great injury, for it has bereft me of you, whom I loved above all men, then after you, Lancelot, whom others feared so much that, if Mordred had known that he was in my favor just as he was formerly, he would never have been so bold as to undertake such a disloyalty as he has begun. Now, it is my belief, I shall have a lack of valiant men, both of you and of those on whom I relied most in times of great need, for the disloyal traitor has assembled all the powerful in my lands to come against me. Ah, God! If now I had in my company those whom I used to have, I would not fear the whole world, if it were against me."

Such words spoke King Arthur then and there; they made Sir Gawain grieve much. He made an effort to talk as much as he could, and he said:

"Sire, if you have lost Lancelot by my folly, win him back by your wisdom, for you can easily attract him to you, if you will, for he is the man of the greatest merit that I have ever seen and the kindest in the world. He loves you with such a great love that I know truly that he will come to you, if you send for him. You need him badly, it seems to me, and for any reliance you have on me, do not stop, for certainly you will never again see me bear arms, neither you nor anybody else."

When King Arthur heard what Gawain said to him, that he could not escape death, he was so stricken by these words, and he mourned so loudly that there was no one present who did not feel great pity.

140

"Fair nephew," said the king, "can what you say be true, that you are leaving us at this juncture?"

"Sire, yes, indeed," was the answer. "I shall never see the fourth day from now."

"That should I bewail," said the king, "for mine is the greatest loss."

"Sire," said Sir Gawain, "still I advise you to send word to Lancelot to come to your aid. I know for a certainty that he will come as soon as he has your letter, for he loves you much more than you think."

"No," said the king, "for I have wronged him so much that I do not believe any prayer could serve, and therefore I shall make no request of him."

Then the sailors came to the king and said to him:

"Sire, when it is your pleasure, you may go aboard your ship, for we have made ready all that is needful, and the wind has risen, good, and strong, and favorable. If you delayed longer, it would be folly."

Then the king had Sir Gawain taken up and put on the ship, and laid as comfortably as those caring for him could arrange. Then the richest barons went aboard and took with them their arms and horses. The other barons sailed on other ships and their men with them. Thus King Arthur put to sea, wroth with Mordred's great disloyalty toward him, but still more did he lament for Sir Gawain whom he saw grow worse every day and approach his end. That was the grief that touched his heart more than any other; that was the grief that left him no rest, day or night; that was the grief that would not let him eat or drink. But now the tale ceases telling of him and returns to Mordred.

Now the tale tells that Mordred kept on with the siege of the tower of London till the tower was worsened and battered, for the machines were casting stones at it, and there were great blows so that the besieged could not have held out as long as they did, had they not defended themselves so wondrously. Meanwhile, though the siege upon the tower went on, Mordred never ceased sending for the great nobles of Ireland and Scotland and of the foreign lands that did homage to him. When they had come to him, he gave them such fine gifts that they were quite astonished; he conquered their good will so craftily thus that they yielded themselves so entirely to him that they said both in public and in private that they would not fail to aid him against all men, even against King Arthur, if it turned out that fortune brought him back. Thus Mordred drew into his party all the noble men who held lands from King Arthur, and kept them with him over long stretches of time. He could well do so, for King Arthur, before he departed, had left him all his treasures wherever they might be. Besides, the whole world brought and gave him more; they considered their attentions well spent because of his great generosity.

One day, as he was having the tower assaulted, a messenger of his came to him and said to him privately as he stood somewhat off from the others:

"Sire, I have some wondrous news to tell you. King Arthur has landed on this island with his forces and is coming against you with many people. If you wish to wait here for him, you will see him in two days. You cannot fail to have battle, for he is coming on for no other reason. Now, plan what you will do about it, for if you do not get good counsel, you can lose quickly."

When Mordred heard this news, he became much astonished and dismayed, for he greatly feared King Arthur and his attack, and in the same way he was much afraid because of his disloyalty, lest it harm him more than aught else. Then he consulted on this matter with those in whom he had the most confidence, asking what he could do. They said:

"Sire, we can give you no other advice than to assemble your men and go against him, ordering him to vacate this land which you hold legally from its nobles. If he does not wish to quit the land, you have more men than he has who love you well. Fight him confidently and know for sure that his men can never hold out against you, since they are weak and weary and we are fresh and rested. We have not borne arms for some time. Before you leave here, ask your barons whether they agree to fight. We believe that there will be no other outcome than that we have described."

Mordred said that he would act as they advised. He called before him all his barons and all the noble men of the country who were in the city. They came to him and when they had come, he told them that King Arthur was advancing against them with his forces and would be in London within the third day. Those present said to Mordred:

"Sire, what do we care about his coming? You have more men than he has. Go confidently to meet him, for we will risk death rather than not stand by our guarantee of the land which we have given you, and we shall never fail you as long as we can bear arms."

When Mordred saw that they were urging him on to combat, he was exceedingly glad, thanked them all and bade them take up their arms, for there was no reason for delay, and he would like to meet King Arthur before he had hurt the land. Then the news was spread throughout the country, and they said that they would set out the next morning to go against King Arthur. That night all worked and toiled to get ready. The next day, as soon as it was light, they left London; they calculated that they numbered more than ten thousand. Now the tale ceases to tell of them and returns to Queen Guenevere, King Arthur's wife.

Now the tale tells that when Mordred had left London with his army, the people in the tower had learned the news that King Arthur was coming and that their enemies were going to meet him in combat. They told the queen, who was at the news both glad and sorrowful, glad because she saw that she was free and sorrowful on account of the king, who she feared would die in battle. Then she began to think, and was so worried that she knew not what to do. While she was thus thinking, her cousin by chance came before her. When he saw her weeping, he was much distressed and said to her:

"Ah, my lady, what troubles you? For God's sake, tell me, and I will advise you as best I can."

"I will tell you, then," said the queen. "Two things have set me to thinking thus. One is that my lord the king has undertaken this battle and if Mordred wins, he will kill me. If my lord is victorious he will not believe at all that Mordred has not known me carnally, because of the great force that he exerted to have me; I know truly that he will kill me as soon as he can lay hands on me. By this double reasoning you can see clearly that I cannot escape death either from one side or from the other. Now consider whether I can be much at ease."

Her cousin did not know how to advise her in this matter, for he saw death prepared for her on every hand, and he said:

"My lady, God willing, my lord the king will have greater mercy on you than you think. Be not so sorely dismayed, but pray God Our Lord Jesus Christ that He bestow honor and victory in this battle upon him and that he pardon you his wrath, if it is true that he is angry with you."

That night the queen rested little, as she was not at ease, but badly frightened, for she saw safety nowhere. The next day, as soon as it was light, she waked two of her damsels, the ones in whom she had the greatest confidence. When they were dressed and ready, she had each mount on her palfrey, took two squires with her, and caused two pack animals laden with gold and silver to be led out of the tower. So the queen quitted London and went to a forest nearby, where there was an abbey of nuns that her ancestors had established. When she arrived, she was received as nobly as such a lady should be received. She had all the treasure that she had brought with her unloaded there. Then she said to the damsels who had come with her:

"If you like, damsels, you may go away, and if you like, you may remain. As for me, I tell you that I shall stay here and will enter religion among the nuns here, for my mother, who was queen of Tarmelide, and considered a virtuous lady, came here and lived out the rest of her life."

When the damsels heard what the queen said, they wept many tears and said:

"My lady, you will never receive this honor without us."

The queen said that she was very glad of their company. Then the abbess came in. As soon as she saw the queen, she showed her very great joy. The queen at once requested to enter the order there.

"My lady," said the abbess, "if the king had passed on from this world, we would very gladly make you one of our ladies and our companion. But because he still lives, we should not dare receive you, for he would certainly kill us, as soon as he found it out, and, besides, my lady, there is something else. I am sure that if we had received you, you would not be able to hold up under our rules, for there is much severity in them, especially for you who have had all the comforts in the world."

"My lady," said the queen, "if you do not receive me, it will be the worse for you and for me, for if I go on from here, and evil by chance befalls me, the misfortune will be mine, but the king will ask you for my body, be sure of that, for by your fault I will have suffered evil."

The queen spoke so long to the abbess that the latter did not know what to say. The queen drew her aside, and told her of her anguish and fear, because of which she wished to enter religion.

"My lady," said the abbess, "here is what I advise. You will stay here, yes, and if by ill luck Mordred overcomes King Arthur and wins this battle, then you may appropriately take our habit and enter our order completely. If the God of Glory should give your lord victory in this battle and he gained the upper hand and returned here safe and sound, I would make your peace with him, and you would be better received by him than you ever were."

The queen answered the abbess:

"My lady, I believe that this advice is good and loyal, and I will do as you have counseled."

Thus the queen stayed there with the nuns where she had placed herself for fear of King Arthur and of Mordred. Now the tale ceases to tell of her and returns to King Arthur.

Here the tale tells that, when King Arthur had set sail to go to the kingdom of Logres to ruin and destroy Mordred, he had a good brisk wind which bore him across with his people so that they beached beneath the castle of Dover. When they had landed and taken their arms from the ships, the king sent word to the citizens of Dover that they should open their gates and receive him within. This they did most joyfully, and said that they had thought that he was dead.

"Now, know," said King Arthur, "that Mordred perpetrated this disloyal act, for which he shall die, if I ever can make him, as a traitor and perjurer both before God and his liege lord."

That day about the hour of vespers Sir Gawain said to those about him:

"Go tell my lord, my uncle, that he should come speak with me."

One of the knights went to the king and said that Sir Gawain was asking for him. When the king came, he found Sir Gawain so stricken that nobody could draw a word from him. Then the king began to weep bitterly and to lament aloud. When Sir Gawain heard his uncle lamenting so for him, he recognized him, opened his eyes, and said as his strength permitted:

"Sire, I am dying. For God's sake, if you can keep from doing battle against Mordred, keep from it. I tell you truly, if you die by any man's hand, you will die by his. And greet my lady the queen for me. And you, gentlemen, some of whom, please God, will see Lancelot, tell him that I send him greetings more heartfelt than those I have ever sent any man, and that I beg his mercy, and I pray God that He will keep him in the state in which I left him. And I beg him not to fail to come see my tomb as soon as he knows that I am dead. Thus it cannot be that he will not take some pity on me."

Then he said to the king:

"Sire, I request that you have me buried at Camelot with my brothers, and I want to be placed in that same tomb where the body of Gaheriet was laid, for he was the man I loved most in the world. And have this carved on the tombstone: 'Here lie Gaheriet and Gawain, whom Lancelot slew through Gawain's mad hatred.' I desire that the inscription be such so that I may be blamed for my death as I have deserved."

The king, who was grieving sorely, when he heard what Sir Gawain was saying, asked him:

"What, fair nephew, have you then come to your death through Lancelot?"

"Sire, yes, by the wound that he made in my head. It would have been healed, but the Romans opened it for me in the battle with them."

After those words, no one heard him say another word, save only, "Jesus Christ, Father, do not judge me in accordance with my evil deeds."

Then he left this world with his hands crossed on his chest. The king wept, and lamented aloud, and swooned upon him many times, and cried that he was weary, weak, and full of dolor, and he said:

"Ah, Fortune, spiteful and inconstant being, the most treacherous thing on earth, why were you ever so kind to me and so friendly to make me pay so dearly in the end? Long ago you were a mother to me; now you have become a stepmother, and to make me die of grief, you have called death to your aid so that in two ways you have put me to shame, through my friends and through my lands. Oh, villainous death, you should never have such a man as my nephew, who surpassed all others in goodness."

Greatly was King Arthur troubled by this death, and so overwhelming was his sorrow that he knew not what he should say. He swooned so often that the barons feared that he might die among them. They carried him away into a chamber because they did not wish him to see the body, for as long as he beheld it, he would not cease his complaint. All day long the lamentations in the castle were so loud that you could not have heard the thunder of God. Men and women all wept as if each were a cousin-german of Sir Gawain. It was no wonder, for Sir Gawain had been the knight most loved in the world by many sorts of people. They did every honor possible to his body, and put it in silken cloths embroidered with gold and precious stones. That night there was such a great illumination that you would have thought the castle was on fire.

In the morning, after day broke, King Arthur, who saw himself laden with many cares, took one hundred knights and had them armed and had a horse-borne bier prepared, and Sir Gawain's body placed on it, and he said:

"You will take my nephew to Camelot, and there you will have him buried as he requested and put into Gaheriet's tomb."

While he was speaking thus, he wept so bitterly that those present were no less moved by his grief than they were by the death of Sir Gawain. Then the hundred knights mounted, and in the funeral procession there were more than a thousand others, who all wailed and cried after the corpse and said:

"Ah, good knight and true, courteous and kind, may death be cursed who took your company from us!"

Thus all the people wept after the body of Sir Gawain. When they had accompanied the body a long way, the king stopped and said to those who were to carry on the body:

"I can go no further; go on to Camelot and do what I have told you."

Then the king turned about, grieving fearfully, and he said to his men:

"Now, my lords, it will appear what you can do henceforth, for you have lost him who was your father and a shield in all needs. Ah, God, I fear that soon we shall suffer without his help." Thus spoke the king as he rode away.

Those who were to take the body rode all day, till adventure brought them to a castle named Beloé; its lord was a knight who had not loved Sir Gawain, but had hated him from envy, because he saw that Sir Gawain was a better knight than he. Those who bore the body alighted before the main hall. There was none who did not have a very heavy heart. Then the lady of the castle appeared who asked them who that knight was. They said that it was Sir Gawain, King Arthur's nephew. When the lady heard those words she ran toward the body as though out of her mind, and swooned upon it. When she recovered from it, she said:

"Ah, Sir Gawain, so great is the pity of your death, especially for ladies and damsels! I lose much more than any other, for I am losing the man I loved most in the world, and may all those here know that I have never loved any save him, and never again will I love another as long as I live."

At these words the lord of the castle came out of his room, and was most angry at the grief that she was exhibiting. Then he ran into another room, took his sword, came toward the corpse, struck his wife, who was lying on it so that he cut through her shoulder and half a foot into her body. The lady cried:

"Ah, Sir Gawain, I have died for you. For God's sake, my lords who are present here, I pray you to carry my body where you are bearing his so that those who will see our tombs will know that I died for him."

The knights did not hear much of what the lady said, for they were too much shocked to see her killed in such a misadventure. They rushed upon the knight, seized his sword, and one of the knights said to him wrathfully:

"Certainly, sir knight, you have brought shame upon us when you killed this lady before us for no reason. So help me God, never again will you strike a lady and remember doing so."

Then he took the sword and dealt the lord of the castle such a blow that the wound was mortal. The man, who felt wounded to death, wanted to turn in flight. His adversary would not let him, but aimed another blow which stretched him dead on the floor of the hall. Then a knight who was present cried:

"Alas! Alas! This knight has killed my lord."

He spread the word throughout the town; the people leaped to arms and said that unlucky was the day the knights came, for they would sell the life of their lord very dearly. They came to the hall where the strangers were and attacked them. The knights conveying Sir Gawain's body, who

147

were good knights and friends, defended themselves so well that the townspeople considered the attack that they had undertaken to be foolish. They were quickly driven from the hall.

The strangers remained there that night and ate and drank what they found there. In the morning they prepared a bier and carried away with them the lady of the castle. They rode on till they came to Camelot. When the people of the city knew that it was the body of Sir Gawain, they were sad and very downcast because of his death. They said that now they were completely destroyed. The body was conveyed to the main church and placed in the middle thereof. When the common people of the city learned that Sir Gawain's body had been brought, so many came that no one could number them.

When the third hour came and the body had received its rightful treatment, they put it in the tomb with Gaheriet, and inscribed upon the tomb:

"Here lie the two brothers, Sir Gawain and Gaheriet, whom Lancelot of the Lake slew because of the mad hatred of Sir Gawain."

Thus was Gawain buried with Gaheriet, his brother; the people of the country mourned loudly because of the death of Sir Gawain.

But now the tale ceases to tell of Sir Gawain and of the Lady of Beloé, and the story goes back to tell of King Arthur and his company.

XVIII
The Last Campaign

Now the tale tells that, when King Arthur had left Sir Gawain's body, which he had sent to Camelot, he came back to Dover Castle and tarried there all that day. The next day he departed and set off to fight Mordred. He rode with his army, and lay that night on the edge of a forest. When he had gone to bed and fallen asleep, it seemed to him in his slumber that Sir Gawain came before him, handsomer than he had ever before seen him at any time. A multitude of poor people followed after him, and they were all saying:

"King Arthur, we have won for Sir Gawain the house of God, because of the great good that he has done us. Do as he has done, and thus you will act wisely."

The king answered that he would be glad to do so; then he ran to his nephew, and embraced him, and Sir Gawain said, weeping:

148

"Sire, take care not to go into battle against Mordred; if you fight him, you will die in combat or you will be wounded unto death."

"It is certain," said the king, "that I shall fight him, even if I am to die for it. I should be recreant indeed if I did not defend my land against a traitor."

Sir Gawain, then departing with the greatest lamentations, said to the king, his uncle:

"Ah, sire, what grief and what a pity when you hasten to your end!" Then he came back to the king and said to him: "Sire, send for Lancelot, for know truly that if you have him in your company, Mordred can never hold out against you. If you do not send for him in your need, you cannot escape without death."

The king said that he would never send for him, because he had done him so much wrong that he did not believe that Lancelot would heed his summons. Sir Gawain turned away tearfully and said:

"Sire, know that it will be a great pity for all upright men."

So it befell King Arthur as he slept.

In the morning, when he awoke, he made the sign of the cross upon his face and said:

"Ah, fair Lord God Jesus Christ, who have given me so many honors since I first wore a crown and came to hold lands, fair sweet Lord, in your mercy, do not allow my honor to be lost in this battle, but give me victory over my enemies who are perjured and disloyal toward me."

When the king had said this, he rose and went to hear the mass of the Holy Ghost, and when he had heard it through, he had all his host break their fast lightly, because he did not know at what hour he might encounter Mordred's men. When they had eaten, they set out and rode all day in good order and leisurely, so that their horses would not be too tired whenever they might come to battle. That evening they encamped on Lovedon Meadow and were undisturbed. The king lay alone in his tent except for his chamberlains.

When he had fallen asleep, it seemed to him that a lady came before him, the most beautiful that he had ever seen in the world. She raised him from the earth and carried him up to the highest mountain he had ever seen. There she set him on a wheel. On that wheel there were seats, some going up and some going down. The king looked to see at what place on the wheel he was seated and saw that it was the highest seat. The lady asked:

"Arthur, where are you?"

"My lady," said he, "I am on a high wheel, but I do not know what it is."

"It is the wheel of fortune," she said, and then she asked, "Arthur, what do you see?"

"My lady, it seems to me that I see the whole world."

"True," she said. "You see it, there is very little of which you have not been the lord until now; you have been the most powerful king in all the circumference that you see. But such is earthly pride that there is none so high but that he must fall from power over the world."

Then she took him and cast him down to the ground so feloniously that in the fall it seemed to Arthur that he was broken to bits and that he lost power over his body and limbs.

Thus King Arthur saw the misfortunes which were to be his in the future. In the morning, when he was up, he heard mass before he was armed, and made his confession to an archbishop the best he could for all the sins of which he felt guilty toward his Creator. When he had confessed and had cried out for mercy, he related the two visions that had appeared to him on the two nights before. When the archbishop heard them, he said to the king:

"Ah, sire, for the safety of your soul, your body, and your kingdom, turn back to Dover with all your people and send word to Lancelot to come to your aid. He will gladly come. If you do battle with Mordred at this moment, you will be mortally wounded or killed, and we shall suffer such harm that it will last as long as the world lasts. King Arthur, all this will befall you if you do battle with Mordred."

"My lord," said the king, "it is a wonder when you forbid me to do that from which I cannot turn aside."

"You must do as I say," said the archbishop, "if you do not wish to be put to shame."

So spoke the archbishop to King Arthur, like one who thought himself able to prevent the king from carrying out his will, but that was not to be, for the king swore on the soul of Utherpendragon, his father, that he would never turn back, but would go into combat against Mordred.

"Sire," said the archbishop, "it is a pity that I cannot bend your will."

The king told him to be silent, for he would not give up doing his will for all the honors in the world.

That day the king rode toward Salisbury Plain as straight as he ever could, like one who knew that on the plain would take place the great mortal battle of which Merlin and the other soothsayers had often spoken.

When King Arthur had marched out on the plain, he told his people that they would encamp there, for there he would await Mordred. They did as he commanded; they pitched camp quickly and made ready as best they could.

150

That evening after supper King Arthur went out with the archbishop to take the air on the plain. They came to a tall, hard rock. The king looked up high on the rock and saw letters carved. At once he looked at the archbishop and said:

"My lord, you may see a marvel; on this rock there are letters carved into it long ago; now see what they say."

The archbishop looked at the letters and read:

"On this plain will take place the mortal battle through which the kingdom of Logres will be left an orphan."

"Sire," he said to the king, "now know what they mean. If you fight Mordred, the kingdom of Logres will be orphaned, for you will die in battle or you will be wounded unto death. You cannot depart from it otherwise, and so that you may better believe that in this message there is naught but truth, I tell you that Merlin himself cut these letters. In all he ever said, there was naught but truth. He had certain knowledge of things to come."

"My lord," said King Arthur, "I see enough so that, if I had not advanced so far, I would turn back, whatever eagerness I had had up till now. But now may Jesus Christ come to our aid, for I shall never leave off until Our Lord has given victory either to me or to Mordred. If I come to harm, it will be through my sin and my excessive hatred because I have a greater number of good knights than Mordred."

So spoke King Arthur, more dismayed and more frightened than was customary with him, because he had seen so many things foretelling his death. The archbishop wept tenderly because he could not dissuade the king. The king returned to his tent, and as he returned, a youth appeared before him and said:

"King Arthur, I do not greet you, for my liege is your mortal enemy; that is Mordred, king of the kingdom of Logres. He warns you through me that you have unreasonably invaded his land, but if you will give your word as a king that you will go away in the morning, you and your men, to the land whence you came, he will allow so much and do you no harm; and if you will not do this, he warns you that there will be battle tomorrow. Now send him your message telling what you will do, for he does not desire your destruction, if you will quit his land."

The king heard the warning through, and said to the youth:

"Go tell your lord that this land, which is mine by right of inheritance, I will not quit for him at all, but I shall stay on it as my own to defend it and to eject him from it as a perjurer, and let perjured Mordred know that he will die by my hand; tell him this in my name. I would rather fight him than not, even if he were to kill me."

After this speech, the youth did not stay, but left without asking leave and rode till he came before Mordred and told him word for word what King Arthur had replied and said to him:

"Sire, know for sure that you cannot fail to have battle, if you dare await him tomorrow."

"I shall wait for him," said Mordred, "without fail, for I desire nothing so much as a pitched battle against him."

Thus was fixed the battle in which many a valiant man died without having deserved it. That night King Arthur's men were in great dread, for they knew well that they had many less men than Mordred had on his side. That is why they feared to fight them. Mordred had pleaded with the Saxons until they came to help him. They were great, lusty folk, but they were not so hardened to battle as King Arthur's folk. They had turned toward Mordred, and the highest men in Saxony had done homage to him, because at this moment they hoped to avenge many a great hurt that King Arthur had done them during his time.

Thus, great forces were drawn up on either side. As soon as day appeared, King Arthur rose and heard mass, then armed himself and ordered his people under arms. The king established ten divisions; the first was led by Sir Ywain, the second by King Yon, the third by King Karados, the fourth by King Kabarentin, the fifth by King Aguisant, the sixth by Girflet, the seventh by Lucan the Butler, the eighth by Sagremor the Desreez, the ninth by Guivret. King Arthur led the last, and in that was the greatest strength of his army, in which those farther forward put their hope, for in it were many valiant men who could not easily be defeated, unless overwhelming forces came upon them.

When King Arthur had thus assembled and established all his divisions, he prayed each high man to think on doing his best, for if he could come out victor from this battle, he would never find anyone who dared rebel against him.

In this wise the king ordered his divisions. Mordred acted in like manner, but, because he had more men than King Arthur, he put them into twenty divisions and in each as many people as was proper and a good knight as a leader. In the last he put his greatest strength, and gathered together the knights whom he trusted most, and was its leader. He said that with this division he would attack King Arthur, for his spies had told him already that the king was leading the last of his divisions. In the first two divisions Mordred had no knight who was not from Saxony; in the next two were the Scots, afterward there were the Welsh, who put their men into two divisions, and finally there were the men of North

Wales in three divisions. Thus Mordred had arranged the knights from ten kingdoms.

They rode in battle order till they came out on the great Salisbury Plain and saw the divisions of King Arthur and the banners which waved in the wind. King Arthur's host, all on horseback, waited until Mordred's men came up. When they were so close that they were about to clash, you could have seen lances lowered. Before all others among the Saxons came Arcan, the brother of the Saxon king, in full armor on a war-horse. When Sir Ywain, who was at the van of his companions awaiting the first shock, saw him, he spurred out with his lance down. Arcan struck Sir Ywain and broke his spear. Sir Ywain struck him so hard that he pierced his shield and put his spear head into his body. His aim was good, and he bore him off his horse onto the ground. In his fall, the lance broke so that the man lay stretched on the ground wounded unto death. Then a relative of Sir Ywain shouted for many to hear.

"Now Saxony is despoiled of its best heir!"

Then the divisions advanced, King Arthur's first one against the two from Saxony. You could have seen, as they met, many a fine lance-blow and many a good knight brought to earth, and many a good horse running wild about the field, for there was nobody to hold them. You could have seen very soon the ground covered with knights, some dead, some wounded.

So began the battle on the plains of Salisbury, by which the kingdom of Logres was borne toward destruction, and so were many others, for afterward there were not as many valiant men as there were before. After their death the land lay wasted and pillaged, bereft of good lords, for they were all slain in great pain and anguish.

The battle was begun, great and marvelous. When those in the van had broken their spears, they set their hands to their swords, and struck such great blows that they bathed their swords in brains beneath the helmets. Sir Ywain did truly well that day and harmed the Saxons much. When the king of the Saxons had looked on a while, he said to himself:

"If that man lives long, we are defeated."

He charged through the press against Sir Ywain as hard as his horse could run, and with all his strength struck him so hard that the shield did not prevent his putting his spear into Sir Ywain's left side, but he did not mortally wound him. As he was carried on by, Sir Ywain struck him with his sharp sword so that he made his head fly off, and his body fall to the earth. When the Saxons saw their lord on the ground, they began to lament loudly, and when the men of Logres saw the duel that they had begun, heeding nothing, they charged, swords drawn. They began slaying the Saxons and did such great destruction that the Saxons soon had to turn and flee. There was not one of them without a wound, great or small. But they were more discomfited by the death of their lord than by anything else. When the Saxons had quitted the field in flight, pursued by the men from Logres, they fell back on the Irish, who spurred forward to aid them against Sir Ywain's men. Many of the latter died then because the attackers were fresh and rested. But they were hardy fighters who would rather die than turn about. They received them as best they could despite being weary and worn by travail. Sir Ywain during this charge was carried from his horse and wounded by two spears. He would have been killed at this moment and all his companions cut to pieces and killed if King Yon, who was leading the second division, had not succored them as quickly as possible with all the men at his command. They hit each other so mortally that they put lances into bodies, felled each other from their horses so that one could soon have seen the plain covered with them, some wounded, others killed. King Yon, who rode up and down dealing blows, finally reached the spot on the field where he found Sir Ywain afoot amidst the enemy trying to get on his horse, without being able to do so because the enemy pressed him too hard. When the king saw this, he charged on those busy trying to kill Sir Ywain, and dealt out blows wherever he could reach them. Thus he scattered and separated them whether they liked it or not, and forced them back till Sir Ywain was on a horse that the king himself gave him.

When Sir Ywain had remounted, he entered the mêlée again, like the courageous man he was, and King Yon said to him:

"My lord, watch out the best you can, if you do not want to die."

Sir Ywain said that he had never feared death except on that day, and added, "I wonder how that can be, for never before could fear bring me to dismay."

Then they went back into the battle and began again to deal hard blows so fast that it seemed as if they had not struck once. They did so much with their prowess that the Irish were thrown into a panic and were fleeing in fright when an Irish knight charged, with a sharp pointed spear in his hand, and struck King Yon so hard that his armor did not save him from having the head and shaft run into his body. The blow was true, and cast him on the ground so badly wounded that he needed no surgeon. When Sir Ywain saw it, he was sorely grieved and said:

"Ah! God! What a pity about this valiant knight, dead so soon! Ah! Round Table, your high station will be brought low today, for it seems to me that today you will be shorn of those whom you have fed and who till now have upheld the high renown that has been yours."

154

Such words spoke Sir Ywain when he saw King Yon stretched on the ground. He rushed upon the man who had killed him, and struck him so hard that he split him down to the teeth, so that he fell dead on the ground, and said:

"This man is dead, but thereby life has not been restored to that other noble man."

When King Yon's knights saw that their lord was dead they cried, "Alas, woe is ours," and because of their weeping, they left off the pursuit. When those who were fleeing before them saw that their pursurers had halted over the body, they knew at once that he for whom they wept had been some high personage, and their panic had not been such but that they turned about at once and charged on those who were mourning and rained blows on them so mortally that they killed many and would have killed them all if the third division had not come to their relief, as soon as they saw that they were being dealt with murderously. When King Karados, who was leading the third division, learned that their mourning was for King Yon, whom those men had slain, he said to his men:

"Gentlemen, we are going into this battle; I do not know what will become of me. If I happen to be killed, I beg you for God's sake never to heed the loss, for your enemies could take heart and courage."

So spoke King Karados when he went into battle. He did so well that nobody who saw him could consider him a coward. King Karados' men killed so many that, before their enemies had aid, you could see the whole place covered with corpses. When the high barons of Scotland saw their companions handled so roughly, they could not endure the sight, and they charged on King Karados' men. Heliades, who was lord over Scotland, since Mordred had given it to him as his fief, headed for King Karados, who was better mounted and more richly caparisoned than any of his followers. Like one bold enough to meet the best knight in the world, the king did not refuse combat. Their spears struck so hard that they pierced the shields, and the shock was so great that the sharp lances ran into their bodies so that the heads came out beyond their bodies. The knights fell to the ground so skewered that neither of them could taunt the other, for they were both wounded unto death. To rescue them, their men came out from both directions, each side aiding its own leader and hampering those opposed. King Karados' men prevailed, and they carried off Heliades by main might, but they found that his soul had left his body since the spear had been driven through his body. Some others disarmed King Karados and asked him how he was; he told them:

"I pray you only to avenge my death, for I know that I shall never see the ninth hour. For God's sake, pretend that it is not so, for our men could be quickly discouraged; thus the loss might be greater, but do this for me: take off my coat of mail and carry me on my shield to yon hill. I will at least die more comfortably there than I would here."

They obeyed his commands; lamenting much, they carried him to the height, for they loved their lord with a great love. When they had placed him beneath a tree, he said to them:

"Go into the battle and leave me here with four squires for a guard, and avenge my death however you can. If it happens that any of you escape, I beg you to carry my body to Camelot to the church where Sir Gawain lies."

They said that they would gladly do so, and then asked him, "Sire, do you think that there will be as great a defeat in this battle as you say?"

"I tell you," he replied, "that since Christianity came to the kingdom of Logres, there has been no battle where so many valiant knights died as will die in this one. It is the last that there will be in King Arthur's time."

After they heard these words, they left him and went back to the battle. King Karados' men and King Yon's did so well that they defeated the Scots, Irish, and Saxons. King Arthur's men in these three divisions were so mauled that more than half lay dead upon the ground. By the great load that they had borne, they had destroyed six of Mordred's divisions and had gone so far that they encountered the divisions that had come from the kingdom of Wales. In those two divisions were many brave men who longed to get into the battle, and were very sorry to have rested so long. They received King Arthur's men so well that few remained in their saddles, because these Welsh had done nothing and King Arthur's men were worn and battered from giving and receiving blows. In this encounter, Sir Ywain was brought down, so weary and so tormented that he lay long in a faint. The hunting down of King Arthur's men began at once; more than five-hundred knights passed over Sir Ywain in that rush. They hurt him so that, though he had suffered more anguish on that day, he suffered a great deal at this moment, and that was what weakened him most, and deprived him most of vigor and strength. So King Arthur's men were put to flight. When King Kabarentin of Cornwall saw that they were getting the worst of it, he said to his men:

"Now, at them! Our men are being defeated."

Then, the fourth of King Arthur's divisions stirred. You could have heard, as they advanced, war cries of the different peoples, and you could have seen knights falling to earth and staggering, some dead, others wounded. You never saw an encounter more laden with pain than that one was, because the combatants hated one another mortally. When the

156

lances were broken, they put their hands to their swords and dealt one another heavy blows, so that helmets were knocked to pieces and shields were cut up. They brought down one another's horses; each man pressed his opponent to the death. It was not long before Mordred sent two divisions to aid his people. When King Aguisant, who commanded the fifth division, saw them spreading over the field, he said to his people who surrounded him:

"Now let us go over that way, so that we can fight those who have just left the main band of their people, and take care not to touch any of the others, before you reach them. When you get there, hit them so that they will be astounded."

As he commanded, so they did, for they passed on beyond those at whom he had pointed, and went to attack the divisions that had left Mordred. As their lances hit their marks, you would have heard such a great din that one could not have heard the thunder of God. You could have seen more than five hundred men on the ground after the onslaught, and the men on Mordred's side were at the beginning badly hurt. So in two spots the battle was carried on more cruelly than there was any need for.

When Aguisant's men had broken their lances, they drew their swords and rushed upon their enemies and struck them wherever they could reach them. Those who were attacked defended themselves well and slew many. While King Aguisant was riding about wielding his sword, he looked down and saw Sir Ywain, covered with wounds, trying to get on a horse, but his enemies had beaten him down twice or thrice. When the king saw Sir Ywain, he rode that way with all the speed that he could get from his horse. There were four who sought to kill Sir Ywain. The king charged as he came and struck one man so that his helmet did not keep the steel from having a drink amidst his brains. He kept pushing his attack; they all marveled whence such prowess came. Aguisant's valor accomplished so much that he freed Sir Ywain from all those who had attacked him. He gave him a horse, and made him get on it. When Ywain was remounted, tired as he was, he rushed into the battle and did so much after what he had done before, that all were struck with wonder.

All divisions were in combat before the third hour, except the last two, the one where King Arthur was and the one that Mordred was leading. The king had had a boy climb a hill to see how large Mordred's division, the last, might be. When the lad was on the hill and had seen what the king had ordered him to see, he came back to the king and told him privately:

"Sire, there are at least twice as many men in his division as in yours."

157

"Really," said the king, "there is great mischief there. Now may God help us, for otherwise we shall be dead or brought low." Then he pined for Sir Gawain, his nephew, and said, "Ah, fair nephew, now I suffer for lack of you and Lancelot. Would to God that you two were in armor beside me. We should certainly win this battle with God's help and with the prowess that I know is in you. But, fair sweet nephew, now I may consider myself foolish for not believing you when you told me to send word to Lancelot to come help me and succor me against Mordred, for I know if I had sent for him he would have come gladly and with no rancor."

King Arthur spoke these words in great dismay; his heart told him truly a part of the evils to come for him and his company. He was, though, very well armed and very richly armed. Then he came to his knights of the Round Table, of whom there must have been in his company seventy-two.

"My lords," he said, "this is the most fearful battle that I have ever seen. For God's sake, you brothers and companions of the Round Table, keep close to one another, for, if you do so, nobody can easily defeat you. There are two of them for one of us, and they are well trained in battle, wherefore they are the more to be feared."

"Sire," they said, "be not dismayed, but ride out confidently, for you can already see Mordred coming at full speed toward you. Be not afraid, for from too much fear no good can come to you or to us."

Then the king's standard was put forward, and more than a hundred knights were set to guard it.

Mordred, who had selected four hundred of the hardest in his company said to them:

"You will separate from us, and go straight to that hill. When you come to it, ride around it as quietly as you can through that valley. Then head for the standard, digging in your spurs so hard that none of those around it will be left on horses, but all beaten to the ground. If you can do this, I tell you truly that the king's men will be in such disarray that they will never hold out but will turn tail in flight, since they will have no rallying point."

They said that they would gladly carry out his commands. Then they charged upon the king's division. It would have seemed to you that at the shock of their meeting the whole earth was collapsing, for the uproar from the felling of the knights was so great that one could have heard the noise two leagues away. King Arthur, who recognized Mordred, headed against him, and Mordred came on, too. They struck each other like men who are valiant and bold. Mordred hit the king first, so that he

158

pierced his shield, but the hauberk was strong; not a link broke. The lance flew to pieces at the shock. The king was not stirred from his seat at all. And the king, who was strong and tough and used to handling a lance, struck Mordred with such great force that he bore him to earth along with his horse in a heap. But he did not hurt him otherwise, for Mordred's armor was too good. Then King Arthur's men sprang from their ranks and sought to take Mordred prisoner, but rushing to rescue him you could have seen two thousand men clothed in iron, none of whom hesitated to put his body in mortal risk for love of Mordred. You could have seen many a blow dealt and taken, and knights dying beyond all count. There was around the fallen man such a vicious struggle that you could soon have seen more than one-hundred men lying on the earth, all killed or mortally wounded. However, because the forces kept growing around Mordred, he was remounted despite all his enemies, but first he had three blows from the king's own hand. Any other knight would have considered himself badly hampered by the least of these. But Mordred was a good knight and bold. He rushed upon King Arthur to have his vengeance, for it greatly angered him to be thus brought down among his people. The king did not refuse combat, but turned his horse's head toward him. The strokes of their sharp swords were heavy, and they were made so dizzy that they could hardly stay in their saddles, and if they had not both clung to their horses' necks, they would have fallen off. But the horses were strong, and they carried their riders on nearly a furlong.

Then the general battle began again great and marvelous. Galegantin the Welshman, who was a valiant and bold knight, charged upon Mordred, who was furious and struck his attacker with all his might so that his head flew from his shoulders. It was a great pity for he had been most loyal to King Arthur. When King Arthur saw the fall of Galegantin, he was not happy and declared that he would avenge him if he could. He bore down again upon Mordred, and as he was about to strike him, a knight from Northumberland caught him as he passed. He hit him on the left side where the shield was no protection. He could have very badly wounded him, if the hauberk had not been so strong. But it held up and not a link broke. The blow was well aimed, and carried the king beneath his horse's belly. When Sir Ywain, who was near at hand saw this blow, he cried:

"Ah, God, what a grievous thing is this, when so valiant a man is brought down by such vile means." Then he took after the knight from Northumberland and struck him so hard with a short thick spear that no armor kept spear tip and shaft from going into his body. The spear broke when the knight fell. Then Sir Ywain came to the king and got him on

159

horseback in spite of all his enemies. And Mordred, who was so angry that he almost went out of his wits because King Arthur had been re-mounted, aimed at Sir Ywain, holding his sword in both hands. The blow was heavy and came from above; it split Sir Ywain's helmet and iron hood and his head down to his teeth. It felled him to the earth. The pity of it was heart-rendering, for at that time Sir Ywain was held to be one of the good knights in the world and the man of greatest merit.

When King Arthur saw this blow, he said:

"Ah, God, why do you allow what I see, for the worst traitor on earth has killed one of the most valiant men in the world."

"Sire," answered Sagremor the Desreez, "that is the play of fortune; now you may see that she is selling you dearly the great estates and the great honors that you have had for a long time, for she is carrying off your best friends. God grant that we have nothing worse."

While they were speaking of Sir Ywain, they heard behind them a great outcry, for Mordred's four hundred knights were shouting as they approached the standard, and King Arthur's men were, also. You could have seen, at their encounter, lances breaking and knights falling. But King Arthur's men, who were good knights and experienced, received the four hundred so well that they brought down more than a hundred during the charge. Both sides drew their swords, and struck back and forth with all their might, and killed one another whenever they could. King Arthur's men who were guarding the standard did so well at that attack that out of Mordred's four hundred knights only twenty escaped without being slain and cut to pieces, there where they fought, before the ninth hour. If you had then been on the field where the battle was, you would have seen the whole place littered with the dead and a great many wounded.

Shortly after the ninth hour the battle was coming to an end in such wise that of all those who met on the plain, who had numbered more than one hundred thousand, there were not more than three hundred left who were not among the dead. It had so befallen the knights of the Round Table that they were all killed except four, for they had abandoned them-selves the most freely because the need that they saw was so great. Of the four who remained one was King Arthur, the second Lucan the Butler, the third Girflet, and the fourth Sagremor the Desreez. But Sagremor had a body wound so bad that he could hardly sit in his saddle. They gathered their men together and said that they would rather lie there dead than that the others should have the victory. Mordred rushed upon Sagremor and hit him so hard, with the king looking on, that he made his head fly off onto the field. When the king saw that blow, he lamented:

"Ah, God! Why do you let me fall so far from earthly glory? To avenge that blow, I vow to God that here Mordred or I must die."

He held a stout and sturdy spear and he charged at as fast a gallop as he could get from his horse. Mordred, who knew well that the king meant only to kill him, did not refuse combat, but swung his horse's head around. The king, who came on with all his might, struck him so hard that he broke the links in the traitor's coat of mail and thrust his spear head into his body. The story says that after the spear was pulled out a ray of sunlight passed through the wound so clearly that Girflet saw it, concerning which the natives of the country said that it was a sign of the wrath of God. When Mordred saw himself so wounded, he understood that the wound was mortal. He struck the king so hard on the helmet that nothing stopped his making the king feel the sword on his skull, of which it cut away a piece. King Arthur was so stunned by that blow that he fell down from his horse to the earth, and Mordred fell too. Both were so stricken that neither had power to rise but lay there side by side. Thus the father killed the son, and the son mortally wounded the father.

XIX
The Death of King Arthur

When King Arthur's men saw him lying there, they were so torn by grief and anger that no man's heart can conceive the pain they suffered.

"Oh! God," they said, "why did you permit this battle?"

Then they rushed upon Mordred's men, who also charged, and the mortal struggle began again so that, before the hour of vespers, all were slain except Lucan the Butler and Girflet. When these two who were left saw that the battle had come out thus, they began to weep bitterly and said:

"Oh, God, was there ever a mortal man who saw such grievous things! Ah, battle, in this country and in others you have made orphans and widows. Ah, day, why did you ever break to lay such great poverty upon the kingdom of Great Britain, whose heirs were renowned for prowess and who lie dead, destroyed with such dolor? Ah, God, what more can you take from us? We see here dead all our friends."

When they had lamented thus for some time, they came to King Arthur where he lay, and they asked him:

"Sire, how do you feel?"

"We have only to get to horse and depart from this place," was his answer. "I see my end at hand, and I would not die among my enemies."

Then he mounted on a horse very easily; thus, all there left the field and rode straight toward the sea until they came to a chapel which was called the Black Chapel. A hermit, who had his lodging quite near in a grove, said mass there daily. The king alighted, and so did the others, and took the saddles and bridles off their horses. The king went in, and knelt before the altar, and began saying his prayers as he had learned them. He remained thus till morning without ever moving away. His prayer to Our Lord did not end until he had gained mercy for his men who had been killed that day. While he prayed, he wept so bitterly that those with him heard his sobs.

All night long King Arthur was at his prayers and orisons. The next day, it happened that Lucan the Butler was behind him. He had been looking at the king who did not stir. Then he said as he too wept:

"Ah, King Arthur, for you there is such overwhelming grief!"

When the king heard these words, he rose with difficulty as one weighed down by armor; he took Lucan, who was disarmed, and embraced him and pressed him to him with such force that he crushed his heart within him, so that it was impossible for him to say a word; instead his soul departed from his body. When the king had gone on thus a long time, he loosed his hold, for he did not believe that Lucan was dead. When Girflet had looked at Lucan for some time, he saw that he did not stir. Then he perceived that he was dead and that the king had killed him. Then his lamentation began once more.

"Ah, sire," he cried, "how ill you acted, for you have killed Lucan!"

When the king heard him, he leaped up and looked about him and saw his butler lying dead on the floor. Then his mourning increased and he answered Girflet like a man aggrieved:

"Girflet, fortune, which was a mother to me so long, has become a stepmother. She makes me wear out the last bit of my life in grief and anger and sadness."

Then he told Girflet to put on the saddles and bridles, which was done. The king mounted and rode toward the sea till it was noon. He alighted by the shore and ungirded the sword and drew it from its sheath. When he had looked long upon it, he said:

"Oh, Excalibur, good, rich sword, the best in this world except for the one with the Strange Hangings, now you will lose your master. Where will you find a man by whom you may be so well employed as by me, unless you come into the hands of Lancelot? Oh, Lancelot, man of most merit in the world and best of knights, would to Jesus Christ that

162

you held this sword in your hands and that I knew it. Then indeed my soul would be more at ease forever after."

Then the king called Girflet and said to him:

"Go upon that hill where you will find a lake and throw my sword into it, for I do not wish it to remain in this kingdom until the wicked heirs who will remain hereafter secure possession of it."

"Sire," said Girflet, "I will obey your command, but if it pleased you, I should much prefer that you gave it to me."

"No, I will not," said the king, "for it would not be well used by you."

Then Girflet climbed the hill, and when he came to the lake he drew the sword from its scabbard and began to look at it. It seemed to him so good and so beautiful that it was his opinion that it would be too great a pity if he threw it in the lake as the king commanded, for thus it would be lost. It would be better that he should throw in his own and tell the king that he had obeyed him. Then he ungirded his sword and threw it in the lake, and hid the other in the grass. Then he returned to the king and said to him:

"Sire, I have done your bidding, for I have thrown your sword in the lake."

"What did you see?" asked the king.

"Sire," Girflet answered, "I saw nothing but good."

"Ah," said the king, "you torment me. Go back and throw it in, for you have not yet done so."

Girflet went back at once to the lake, drew the sword from the sheath and said that it would be too great a pity if it was thus lost. So he thought that he would throw in the scabbard and keep the sword, for it could be useful to him or someone else. He took up the scabbard and threw it into the lake without delay. Then he took the sword and hid it beneath a tree and returned at once to the king and said:

"Sire, now I have carried out your order."

"And what did you see?"

"Sire, I saw nothing but what I should."

"Ah," said the king, "you have not yet thrown it in. Why do you torment me so? Go, throw it in; you will find out what will happen, for it will not be lost without some great wonder."

When Girflet saw that he had to obey, he went back where the sword was, took it up, and began to look at it with longing and to lament:

"Good, beautiful sword, it is such a pity about you, that you do not fall into the hands of some valiant man!"

Then he cast it into the deepest part of the lake as far out from him

163

as he could. As it was coming down toward the water he saw a hand issue from the lake and show itself up to the elbow, but he saw naught of the body to which the hand belonged. The hand took the sword by the hilt and cut upward with it three or four times.

When Girflet had gazed on this action, the hand plunged back into the water with the sword. He waited there a long time to learn whether it would make some other showing. When he saw that he was wasting his time, he left the lake and returned to the king. He told that he had thrown the sword into the lake, and related what he had seen.

"By God," said the king, "I thought rightly that my end was near at hand."

Then he began to think, and, as he thought, tears came to his eyes. When he had been thus long in thought he said to Girflet.

"You must leave here and separate from me with such a fate that you will never see me again as long as you live."

"I shall never leave you with such an agreement," said Girflet.

"Yes, you will," said the king, "or else I shall hate you with a mortal hatred."

"Sire," said Girflet, "how could I leave you here all alone and go away? You tell me, besides, that I shall never see you again."

"You must do what I tell you," said the king. "Go away quickly, for there must be no delay. I beg you by that love that there has been between you and me."

When Girflet heard the king entreating him so gently, he answered:

"Sire, I will do what you command, sorely grieving, but only if you please, tell me whether you think I shall ever see you again."

"No," said the king, "be sure of that."

"And where do you think of going, please, sire?"

"I will not tell you that," said the king.

When Girflet saw that he would learn nothing more, he got on his horse and left the king. As soon as he had left, a hard, wondrous rain began to fall that lasted until he reached a hill half a league from the king. There he stopped beneath a tree until the rain was over. He began to look in the direction where he had left the king. Then he saw coming over the sea a ship which was full of ladies. When the ship came to shore just where the king was, they came to the ship's side, and the lady who ruled the others held Morgan, King Arthur's sister, by the hand and began to call to the king to come aboard the ship. The king, as soon as he saw Morgan, his sister, rose to his feet from the ground where he was sitting, and boarded the ship, and drew his horse on after him, and took his arms along.

164

When Girflet, who was on the hill, had observed all this, he went back as fast as his horse could gallop, and came to the shore. From there he saw King Arthur among the ladies and recognized Morgan the Fay, for he had often seen her. In that short time the ship had pulled away from the shore more than the length of eight cross-bow shots. When Girflet saw that he had thus lost the king, he alighted on the shore, and mourned loudly. He stayed there all that day and all night long without ever eating or drinking, and he had had no food or drink the day before.

In the morning after it had got light and the sun was up, and the birds had begun to sing, Girflet was still plunged in grief and vexation. Sorrowful as he was, he got on his horse, and set off from there. He rode till he came to a grove near there. There was in this grove a hermit with whom he was well acquainted. He went to his hermitage and stayed there two days, because he was quite ill from the great grief that he had had. He told the holy man about what he had seen happen to King Arthur.

On the third day he left and thought that he would go to the Black Chapel to learn whether Lucan the Butler had yet been buried. When he arrived there about noon, he dismounted at the entrance, tied his horse to a tree, and then went inside. He found before the altar two tombs, very rich and very beautiful, but one was much richer and handsomer than the other. On the less beautiful there was an inscription which read:

"Here lies Lucan the Butler, whom King Arthur crushed in his arms."

On the other tomb, that was so marvelous and rich, there were letters that said:

"Here lies King Arthur, who by his valor made twelve kingdoms subject to him."

When he saw this, he fainted upon the tomb. When he recovered from his swoon, he kissed the tomb very sweetly, and began to lament aloud and stayed there till evening when the holy man came to serve at the altar. When the holy man had come, Girflet asked him at once:

"Is it true, sir, that King Arthur lies here?"

"Yes, my good friend, he truly lies here. I do not know who the ladies were that brought him!"

Girflet immediately concluded that they were the ones who had taken him aboard the ship. He said that since his lord had departed from this world, he would no longer remain among men. He begged the hermit until the latter accepted him in his company. Thus Girflet became a hermit and served in the Black Chapel, but it was not for long; after King Arthur's death he lived only eighteen days.

While Girflet was residing in the hermitage, Mordred's two sons came forward. They had remained at Winchester to guard the city, if need were; their father had left them there. These two sons were good, experienced knights. As soon as they learned of the death of Mordred and King Arthur and the other noble men who had been in the battle, they took everybody from Winchester and rode over the land about them in every direction. They could do so freely because they found no one to oppose them, for all valiant men and good knights had died in the battle. When the queen heard of the death of King Arthur and she had been told these fellows were going about seizing the land, she was afraid that they would kill her if they could lay hands on her. So she at once assumed the habit of the nuns.

While these things were happening, a messenger came to Lancelot in the city of Gaunes from the kingdom of Logres, and told him the whole truth about King Arthur, how he had died in battle and how Mordred's two sons had seized the land after King Arthur's death. When Lancelot heard this news, he was troubled and angry, for he had loved King Arthur sincerely. The other good knights at Gaunes were also angered. Lancelot considered with the two kings what he might do about the matter, for he hated nobody more than he did Mordred and his children.

"My lord," said Bohort, "I will give you my opinion as to what we should do. We will send for our men from near and far; we will leave the kingdom of Gaunes, and pass over to Great Britain. When we are there, if Mordred's sons do not flee, they can be certain of death."

"You wish us to act thus?" asked Lancelot.

"My lord," said Bohort, "we see no other way to avenge ourselves."

Then they sent for their men from near and far in the kingdom of Benwick and Gaunes, so that in a fortnight more than twenty thousand had assembled; some on foot, some on horseback. They were brought together in the city of Gaunes. The knights and noble men of the country had come. King Bohort and King Lionel and Lancelot and Hector with their companions set out at once from the kingdom of Gaunes and rode daily till they came to the sea. They found their ships ready, went aboard, and with a good wind landed the same day on British soil. When they were safe and sound ashore, they were in high spirits and encamped on the coast and rejoiced greatly.

The next day Mordred's two sons received the news that Lancelot had landed in their country and had brought many men with him. When they heard the news, they were sorely dismayed, for they feared nobody as much as they feared Lancelot. They consulted among themselves as to what they should do. Finally they agreed that they would take their men and go fight Lancelot in a pitched battle. To whomever God gave victory, let him have it, for they preferred dying in battle to going in flight through the country. As they planned, they also acted, for they sent out at once for their men and gathered them at Winchester. They had already made such progress in a short time that all the noble men of the country had done them homage. When they had assembled their men, as I have described to you, they rode out of Winchester on a Tuesday morning. A messenger at once told them that Lancelot was coming upon them with an army and was near there, five English leagues away; they could be sure of doing battle by the third hour. When they heard this news, they said that they would fight where they were and wait for Lancelot and his men, since they could not do otherwise than fight. They then got off their horses to let them rest. Thus the people from Winchester had halted.

Lancelot was riding up with his company, but nobody could have been more troubled and sadder, for the very next day that battle was to be done, news was brought him that his lady the queen had died and quit this world three days before. It had happened just as it was reported to him, for the queen had recently left this world. But never did a lady of high degree make a finer end or more noble repentance, nor more fervently cry for mercy from Our Lord than she did. Lancelot was most grieved and tormented when he knew the truth.

He rode toward Winchester in great ire. When those waiting for his host saw them coming, they got on their horses and attacked them in full battle order. At the shock you could have seen many a knight unhorsed and going to his death, and many a horse killed and many running riderless while their masters lay on the ground after their souls had departed from their bodies. The battle lasted till the ninth hour, for there were large forces on both sides. About then it happened that the elder of Mordred's two sons, whose name was Melehan, held a short, thick spear which had a tempered tip well sharpened. He charged on King Lionel at full speed, and struck him with all his might so hard that the shield and the coat of mail did not prevent his putting the lance into his body. He hit so true and hard that the king was borne from his horse. At his fall the lance broke, so that the head with a great piece of the shaft remained in Lionel's body. Bohort saw this blow and recognized that his brother was mortally wounded. He was so stricken with grief that he thought he should die of it. He charged at Melehan with drawn sword and struck him on the helmet like a man who has delivered many a mighty blow. He cut through his helmet and iron hood and split them down to his teeth. He twisted his sword out, and cast Melehan down dead, sprawling on the ground. When Bohort saw him thus, he looked at him and said:

"Traitor, disloyal hound, your death is but a poor return to me for

167

the harm you have done me! You have put a sorrow into my heart that will never again come out of it."

Then he galloped over where the press was greatest. He began to knock down and kill everyone he reached before him, so that no one saw him without marveling. When the knights from Gaunes saw King Lionel fall, they dismounted by him and carried him out of the press to the shade of an elm tree. When they saw him so badly wounded, there was no one who was not greatly troubled, but they dared not lament aloud lest their enemies should perceive it.

Thus the battle went on fierce and stubborn till the ninth hour, so even that one could hardly say which was the better party. After that hour Lancelot came into the fighting. He met the younger son of Mordred and recognized him by his armor, for he was bearing arms like those his father was accustomed to bear. Lancelot, who mortally hated him, rode at him with drawn sword. The man did not flee, but threw his shield up before him, as soon as he saw Lancelot coming. Lancelot struck him with all his might, so that he split the shield down to its knob and cut off the wrist with which Mordred's son was holding it. When the man felt himself maimed, he turned in flight, but Lancelot was so close upon him that he had neither power nor time to defend himself. Lancelot dealt him such a heavy blow that he made his head with the helmet still on fly more than half the length of a lance from his body.

When the others saw this son of Mordred dead after the other, they no longer knew where to find shelter. They turned and fled to save their lives, each man as he could, and headed toward a forest near there, less than two English leagues away. Lancelot's men were on their heels, killing all they could, for they hated them mortally; so they slaughtered them like so many dumb animals. Lancelot went felling them and killing them so thickly that after him you could have followed his trail by those he beat to the earth.

He went on thus till he came upon the Earl of Gower, whom he knew to be a traitor and felon and who had brought many vexations to many a noble man. He shouted at him, as soon as he saw him:

"Ah, traitor! Now you have gone on till you have come to your death, for nothing can save you."

The fellow looked around in haste, and when he saw that it was Lancelot who was threatening him as he followed him with drawn sword, he saw clearly that he was done for if Lancelot could reach him. So he set spurs into his horse and fled as fast as he could. He was well mounted and so was Lancelot. The chase went on in this manner and lasted till they were a good half league within the forest. Then the earl's horse collapsed and fell dead beneath him. Lancelot, who was close upon him, saw him afoot on the ground. He spurred at him, armed as he was, and struck him on the helmet so hard that he put his sword among his teeth. The earl fell down, like a man to whom death brings anguish. Lancelot did not even look at him, but rode on at great speed. When he thought he was returning to his men, he was advancing farther and farther into the depths of the forest.

He went on thus wandering back and forth, as adventure led him until he came after the hour of vespers to a glade. Then he saw a youth on foot who was coming from the direction of Winchester. When the boy saw him, he thought that he was one of the men from Logres and that he had fled from the battle.

"My lord," he said, "I come from the battle where it has been a dolorous day for our men; to my knowledge not a single one has got away. Nevertheless, the fellows from over there are in a bad humor because of King Lionel, who has been killed."

"What!" said Lancelot. "Has he been killed, truly?"

"Yes, my lord," said the lad, "I saw him dead."

"That is a pity," said Lancelot. "He was a noble man and a good knight."

Then he began to weep bitterly, so that his cheeks were wet beneath his helmet.

"My lord," said the youth, "it is late now, and you are far from people and houses. Where do you think you will lie tonight?"

"I know not," said Lancelot. "It matters not where I lie."

When the lad saw that he could get no more from him, he ran off at once. Lancelot, however, went riding through the forest mourning bitterly, and he said that now nothing was left to him when he had lost his lady and his cousin.

In such bitterness and such grief Lancelot rode all night wherever chance or adventure might take him. In the morning he happened upon a mountain full of rocks where there was a hermitage quite remote from every living man. He turned his horse's head in that direction and thought that he would go see the spot to learn who inhabited it. He went up along a path until he arrived at the establishment, which was very poor. There was a small, old chapel there. He alighted at the entrance, and took off his helmet and then went in and found before the altar two holy men dressed in white robes. They seemed like priests, and so they were. He greeted them, and on hearing him speak, they returned his greeting. Then, when they had faced about, they ran to him with outstretched arms and gave him kisses and expressed great joy. Then Lancelot asked who they were.

"Do you not know us?" they asked.

He looked at them closely and saw that one was the Archbishop of Canterbury, the same one who had been to so many pains to make peace between King Arthur and the queen. The other was Bleobeeris, Lancelot's cousin. Then he was very glad, and he asked:

"Good my lords, when did you come here? It pleases me much to have found you."

They said that they had come there just after the dolorous day, the day on which the battle took place on Salisbury Plain.

"We can tell you that, to our knowledge, of all our companions only King Arthur, Girflet, and Lucan the Butler were left, but we know not what became of them. Chance brought us here. We found a hermit here who welcomed us. He has since died, and we have stayed on after him. Thus we will spend the rest of our lives, God willing, in the service of Our Lord Jesus Christ and will pray him to forgive our sins. What will you do, my lord, who till now have been the best knight in the world?"

"I will tell you," answered Lancelot. "You have been my companions in worldly delights; now I will join your company in this spot and in this life, and never again will I move from here as long as I live. If you do not accept me here, I will become a hermit elsewhere."

When the others heard him, they were very, very glad. They thanked God sincerely and stretched their hands toward heaven. So Lancelot remained there with the holy men. But now the tale ceases to tell of him and returns to his cousins.

Now the tale tells that, when the battle of Winchester was ended and the men with Mordred's sons had fled, if they could, or were killed, King Bohort entered Winchester with all the power of his people, whether those within liked it or not. When he learned for a certainty that his brother Lionel was dead, he lamented so bitterly that I could scarcely describe his despair. He had the body buried in the city of Winchester as one should do for a king's body. After the burial, he had Lancelot sought far and wide in every direction, but nobody could find him. When Bohort saw that he could not be found, he said to Hector:

"Hector, cousin mine, since my lord is lost thus, I wish to go to our country; you will come with me. When we are there, take whichever of the two kingdoms best pleases you, for you will have at your pleasure whichever you like."

Hector said that he now had no desire to leave the kingdom of Logres, but would stay on a while longer.

"And when I leave, I will go straight to you, for you are the man I most love in the world, and I ought rightfully to do so."

Thus Bohort departed from the kingdom of Logres and went back to his country with his men. Hector rode through the country, forward one hour, and back the next, until he chanced on the hermitage where Lancelot was residing. The archbishop had given him such instruction that Lancelot had become a priest, and sang mass every day. He maintained such strict abstinence that he ate only bread and water and roots that he dug in the brush. When the two brothers saw each other, many tears were shed by both, for they loved each other with a true love, and Hector said to Lancelot:

"My lord, since I have found you here in such noble service as the service of Jesus Christ, I am a man who will never leave in his lifetime, but I will be of your company every day of my life."

When those who lived there heard him, they were most joyous at having so good a knight offer himself for the service of Our Lord, and they received him into their company. Thus the two brothers were in the hermitage together and were every day attentive to the service of Jesus Christ. Lancelot lived four years in such a manner that there was not a man born who could have suffered pain and travail as he suffered from fasting and vigils and from being at prayers from the moment he woke in the morning. In the fourth year Hector died and passed on from this world and was buried there at the hermitage.

On the fifteenth day before May Lancelot went to bed ill. When he felt that he had to die, he begged the archbishop and Bleobeeris to carry his body as soon as he was dead to Joyous Guard and put him in the tomb where Galeholt, lord of the Distant Isles, had been placed. They gave their word as brothers to do all that. Lancelot lived four days after making this request and passed on from this world on the fifth day. At the moment when his soul left his body the archbishop and Bleobeeris were not there, but were sleeping outside under a tree. Bleobeeris happened to awaken first and saw that the archbishop was sleeping beside him. In his sleep the archbishop was seeing a vision of some sort and was showing the greatest joy in the world and was saying:

"Ah, God, blessed be thy name! Now I see all I wished to see."

When Bleobeeris saw that his companion was sleeping and laughing and talking, he marveled not a little, was even at once afraid that the devil had got into him. Then he woke him gently, and when the archbishop had opened his eyes and saw Bleobeeris, he said to him:

"Ah, brother, why did you pull me from the great joy I was in?"

And Bleobeeris asked him what joy that was.

171

"I was," he said, "in such great joy and in so great a company of angels that I have never seen so many people anywhere I have been, and they were bearing up to heaven the soul of our brother Lancelot. Now let us go see if he has died."

"Let us go," said Bleobeeris.

They went straight to the place where Lancelot was, and found that his soul had gone away.

"Oh, God," said the archbishop, "blessed by thy name! Now, I know truly that the angels as I saw them were celebrating for this our brother. Now I know well that penitence is of greater value than aught else; I shall never leave off penitence as long as I live. Now we must carry his body to Joyous Guard, for while he lived, we gave our word to do so."

"That is true," said Bleobeeris.

Then they prepared a bier, and when it was ready, they placed Lancelot's body on it, and then they took it, one on one side and the other on the other and walked for days in great travail and pain till they came to Joyous Guard. When the people of Joyous Guard learned that it was Lancelot's body, they went out to meet it and received it with tears and lamentations. About the body you could have heard such great wailing and sobbing that hardly could you have heard the thunder of God. They went down into the main church of the castle and did the body as great honor as they could and should do to so noble a man as Lancelot had been.

The very day that the body was brought there, King Bohort alighted at the castle accompanied only by a single knight and a squire. When he learned that the body was in the church he went there, and had it uncovered, and looked at it to make sure that it was his lord. When he had recognized him, he swooned upon the body and then began to lament and wail so bitterly that nobody ever saw greater lamentation. That day great was the grief in the castle. At night they had Galeholt's tomb opened; it was so rich that there was none richer. The next day they laid Lancelot's body within it. Afterward they had an inscription cut, which read:

"Here lies the body of Galeholt, lord of the Distant Isles, and with him rests Lancelot of the Lake, who was the best knight ever to enter the kingdom of Logres, excepting only Galahad his son."

When the body was buried, you could have seen the people of the castle kissing his tomb. Then they asked King Bohort how he had come at the right time for Lancelot's burial.

"Truly," said King Bohort, "a religious hermit who lives in the kingdom of Gaunes told me that, if I were on this very day in this castle, I would find Lancelot dead or alive. But, for God's sake, if you know where he has lived since I last saw him, tell me."

The archbishop at once told of Lancelot's life and ending. When King Bohort had listened to him, he responded:

"My lord, since he was with you to the end, I am the man who, in his stead, will be your companion as long as I live, for I will go away with you and spend the rest of my life in the hermitage."

The archbishop thanked Our Lord for that most tenderly.

On the next day King Bohort left Joyous Guard and sent away his knight and his squire, and through them told his liege men to make whomever they liked king, for he would never again return. Thus King Bohort went away with the archbishop and Bleobeeris and lived out the rest of his days in the love of Our Lord.

Here Master Walter Map ceases to tell the *History of Lancelot*, for he has brought it to its end according to the events that happened, and here finishes his book so completely that after this nothing but falsehoods could be told.